THE
SATISFIED
SOUL

JOHN PIPER

120 DAILY MEDITATIONS

THE
SATISFIED
SOUL

Showing the Supremacy of God in All of Life

MULTNOMAH

THE SATISFIED SOUL

Hardcover ISBN 978-1-60142-999-5
eBook ISBN 978-0-7352-8967-3

Copyright © 2017 by Desiring God Foundation

These meditations originally appeared in John Piper's *Pierced by the Word*, *Life as a Vapor*, and *A Godward Heart*.

Cover design by Kristopher K. Orr; cover photography by Anthony Heflin, 500px

Published in the United States by Multnomah, an imprint of the Crown Publishing Group, a division of Penguin Random House LLC, New York.

MULTNOMAH® and its mountain colophon are registered trademarks of Penguin Random House LLC.

Library of Congress Cataloging-in-Publication Data
Names: Piper, John, 1946– author.
Title: The satisfied soul : showing the supremacy of God in all of life / John Piper.
Description: First Edition. | Colorado Springs : Multnomah, 2017. | "120 daily meditations."
Identifiers: LCCN 2017031411| ISBN 9781601429995 (hardcover) | ISBN 9780735289673 (electronic)
Subjects: LCSH: Meditations.
Classification: LCC BV4832.3 .P573 2017 | DDC 242–dc23 LC record available at https://lccn.loc.gov/2017031411

Printed in the United States of America
2019

10 9 8 7 6 5 4 3 2

SPECIAL SALES

To those who long for a satisfied soul.

Satisfy us in the morning with your steadfast love.
PSALM 90:14

Contents

Contents   ix

A Word to the Reader

One of the reasons I put together collections of short meditations is that my life has been changed as much by paragraphs as by books. Books on one topic are valuable. They let the author explore all the angles of an insight. But where do the insights themselves come from? Usually they come from paragraphs. Even sentences. For reasons not entirely explainable, God can make a single paragraph life changing.

Perhaps some evening your soul is hungry. Not for anything in particular, just a soul-hunger. A longing. Something is needed beyond what television is going to give. Something about God, or about the meaning of your life, or about eternity. You're tired and you know that you probably can't stay awake to read twenty pages. So you pick up a book that you know focuses on eternal things, a Godward book. And three minutes later you have seen something, and you will never be the same again.

It may take a lifetime to sound the depths of what you just saw. But the seeing happens in an instant. It's as if God takes the paragraph in his fingers and uses it to adjust the lens on the eye of your soul, and something wonderful comes into focus that you had never seen before.

Isn't it amazing to think about the relationship between God's focusing fingers and the human activity of writing and reading? You may have read that same paragraph before—perhaps just the other evening. But this time, God put his fingers on it and turned the lens just one more focusing notch. What this means is that I should pray as a writer, and you should pray as a reader. We should ask God to do this focusing.

I think of your reading and my writing as a kind of partnership in the pursuit of a Godward miracle. I write, you read, but God gives the sight. What we both want is this miracle of seeing—seeing life-changing things about God and life and eternity.

In one of his letters, the apostle Paul said, "By reading you can perceive my insight into the mystery of Christ" (Ephesians 3:4, author's translation). But was reading enough? A few sentences later he prayed, "That you may have strength to...know the love of Christ" (Ephesians 3:18–19). Something more was needed than reading. Something from God—he called it "strength to know." Earlier he had prayed that the eyes of his readers' hearts would be "enlightened that you may know" (Ephesians 1:18). Something from God is needed—in answer to prayer. This is what I meant when I said that God takes a human paragraph and puts his fingers on the lens of the eye of your soul. The slightest turn, and we are made strong with sight. We are never the same again.

So I have written. And you are reading. And God is ready to act. My words are not Scripture. They are not infallible like God's words. But my earnest aim in all I write is to be faithful to God's written Word in the Bible. To point to God and his Son and his works and his ways. My aim is a Godward book in the hope that God would put his fingers on its paragraphs and turn the lens of the eye of your soul, ever so delicately, and bring glories into focus.

This is how God forms us into his image. "Beholding the glory of the Lord, [we] are being transformed into the same image from one degree of glory to another" (2 Corinthians 3:18). This is our aim: from a Godward paragraph, to a sight of glory, to *A Satisfied Soul.*

꩜

I have enjoyed a long and happy relationship with Multnomah Books—especially in bringing my shorter writings to publication. *A Satisfied Soul* is a continuation of what we began in *A Godward Life, Book One* (2001, 2015), and continued in *A Godward Life, Book Two* (2003, which became *Taste and See*, 2005, 2016), *Pierced by the Word* (2003), *Life as a Vapor* (2004), and *A Godward Heart* (2014).

A Satisfied Soul is now the third volume of 120 (or more) readings, alongside *A Godward Life* and *Taste and See*. The three together combine for 365 daily readings, one for every day of the year, if you like. This new volume is a compilation of the three previously published smaller books (*Pierced by the Word*, *Life as a Vapor*, and *A Godward Heart*). Multnomah and the team at Desiring God thought it would serve readers to bring those three smaller devotionals together in this one volume to complement *A Godward Life* and *Taste and See*. I am thankful for this publishing partnership for the sake of spreading what I pray will prove to be life-changing, Christ-exalting paragraphs.

1

THE MORNING I HEARD
THE VOICE OF GOD

When God's Word Gets Personal

Let me tell you about a most wonderful experience I had early Monday morning, March 19, 2007, a little after six o'clock. God actually spoke to me. There is no doubt that it was God. I heard the words in my head just as clearly as when a memory of a conversation passes across your consciousness. The words were in English, but they had about them an absolutely self-authenticating ring of truth. I know beyond the shadow of a doubt that God still speaks today.

I couldn't sleep for some reason. I was at Shalom House in northern Minnesota on a staff couples' retreat. It was about 5:30 in the morning. I lay there, wondering if I should get up or wait till I got sleepy again. In his mercy, God moved me out of bed. It was mostly dark, but I managed to find my clothing, get dressed, grab my briefcase, and slip out of the room without waking up Noël. In the main room below, it was totally quiet. No one else seemed to be up. So I sat down on a couch in the corner to pray.

As I prayed and mused, suddenly it happened. God said, *"Come and see what I have done."* There was not the slightest doubt in my mind that these were the very words of God, in this very moment. At this very place in the twenty-first century, God was speaking to me with absolute authority and self-evidencing reality. I paused to let this sink in. There was a sweetness about it. Time seemed to matter little. God was near. He had me in his sights. He had something to say to me. When God draws near, hurry ceases. Time slows down.

I wondered what he meant by "come and see." Would he take me somewhere, as he did Paul into heaven to see what can't be spoken? Did "see" mean that I would have a vision of some great deed of God that no one has seen? I am not sure how much time elapsed between God's initial word, *"Come and see what I have done,"* and his next words. It doesn't matter. I was being enveloped in the love of his personal communication. The God of the universe was speaking to me.

Then he said, as clearly as any words have ever come into my mind, *"I am awesome in my deeds toward the children of man."* My heart leaped up, "Yes, Lord! You are awesome in your deeds. Yes, to all men whether they see it or not. Yes! Now what will you show me?"

The words came again. Just as clear as before, but increasingly specific: *"I turned the sea into dry land; they passed through the river on foot. There they rejoiced in me, who rules by my might forever."* Suddenly I realized God was taking me back several thousand years to the time when he dried up the Red Sea and the Jordan River. I was being transported by his word back into history to those great deeds. This is what he meant by "come and see." He was transporting me back by his words to those two glorious deeds before the children of men. These were the "awesome deeds" he referred to. God himself was narrating the mighty works of God. He was doing it for me. He was doing it with words that were resounding in my own mind.

There settled over me a wonderful reverence. A palpable peace came down. This was a holy moment and a holy corner of the world in northern Minnesota. God Almighty had come down and was giving me the stillness and the openness and the willingness to hear his very voice. As I marveled at his power to dry the sea and the river, he spoke again. *"I keep watch over the nations—let not the rebellious exalt themselves."*

This was breathtaking. It was very serious. It was almost a rebuke, at least a warning. He may as well have taken me by the collar of my shirt, lifted me off the ground with one hand, and said with an incomparable mixture of fierceness and love, "Never, never, never exalt yourself. Never rebel against me."

I sat staring at nothing. My mind was full of the global glory of God. *"I keep watch over the nations."* He had said this to me. It was not just that he had said it. Yes, that is glorious. But he had said this to me. The very words of God were in my head. They were there in my head just as much as the words I am writing at this moment are in my head. They were heard as clearly as if at this moment I recalled that my wife said, "Come down for supper whenever you are ready." I know those are the words of my wife. And I know these are the words of God.

Think of it. Marvel at this. Stand in awe of this. The God who keeps watch over the nations, like some people keep watch over cattle or stock markets or construction sites—this God still speaks in the twenty-first century. I heard his very words. He spoke personally to me.

What effect did this have on me? It filled me with a fresh sense of God's reality. It assured me more deeply that he acts in history and in our time. It strengthened my faith that he is for me and cares about me and will use his global power to watch over me. Why else would he come and tell me these things?

It has increased my love for the Bible as God's very Word, because it was through the Bible that I heard these divine words, and through the Bible I have experiences like this almost every day. The very God of the universe speaks on every page into my mind—and your mind. We hear his very words. God himself has multiplied his wondrous deeds and thoughts toward us; none can compare with him! "I will proclaim and tell of them, yet they are more than can be told" (Psalm 40:5).

And best of all, they are available to all. If you would like to hear the very same words I heard on the couch in northern Minnesota, read Psalm 66:5–7. That is where I heard them. Oh how precious is the Bible. It is the very Word of God. In it God speaks in the twenty-first century.

This is the very voice of God. By this voice, he speaks with absolute truth and personal force. By this voice, he reveals his all-surpassing beauty. By this voice, he reveals the deepest secrets of our hearts. No voice anywhere anytime can reach as deep or lift as high or carry as far as the voice of God that we hear in the Bible.

It is a great wonder that God still speaks today through the Bible with greater force and greater glory and greater assurance and greater sweetness and greater hope and greater guidance and greater transforming power and greater Christ-exalting truth than can be heard through any voice in any human soul on the planet from outside the Bible.

The great need of our time is for people to experience the living reality of God by hearing his word personally and "transformingly" in Scripture. Something is incredibly wrong when words that claim to be from God from outside Scripture are more powerful and more affecting to us than the inspired Word of God.

Let us cry with the psalmist, "Incline my heart to your testimonies" (Psalm 119:36). "Open my eyes, that I may behold wondrous things out of your law" (Psalm 119:18). Grant that the eyes of our hearts would be enlightened to know our hope and our inheritance and the love of Christ that passes knowledge and be filled with all the fullness of God (Ephesians 1:18; 3:19). *O God, don't let us be so deaf to your Word and so unaffected with its ineffable, evidential excellency that we celebrate lesser things.*

2

WHAT DOES IT MEAN
TO SEEK THE LORD?

A Meditation on Psalm 105:4

Seek the Lord and his strength;
seek his presence continually!

—PSALM 105:4

Seeking the Lord means seeking his presence. *Presence* is a common translation of the Hebrew word for "face." Literally, we are to seek his face. But this is the Hebraic way of having access to God. To be before his face is to be in his presence.

But aren't his children always in his presence? Yes and no. Yes in two senses: First, it's yes in the sense that God is omnipresent and therefore always near everything and everyone. "He upholds the universe by the word of his power" (Hebrews 1:3). His power is ever present in sustaining and governing all things.

And second, yes, he is always present with his children in the sense of his covenant commitment to always stand by us and work for us and turn everything for our good. "Behold, I am with you always, to the end of the age" (Matthew 28:20). "I will never leave you nor forsake you" (Hebrews 13:5).

But there is a sense in which God's presence is not with us always. For this reason, the Bible repeatedly calls us to "seek the Lord...seek his presence continually." God's *manifest, conscious, trusted* presence is not our constant experience. There are seasons when we become neglectful of the Lord and give him no thought and do not put trust in him, and we find him "unmanifested"—that is, unperceived as great and beautiful and valuable by the eyes of our hearts.

His face—the brightness of his personal character—is hidden behind the curtain of our carnal desires. This condition is always ready to overtake us. That is why we are told to "seek his presence *continually.*" God calls us to enjoy continual consciousness of his supreme greatness and beauty and worth.

This happens through seeking. Continual seeking. But what does that mean practically? Both the Old and New Testaments say it means to set the mind and heart on God. It is the conscious fixing or focusing of our mind's attention and our heart's affection on God.

> Now set *your mind and heart* to seek the Lord your God.
> (1 Chronicles 22:19)

> If then you have been raised with Christ, *seek* the things that are above, where Christ is, seated at the right hand of God. *Set your minds* on things that are above, not on things that are on earth.
> (Colossians 3:1–2)

This setting of the mind is the opposite of mental coasting. It is a conscious choice to direct the heart toward God. That is what Paul prayed for the church: "May the Lord direct your hearts to the love of God and to the steadfastness of Christ" (2 Thessalonians 3:5). It is a conscious effort on our part. But that effort to seek God is a gift from God.

We do not make this mental and emotional effort to seek God because he is lost. That's why we would seek a coin or a sheep. But God is not lost. Nevertheless, there is always something through which or around which we must go to meet him consciously. This going through or around is what seeking is. He is often hidden. Veiled. We must go through mediators and around obstacles.

The heavens are telling the glory of God. So we can seek him through that. He reveals himself in his Word. So we can seek him through that. He shows himself to us in the evidences of grace in other people. So we can seek him through that. The seeking is the conscious effort to get through the natural means to God himself—to constantly set our minds toward God in all our experiences, to direct our minds and hearts toward him through the means of his revelation. This is what seeking God means.

And there are endless obstacles we must get around in order to see him clearly, and so that we can be in the light of his presence. We must flee every spiritually dulling activity. We must run from it and get around it. It is blocking our way.

We know what makes us vitally sensitive to God's appearances in the world and in the Word. And we know what dulls us and blinds us and makes us not even want to seek him. These things we must move away from and go around if we would see God. That is what seeking God involves.

And as we direct our minds and hearts Godward in all our experiences, we cry out to him. This too is what seeking him means.

Seek the LORD while he may be found; *call* upon him while he is near. (Isaiah 55:6)

Seek God and *plead* with the Almighty for mercy. (Job 8:5)

Seeking involves calling and pleading. *O Lord, open my eyes. O Lord, pull back the curtain of my own blindness. Lord, have mercy and reveal yourself. I long to see your face.*

The great obstacle to seeking the Lord is pride. "In the *pride* of his face the wicked does *not seek* him" (Psalm 10:4). Therefore, humility is essential to seeking the Lord.

The great promise to those who seek the Lord is that he will be found. "If you seek him, he will be found by you" (1 Chronicles 28:9). And when he is found, there is great reward. "Whoever would draw near to God must believe that he exists and that *he rewards those who seek him*" (Hebrews 11:6). God himself is our greatest reward. And when we have him, we have everything. Therefore, "Seek the LORD and his strength; seek his presence continually!"

3

GLORIFYING THE GRACE OF GOD

Why Everything Exists

One of the main points of a short book I wrote, called *Spectacular Sins: And Their Global Purpose in the Glory of Christ* (Crossway, 2008), is that sin and God's wrath against it were part of God's plan when he created the world. This is different from saying that God sins or that he approves of sinning.

The main reason for making this point is to exalt the revelation of God's grace in the crucifixion of Jesus to the highest place. This is the point of the universe: the glorification of the grace of God in the apex of its expression in the death of Jesus.

Jesus died for sin (1 Corinthians 15:3). The death of Jesus for sin was planned before the foundation of the world. We know this because the book of Revelation refers to names written "before the foundation of the world in the book of life of the Lamb who was slain" (Revelation 13:8), and because Paul tells us that God saved us by "grace, which he gave us in Christ Jesus before the ages began" (2 Timothy 1:9).

Therefore, since Christ was slain for sin, and since grace is God's response to sin, we know that sin was part of the plan from the beginning. God carries this plan through in a way that maintains full human accountability, full hatred for sin, full divine justice, and full saving love for all who trust Christ. And we don't need to know *how* he does it to believe it and rest in it and worship him for it.

Recently I was pondering Ezra 8 and 9. I saw there another pointer to the truth of God's planning for human sin and divine wrath.

Ezra said, "The hand of our God is for good on all who seek him, and *the power of his wrath* is against all who *forsake him*" (Ezra 8:22). This text leads me to ask, Did God know before creation that his creatures would "forsake him"? Yes, he did. The plan for their redemption was in place before the foundation of the world (Ephesians 1:3–6).

Was Ezra 8:22 true before the foundation of the world? Yes, it was. God did not become holy only after creation. He has always been holy and just. "The power of his wrath is against all who forsake him" because this is, and always has been, the holy and just thing for God to do.

Therefore, since God knew that his creatures would forsake him, he also knew that his power and wrath would be against them. Therefore, this was part of his plan. I'm not saying that fore*knowledge* is the same as pre*planning*. But I am saying that if God knew something would happen and he went ahead to put things in place that let it happen, then he does so for reasons. He does not act on a whim. And those reasons are what I mean by *plan*. He created the world knowing that sin would happen and that he would respond as Ezra 8:22 says he does. And thus he planned for it.

This planning is what Paul meant in Romans 9:22 when he said that God was "desiring to show his *wrath* and to make known his *power*." And if you ask Paul why God would go forward with this plan, his most ultimate answer is in the next verse: "In order to make known the riches of his glory for vessels of mercy" (Romans 9:23).

God knew that the revelation of his wrath and power against sin would make the riches of his glory shine all the brighter and taste all the sweeter for the vessels of mercy.

"The riches of his glory" are the riches we inherit when we see his glory in all the fullness that we can bear (Ephesians 1:18) and are transformed by it (Romans 8:30; 2 Corinthians 3:18; 1 John 3:2). These riches of glory reach their supreme height of wonder and beauty in the death of Jesus as he bore the condemnation of God's wrath and power in our place (Romans 8:3; Galatians 3:13).

In other words, God's plan that there be sin and wrath in the universe was ultimately to bring about "the praise of his glorious grace" in the death of Christ (Ephesians 1:6).

What is at stake in the sovereignty of God over sin is the ultimate aim of the universe, namely, the exaltation of the Son of God in the greatest act of wrath-removing, sin-forgiving, justice-vindicating grace that ever was or ever could be. The praise of the glory of God's grace in the death of Christ for sinners is the ultimate goal of all things.

This elevates Christ to the supreme place in the universe. When Paul said, "All things were created...for him" (Colossians 1:16), he meant that the entire universe and all the events in it serve to glorify Jesus Christ. And the apex of his glory is the glory of his grace, most clearly seen in his death for sinners like us.

Oh, that God would make the meditations of our hearts go ever deeper into this mystery. And may the words of our mouths and the actions of our hands serve to magnify the infinite worth of Jesus and his death. This is why we exist.

4

How Is God's Passion for His Glory Not Selfishness?

The Source and Sum of Our Joy

The Bible is laden with God's self-exaltation. Repeatedly he says things like, "For my own sake, for my own sake, I do it, for how should my name be profaned? My glory I will not give to another" (Isaiah 48:11). A major question people have when they hear biblical texts about God's passion for his own glory is, How is this not a sinful form of narcissism and megalomania? The answer is that God's passion for his glory is the essence of his love to us. But narcissism and megalomania are not love.

God's love for us is not mainly his making much of us, but his giving us the ability to enjoy making much of him forever. In other words, God's love for us keeps God at the center. God's love for us exalts his value and our satisfaction in it. If God's love made us central and focused mainly on our value, it would distract us from what is most precious, namely, himself.

Love labors and suffers to enthrall us with what is infinitely and eternally satisfying: God. Therefore, God's love labors and suffers to break our bondage to the idol of self and focus our affections on the treasure of God.

To see the God-centeredness of God's love demonstrated in Christ, look with me at the story of Lazarus's sickness and death:

Now a certain man was ill, Lazarus of Bethany, the village of Mary and her sister Martha. It was Mary who anointed the Lord with ointment and wiped his feet with her hair, whose brother Lazarus was ill. So the sisters sent to him, saying, "Lord, he whom you love is ill." But when Jesus heard it he said, "This illness does not lead to death. It is for the glory of God, so that the Son of God may be glorified through it." Now Jesus loved Martha and her sister and Lazarus. So, [therefore] when he heard that Lazarus was ill, he stayed two days longer in the place where he was. (John 11:1–6)

Notice three amazing things:

1. Jesus chose to let Lazarus die. Verse 6 says, "When he heard that Lazarus was ill, he stayed two days longer in the place where he was." There was no hurry. His intention was not to spare the family grief but to raise Lazarus from the dead.

2. He was motivated by a passion for the glory of God displayed in his own glorious power. Verse 4 says, "This illness does not lead to death. It is for the glory of God, so that the Son of God may be glorified through it."

3. Nevertheless, both the decision to let Lazarus die and the motivation to magnify God were expressions of love for Mary and Martha and Lazarus. Verses 5–6 says, "Now Jesus loved Martha and her sister and Lazarus. So...he stayed...where he was."

Oh, how many people today—even Christians—would murmur at Jesus for callously letting Lazarus die and putting him and Mary and Martha and others through the pain of those days. And if they saw that this was motivated by Jesus' desire to magnify the glory of God, many would call this harsh or unloving.

What this shows is how far above the glory of God most people value pain-free lives. For most people, love is whatever puts human value and human well-being at the center. So Jesus' behavior is scarcely intelligible to them.

But let us not tell Jesus what love is. Let us not instruct him how he should love us and make us central. Instead, let us learn from Jesus what love is and what our true well-being is.

Love is doing whatever you need to do, even to the point of dying on the cross, to help people see and savor the glory of God forever and ever. Love keeps God central, because the soul was made for God.

The mission statement of my life goes like this: I exist to spread a passion for the supremacy of God in all things for the joy of all peoples through Jesus Christ. People have asked me, "Shouldn't love be part of it?" My answer to those folks is that this mission statement *is* my definition of love.

Jesus confirms that we are on the right track here by the way he prays for us in John 17. I assume he is indeed praying for us because he says in verse 20, "I do not ask for these only, but also for those who will believe in me through their word." And I hope we would all agree that this prayer is an expression of his love for us (John 13:1). Consider how Jesus prays in the first five verses of John 17:

> When Jesus had spoken these words, he lifted up his eyes to
> heaven, and said, "Father, the hour has come; glorify your Son
> that the Son may glorify you, since you have given him authority
> over all flesh, to give eternal life to all whom you have given him.
> And this is eternal life, that they know you, the only true God,
> and Jesus Christ whom you have sent. I glorified you on earth,
> having accomplished the work that you gave me to do. And now,
> Father, glorify me in your own presence with the glory that I had
> with you before the world existed." (vv. 1–5)

This is the way the Son of God prays when he is loving his people. He prays that his glory be upheld and displayed.

The connection with us comes in verse 24, "Father, I desire that they also, whom you have given me, may be with me where I am, to see my

The Satisfied Soul

glory that you have given me because you loved me before the foundation of the world." The love of Jesus drives him to pray for us and then die for us, *not* that our value may be central, but that his glory may be central and that we may see it and savor it for all eternity. "To see my glory that you have given me"—for that, he let Lazarus die and for that he went to the cross.

The apostle Paul offered one illustration of God loving us this way:

> To keep me from becoming conceited because of the surpassing greatness of the revelations, a thorn was given me in the flesh, a messenger of Satan to harass me, to keep me from becoming conceited. Three times I pleaded with the Lord about this, that it should leave me. But he said to me, "My grace is sufficient for you, for my power is made perfect in weakness." I will boast all the more gladly of my weaknesses, so that the power of Christ may rest upon me. For the sake of Christ, then, I am content with weaknesses, insults, hardships, persecutions, and calamities. For when I am weak, then I am strong. (2 Corinthians 12:7–10)

Jesus' answer to Paul's plea that the painful thorn be removed was no. The reason he gave to help Paul accept this answer was, "My power is made perfect in weakness" (v. 9). In other words, he was saying it was more loving for him to help Paul value the glory of his power than it was for him to take away his thorn.

Many less-God-centered Christians, I fear, would not be happy with that answer. I have heard Christians say, in so many words, "This hurts and you can't be loving if you are going to subject me to this for the rest of my life." In other words, God's love is defined as what brings them the relief they want and makes them, not the glory of Christ, central.

Paul's response was very different: "Therefore I will boast all the more gladly of my weaknesses, so that the power of Christ may rest upon me" (v. 9).

Oh, how we need to see that Christ, not comfort, is our all-satisfying and everlasting treasure. So I conclude that magnifying the supremacy of God in all things and being willing to suffer patiently to help people see and savor this supremacy is the essence of love. It's the essence of God's love. And it's the essence of our love for people. Because the supremacy of God's glory is the source and sum of all full and lasting joy.

5

GALATIANS 4:18 AND "BEING MADE MUCH OF"

Our Satisfaction in God's Supremacy

Galatians 4:18 seems to be in tension with what I often say about "being made much of." I ask, Do I feel more loved by God because he makes much of me, or because, at great cost to himself, he frees me to enjoy making much of him forever?

The point of that question is to expose the deepest foundation of our happiness. Is it God or me?

- Is the deepest basis of my joy God's greatness or my greatness?
- Am I more satisfied praising him or being praised?
- Am I God-centered because of his surpassing value, or am I God-centered because he highlights my surpassing value?
- Would it be heaven to me to see God or to be God?

In other words, the aim of that provocative question is not to deny that God does indeed make much of us in many ways, but rather to make sure he is kept supreme and central in his own love for us instead of making ourselves the supreme value in God's love.

In Galatians, Paul was warning the church that the Judaizers were seeking to win them over in subtle ways. He said, "They make much of you, but for no good purpose. They want to shut you out, that you may make much of them. It is always good to be made much of for a good purpose, and not only when I am present with you" (Galatians 4:17–18).

I am not happy with this translation of that passage, even though I am very happy with the overall translation of the English Standard Version. "Make much of" is not a close rendering of the Greek word *zeloō,* which usually carries the sense of "desire" or "long for" in a fairly strong way, either positively (zeal) or negatively (jealousy).

Here are three examples of the Greek word used as "bad desire," such as jealousy, envy, or covetousness:

- "The patriarchs, jealous *(zēlōsantes)* of Joseph, sold him into Egypt; but God was with him" (Acts 7:9).
- "Love does not envy *(zēloi)* or boast" (1 Corinthians 13:4).
- "You desire and do not have, so you murder. You covet *(zēloute)* and cannot obtain, so you fight and quarrel" (James 4:2).

Here are two examples of the Greek word used as "good desire," like longing for, or proper jealousy, like God's:

- "Earnestly desire *(zēloute)* the higher gifts" (1 Corinthians 12:31).
- "I feel a divine jealousy *(theou zelō)* for you, since I betrothed you to one husband, to present you as a pure virgin to Christ" (2 Corinthians 11:2).

In view of this meaning, the New American Standard Bible has, I think, a better translation of the Galatians passage: "They *eagerly seek* you, not commendably, but they wish to shut you out so that you will *seek* them. But it is good always to *be eagerly sought* in a commendable manner, and not only when I am present with you" (Galatians 4:17–18).

So the point of verse 18 is not that we should seek to be "made much of" but that we should act in such a way that, if we are eagerly sought out, it will be because our behavior is admirable. It is a good thing when people want to be around us or to imitate us because we follow Christ. "Be imitators of me, as I am of Christ" (1 Corinthians 11:1).

The aim is not to be made much of but to draw people into our passion for making much of Christ. So I don't think Galatians 4:17–18 is in tension with my question, "Do I feel more loved by God because he

The Satisfied Soul

makes much of me, or because, at great cost to himself, he frees me to enjoy making much of him forever?" That question aims to accomplish the same thing as these verses. It aims to make God's worth the supreme value in the universe and to show that his love for us is supremely his helping us be satisfied in that forever.

6

"I LOVE JESUS CHRIST"

An Unforgettable Moment in Seminary

One of the most memorable moments of my seminary days was during the school year 1968–69 at Fuller Seminary on the third level of the classroom building just after a class on systematic theology. A group of us were huddled around James Morgan, the young theology teacher who was saying something about the engagement of Christians in social justice. I don't remember what I said, but he looked me right in the eye and said, "John, I love Jesus Christ."

It was like a thunderclap in my heart. A strong, intelligent, mature, socially engaged man had just said out loud in front of a half-dozen men, "I love Jesus Christ." He was not preaching. He was not pronouncing on any issue. He was not singing in church. He was not trying to get a job. He was not being recorded. He was telling me that he loved Jesus.

The echo of that thunderclap is still sounding in my heart. That was forty-five years ago! There are a thousand things I don't remember about those days in seminary, but that afternoon remains unforgettable. And all he said was, "John, I love Jesus Christ."

James Morgan died a year later of stomach cancer, leaving a wife and four small children. His chief legacy in my life was one statement on an afternoon in Pasadena. "I love Jesus Christ."

Loving Jesus is natural and necessary for the children of God. It's natural because it's part of our nature as children of God. "If God were your Father, you would *love* me, for I came from God" (John 8:42). The children of God have the natural disposition to love his Son.

Loving Jesus is also necessary because Paul says that if you don't love Jesus, you will be cursed: "If anyone has no *love* for the Lord, let him be accursed" (1 Corinthians 16:22). Loving Jesus is an essential (not optional) mark of being a beneficiary of God's grace. "Grace be with all who *love* our Lord Jesus Christ with love incorruptible" (Ephesians 6:24). If you hold fast to the love of anything above Jesus, you are not his disciple: "Whoever loves father or mother more than me is not worthy of me, and whoever loves son or daughter more than me is not worthy of me" (Matthew 10:37).

Sometimes people reduce the meaning of love for Jesus to obedience. They quote John 14:15: "If you love me, you will keep my commandments." But that verse does *not* say keeping Jesus' commandments *is* love. It says that keeping his commandments *results* from love. "If you love me [that is the root], you will keep my commandments [that is the fruit]." And the root and the fruit are not the same. Love is something invisible and inside. It is the root that produces the visible fruit of loving others.

So I join James Morgan in saying, "I love Jesus Christ."

And as I say it, I want to make clear what I mean:

- I *admire* Jesus Christ more than any other human or angelic being.
- I *enjoy* his ways and his words more than I enjoy the ways and words of anyone else.
- I *want his approval* more than I want the approval of anyone else.
- I *want to be with him* more than I want to be with anyone else.
- I *feel more grateful* to him for what he has done for me than I do to anyone else.
- I *trust* his words more fully than I trust what anyone else says.
- I am *more glad in his exaltation* than in the exaltation of anyone else, including me.

Would you pray with me that we would love Jesus Christ more than we ever have? And may our Lord Jesus grant that from time to time we would deliver quietly and naturally a thunderclap into the hearts of others with the simple words, "I love Jesus Christ."

"Though you have not seen him, you love him. Though you do not now see him, you believe in him and rejoice with joy that is inexpressible and filled with glory" (1 Peter 1:8).

7

EVERY STEP ON THE CALVARY ROAD WAS LOVE

The Intensity of Christ's Love and the Intentionality of His Death

The love of Christ for us in his dying was as conscious as his suffering was intentional. "By this we know love, that he laid down his life for us" (1 John 3:16). If he was intentional in laying down his life, the intention was for us. It was love to us. "When Jesus knew that his hour had come to depart out of this world to the Father, having loved his own who were in the world, he loved them to the end" (John 13:1). Every step on the Calvary road meant, "I love you."

Therefore, to feel the love of Christ in the laying down of his life, it helps to see how utterly intentional it was. Consider these five ways of seeing Christ's intentionality in dying for us.

First, look at what Jesus said just after that violent moment when Peter tried to cleave the skull of the servant but only cut off his ear.

Jesus said to Peter, "Put your sword back into its place. For all who take the sword will perish by the sword. Do you think that I cannot appeal to my Father, and he will at once send me more than twelve legions of angels? But how then should the Scriptures be fulfilled, that it must be so?" (Matthew 26:52–54).

It is one thing to say that the details of Jesus' death were predicted in the Old Testament. But it is much more to say that Jesus, in that night, himself was making his choices precisely to fulfill those Scriptures.

That is what Jesus said he was doing in Matthew 26:54. In effect he said, "I could escape this misery, but how then should the Scriptures be fulfilled, that it must be so? I am not choosing to take that way out because I know the Scriptures. I know what must take place. It is my choice to fulfill all that is predicted of me in the Word of God."

A second way the intentionality of his love for us is seen is in the repeated expressions of his intention to go to Jerusalem, into the very jaws of the lion.

Speaking to the Twelve as they traveled, Jesus said, "See, we are going up to Jerusalem, and the Son of Man will be delivered over to the chief priests and the scribes, and they will condemn him to death and deliver him over to the Gentiles. And they will mock him and spit on him, and flog him and kill him. And after three days he will rise" (Mark 10:33–34).

Jesus had a clear and all-controlling goal: to die according to the Scriptures. He knew when the time was near and set his face like flint: "When the days drew near for him to be taken up, he set his face to go to Jerusalem" (Luke 9:51).

A third way we see the intentionality of Jesus to suffer for us is in the words he spoke through the mouth of Isaiah the prophet: "I gave my back to those who strike, and my cheeks to those who pull out the beard; I hid not my face from disgrace and spitting" (Isaiah 50:6).

I have to work hard in my imagination to keep before me what iron will this required. Humans recoil from suffering. We recoil a hundred times more from suffering that is caused by unjust, ugly, sniveling, low-down, arrogant people. At every moment of pain and indignity, Jesus chose not to do what would have been immediately just. He gave his back to the flogger. He gave his cheek to slapping. He gave his beard to plucking. He offered his face to spitting. And he was doing it for the very ones causing the pain. He was doing it intentionally for us.

The Satisfied Soul

A fourth way we see the intentionality of Jesus' suffering is in the way Peter explained how this was possible. He said, "When he was reviled, he did not revile in return; when he suffered, he did not threaten, but continued entrusting himself to him who judges justly" (1 Peter 2:23).

The way Jesus handled the injustice of it all was not by saying injustice doesn't matter, but by entrusting his cause to "him who judges justly." God would see that justice is done. That was not Jesus' calling at Calvary. Nor is it our highest calling now. "'Vengeance is mine, I will repay,' says the Lord" (Romans 12:19).

The fifth and perhaps the clearest statement that Jesus makes about his own intentionality to die is in John:

> For this reason the Father loves me, because I lay down my life that I may take it up again. No one takes it from me, but I lay it down of my own accord. I have authority to lay it down, and I have authority to take it up again. This charge I have received from my Father. (John 10:17–18)

Jesus' point in these words is that he is acting completely voluntarily. He is under no constraint from any mere human. Circumstances have not overtaken him. He is not being swept along in the injustice of the moment. He is in control.

Therefore, when John says, "By this we know love, that he laid down his life for us" (1 John 3:16), we should feel the intensity of his love for us to the degree that we see his intentionality to suffer and die. I pray that you will feel it profoundly. And may that profound experience of being loved by Christ have this effect on all of us: "The love of Christ controls us,…he died for all, that those who live might no longer live for themselves but for him who for their sake died and was raised" (2 Corinthians 5:14–15).

8

BE CAREFUL, LEST THE LIGHT IN YOU BE DARKNESS

Pondering a Puzzling Text

> *No one after lighting a lamp puts it in a cellar or*
> *under a basket, but on a stand, so that those who enter*
> *may see the light. Your eye is the lamp of your body.*
> *When your eye is healthy, your whole body is full of*
> *light, but when it is bad, your body is full of darkness.*
> *Therefore be careful lest the light in you be darkness.*
> *If then your whole body is full of light, having no part*
> *dark, it will be wholly bright, as when a lamp with its*
> *rays gives you light.*
>
> —LUKE 11:33–36

Just before these verses, Jesus said, "Something greater than Solomon is here.... Something greater than Jonah is here" (Luke 11:31–32). That is, the wisdom of Jesus exceeds the greatest human wisdom, and the resurrection of Jesus will be greater than the most spectacular human rescues and resuscitations.

Do we see this for what it is—magnificent and compelling—so it becomes the light and joy of our lives?

In the text above, Jesus talks about seeing, and he talks about two lamps. He said this about the first lamp: "No one after lighting a lamp puts it in a cellar or under a basket, but on a stand, so that those who enter may see the light" (v. 33).

I take this to refer to what Jesus had just said about his wisdom and resurrection. He set a lamp in the world—his wise and powerful presence—greater than Solomon and greater than Jonah. "I am the light of the world," he said (John 8:12; 9:5). His greatness is the lamp that must not be hidden or missed.

He said this about the second lamp: "Your eye is the lamp of your body" (Luke 11:34).

I take this to mean that the way the lamp of Jesus becomes a lamp for you is that you see it for what it really is. Your eye becomes the lamp of your body when you see the lamp of his greatness in the world.

Then Jesus elaborated, "When your eye is healthy, your whole body is full of light, but when it is bad, your body is full of darkness" (v. 34). In other words, if your eye sees me for who I really am, then you are full of light; but if you don't see me for who I am, then you are full of darkness.

Then Jesus said, "Therefore be careful lest the light in you be darkness" (v. 35). In other words, there is much that passes for light through the eye that is not light. There are many bright things in the world that keep us from seeing the true light of Christ, just like city lights keep you from seeing the stars.

"Be careful!" he said. This is the only imperative in the text. Be careful what you see! Be careful what you regard as bright and attractive and compelling. If it is not Christ, you will be filled with darkness, no matter how bright it seems for a season. Candles seem bright until the sun comes out. Then they are useless and are put away.

Christ is the glory we were made to see. His light alone will fill us and give the light of life and meaning to every part of our lives. And when that happens, we ourselves will shine and give off the rays of

Christ. "If then your whole body is full of light, having no part dark, it will be wholly bright, as when a lamp with its rays gives you light" (v. 36).

Lord, open the eyes of our hearts to see the supreme greatness of your wisdom and power. Make our eyes good. Heal our blindness. Fill us with the all-pervading, all-exposing, all-purifying, all-pleasing light of your presence.

9

COVERING THE CHASM

The Rebellion of Nudity and the

Meaning of Clothing

The first consequence of Adam's and Eve's sin was that "the eyes of both were opened, and they knew that they were naked. And they sewed fig leaves together and made themselves loincloths" (Genesis 3:7).

Suddenly they were self-conscious about their bodies. Before their rebellion against God, there was no shame. "The man and his wife were both naked and were not ashamed" (Genesis 2:25). Now there is shame. Why?

There is no reason to think it's because they suddenly became ugly. Their beauty wasn't the focus in Genesis 2:25, and their ugliness is not the focus in Genesis 3:7. Why then the shame? Because the foundation of covenant-keeping love collapsed. And with it the sweet, all-trusting security of marriage disappeared forever.

The foundation of covenant-keeping love between a man and a woman is the unbroken covenant between them and God—God governing them for their good, and they enjoying him in that security and relying on him. When they ate from the Tree of the Knowledge of Good and Evil, that covenant was broken and the foundation of their own covenant keeping collapsed.

They experienced this immediately in the corruption of their own covenant love for each other. It happened in two ways. Both relate to the experience of shame. In the first case, the spouse viewing my nakedness is no longer trustworthy, so I am afraid I will be shamed. In the second, I myself am no longer at peace with God, but I feel guilty and defiled and unworthy. I deserve to be shamed.

In the first case, I am self-conscious of my body, and I feel vulnerable to shame because I know Eve has chosen to be independent from God. She has made herself central in the place of God. She is essentially now a selfish person. From this day forward, she will put herself first.

She is no longer a servant. So she is not safe. And I feel vulnerable around her because she is very likely to put me down for her own sake. So suddenly my nakedness is precarious. I don't trust her anymore to love me with pure covenant-keeping love. That's one source of my fear and shame.

The other source is that Adam himself, not just his spouse, has broken covenant with God. If she is rebellious and selfish, and is therefore unsafe, so am I. But the way I experience it in myself is that I feel defiled and guilty and unworthy. That's, in fact, what I am. Before the Fall, what was and what ought to have been were the same. But now, what is and what ought to be are not the same.

I ought to be humbly and gladly submissive to God. But I am not. This huge gap between what I am and what I ought to be colors everything about me, including how I feel about my body. So my wife might be the safest person in the world, but now my own sense of guilt and unworthiness makes me feel vulnerable. The simple, open nakedness of innocence now feels inconsistent with the guilty person that I am. I feel ashamed.

So the shame of nakedness arises from two sources, and both of them are owing to the collapse of the foundation of covenant love in our relationship with God. One is that Eve is no longer reliable to cherish me; she has become selfish and I feel vulnerable that she will put me down for her own selfish ends. The other is that I already know that I am guilty myself, and the nakedness of innocence contradicts my unworthiness. I am ashamed of it.

Scripture says that they tried to cope with this new situation by making clothing: "They sewed fig leaves together and made themselves loincloths" (Genesis 3:7). Adam's and Eve's effort to clothe themselves was a sinful effort to conceal what had really happened. They tried to hide from God (Genesis 3:8). Their nakedness felt too revealing and too vulnerable. So they tried to close the gap between what they were and what they ought to be by covering what is, and presenting themselves in a new way.

So what does it mean that God clothed them with animal skins? Was he confirming their hypocrisy? Was he aiding and abetting their pretense? If they were naked and shame-free before the Fall, and if they put on clothes to minimize their shame after the Fall, then what was God doing by clothing them even better than they could clothe themselves? I think the answer is that he was giving a negative message and a positive message.

Negatively, he was saying, You are not what you were and you are not what you ought to be. The chasm between what you are and what you ought to be is huge. Covering yourself with clothing is a right response to this—not to conceal it, but to confess it. Henceforth, you shall wear clothing, not to conceal that you are not what you should be, but to confess that you are not what you should be.

One practical implication of this is that public nudity today is not a return to innocence but a rebellion against moral reality. God ordains clothes to witness to the glory we have lost, and it is added rebellion to throw them off.

And for those who rebel in the other direction and make clothes themselves a means of power and prestige and attention-getting, God's answer is not a return to nudity but a return to simplicity (1 Timothy 2:9–10; 1 Peter 3:4–5). Clothes are not meant to make people think about what is under them. Clothes are meant to direct attention to what is not under them: merciful hands that serve others in the name of Christ, beautiful feet that carry the gospel where it is needed, and a bright face that has beheld the glory of Jesus.

Now we have already crossed over to the more positive meaning of clothing that God had in his mind when he clothed Adam and Eve with animal skins. That was not only a witness to the glory we lost and a confession that we are not what we should be, but it is also a testimony that God himself would one day make us what we should be. God rejected their own self-clothing. Then he did it himself. He showed mercy with superior clothing.

Together with the other hopeful signs in the context (like the defeat of the serpent in Genesis 3:15), God's mercy points to the day when he will solve the problem of our shame decisively and permanently. He will do it with the blood of his own Son (as there apparently was bloodshed in the killing of the animals of the skins). And he will do it with the clothing of righteousness and the radiance of his glory (Galatians 3:27; Philippians 3:9, 21).

Which means that our clothes are a witness both to our past and present failure *and* to our future glory. They testify to the chasm between what we are and what we should be. And they testify to God's merciful intention to bridge that chasm through Jesus Christ and his death for our sins.

10

DISCERNING IDOLATRY IN DESIRE

Twelve Ways to Recognize the Rise of Covetousness

Most of us realize that enjoying anything other than God, from the best gift to the basest pleasure, can become idolatry. Paul said that covetousness is idolatry (Colossians 3:5). Covetousness means "desiring something other than God in the wrong way." But what does "in the wrong way" mean?

The reason this matters is both vertical and horizontal. Idolatry will destroy our relationship with God. And it will also destroy our relationships with people.

All human relational problems—from marriage and family to friendship to neighbors to classmates to colleagues—are rooted in various forms of idolatry, that is, wanting things other than God in wrong ways.

So here is my effort to think biblically about what those wrong ways are. What makes an enjoyment idolatrous? What turns a desire into covetousness, which is idolatry?

1. *Enjoyment is becoming idolatrous when it is forbidden by God.* For example, adultery and fornication and stealing and lying are forbidden by God. Some people, at times, feel that these are pleasurable, or else they would not do them. No one sins out of duty. But such pleasure is a sign of idolatry.

2. *Enjoyment is becoming idolatrous when it is disproportionate to the worth of what is desired.* Great desire for nongreat things is a sign that we are beginning to make those things idols.

3. *Enjoyment is becoming idolatrous when it is not permeated with gratitude.* When our enjoyment of something tends to make us not think of God, it is moving toward idolatry. But if the enjoyment gives rise to the feeling of gratefulness to God, we are being protected from idolatry. The grateful feeling that we don't deserve this gift or this enjoyment, but have it freely from God's grace, is evidence that idolatry is being checked.

4. *Enjoyment is becoming idolatrous when it does not see in God's gift that God himself is to be desired more than the gift.* If the gift is not awakening a sense that God, the Giver, is better than the gift, it is becoming an idol.

5. *Enjoyment is becoming idolatrous when it is starting to feel like a right, and our delight is becoming a demand.* It may be that the delight is right. It may be that another person ought to give you this delight. It may be right to tell them this. But when all this rises to the level of angry demands or self-pitying resentment, idolatry is rising.

6. *Enjoyment is becoming idolatrous when it draws us away from our duties.* When we find ourselves spending time pursuing an enjoyment, knowing that other things or people should be getting our attention, we are moving into idolatry.

7. *Enjoyment is becoming idolatrous when it awakens a sense of pride that we can experience this delight while others can't.* This is especially true of delights in religious things, like prayer and Bible reading and ministry. It is wonderful to enjoy holy things. It is idolatrous to feel proud that we can.

8. *Enjoyment is becoming idolatrous when it is oblivious or callous to the needs and desires of others.* Holy enjoyment is aware of others' needs and may temporarily leave a good pleasure to help another person have it. One might leave private prayer to be the answer to someone else's.

9. *Enjoyment is becoming idolatrous when it does not desire that Christ be magnified as supremely desirable through the enjoyment.* Enjoying anything but Christ (like his good gifts) runs the inevitable risk of magnifying the gift over the Giver. One evidence that idolatry is not happening is the earnest desire that this not happen.

10. *Enjoyment is becoming idolatrous when it is not working a deeper capacity for holy delight.* We are sinners still. It is idolatrous to be content with sin. So we desire transformation. Some enjoyments shrink our capacities of holy joy. Others enlarge them. Some go either way, depending on how we think about them. When we don't care if an enjoyment is making us more holy, we are moving into idolatry.

11. *Enjoyment is becoming idolatrous when its loss ruins our trust in the goodness of God.* There *can* be sorrow at loss without being idolatrous. But when the sorrow threatens our confidence in God, it signals that the thing lost was becoming an idol.

12. *Enjoyment is becoming idolatrous when its loss paralyzes us emotionally so that we can't relate lovingly to other people.* This is the horizontal effect of losing confidence in God. Again, great sorrow is no sure sign of idolatry. Jesus had great sorrow. But when desire is denied, and the effect is the emotional inability to do what God calls us to do, the warning lights of idolatry are flashing.

For myself and for you, I pray the admonition of John: "Little children, keep yourselves from idols" (1 John 5:21).

11

THE PRECIOUS GIFT
OF BABY TALK

Human Language as the
Path to Knowing God

Human language is precious. It sets us apart from animals. It makes our most sophisticated scientific discoveries and our deepest emotions sharable. Above all, God chose to reveal himself to us through human language in the Bible.

At the fullness of time, he spoke to us by a Son (Hebrews 1:1–2). That Son spoke human language, and he sent his Spirit to lead his apostles into all truth so they could tell the story of the Son in human language. Without this story in human language, we would not know the Son. Therefore, human language is immeasurably precious.

But it is also imperfect for capturing the fullness of God. In 1 Corinthians 13, there are four comparisons between this present time and the age to come after Christ returns.

> Love never ends. As for prophecies, they will pass away; as for
> tongues, they will cease; as for knowledge, it will pass away. For
> we know in part and we prophesy in part, but when the perfect
> comes, the partial will pass away. When I was a child, I spoke like
> a child, I thought like a child, I reasoned like a child. When I
> became a man, I gave up childish ways. For now we see in a mir-

ror dimly, but then face to face. Now I know in part; then I shall know fully, even as I have been fully known. So now faith, hope, and love abide, these three; but the greatest of these is love. (1 Corinthians 13:8–13)

Note the comparisons with this age (now) and the age to come (then):

Now: We know in part.
Then: When the perfect comes, the partial will pass away (vv. 9–10).

Now: I spoke and thought and reasoned like a child.
Then: When I became a man, I gave up childish ways (v. 11).

Now: We see in a mirror dimly.
Then: We will see face to face (v. 12).

Now: I know in part.
Then: I will know fully, even as I am fully known (v. 12).

In this context, we can see what Paul meant by saying, "When I was a child, I spoke like a child, I thought like a child, I reasoned like a child." He was saying that in this age, our human language and thought and reasoning are like baby talk compared to how we will speak and think and reason in the age to come.

When Paul was caught up into heaven and given glimpses of heavenly realities, he said he "heard things that cannot be told, which man may not utter" (2 Corinthians 12:4). Our language is insufficient to carry the greatness of all that God is.

But what a blunder it would be to infer from this that we may despise language or treat it with contempt or carelessness. What a blunder, if we began to belittle true statements about God as cheap or unhelpful or false.

What folly it would be if we scorned prepositions and clauses and phrases and words, as though they were not inexpressibly precious and essential to life.

The main reason this would be folly is that God has chosen to send his Son into our nursery and speak baby talk with us. Jesus Christ became a child with us. There was a time when Jesus himself would have said, "When I was a child, I spoke like a child and thought like a child and reasoned like a child." That is what happened in the Incarnation. He accommodated himself to our baby talk. He stammered with us in the nursery of human life in this age.

Jesus spoke baby talk. The Sermon on the Mount is our baby talk. His high priestly prayer in John 17 is baby talk. "My God, My God, why have you forsaken me?" (Matthew 27:46; Mark 15:34) is baby talk. He spoke infinitely precious, true, glorious baby talk.

More than that, God inspired an entire Bible of baby talk. True baby talk. Infallible baby talk. Baby talk with absolute authority and power. Baby talk that is sweeter than honey and more to be desired than gold (see Psalm 19:10). John Calvin said that "God, in so speaking, lisps with us as nurses are wont to do with little children."* Oh, how precious is the baby talk of God. It is not like grass that withers or flowers that fade. It stands forever (Isaiah 40:8).

There will be another language and thought and reasoning in the age to come. And we will see things that could not have been expressed in our present baby talk. But when God sent his Son into our human nursery, talking baby talk and dying for the toddlers, he shut the mouths of those who ridicule the possibilities of truth and beauty in the mouth of babes.

And when God inspired a book with baby talk as the infallible inter-

---

* John Calvin, *Institutes of the Christian Religion*, originally published 1536, 1.13.1.

pretation of himself, what shall we say of the children who make light of the gift of human language as the medium of knowing God? Woe to those who despise or belittle or exploit or manipulate this gift to the children of man. It is not a toy in the nursery. It is the breath of life. "The words that I have spoken to you are spirit and life" (John 6:63).

12

LET CHRISTIANS VOTE AS THOUGH NOT VOTING

Political Engagement When the World Is Passing Away

Voting is like marrying and crying and laughing and buying. We should do it, but only as if we were not doing it. That's because "the present form of this world is passing away" and, in God's eyes, "the time has grown very short." Here's the way Paul put it:

> The appointed time has grown very short. From now on, let those who have wives live as though they had none, and those who mourn as though they were not mourning, and those who rejoice as though they were not rejoicing, and those who buy as though they had no goods, and those who deal with the world as though they had no dealings with it. For the present form of this world is passing away. (1 Corinthians 7:29–31)

Let's take these points one at a time and compare them to voting.

1. "Let those who have wives live as though they had none" (v. 29).
This doesn't mean move out of the house, don't have sex, and don't call

her "Honey." Earlier in this chapter Paul said, "The husband should give to his wife her conjugal rights" (1 Corinthians 7:3). He also said to love her the way Christ loved the church, leading and providing and protecting (Ephesians 5:25–30). What it means is that marriage is momentary. It's over at death, and there is no marriage in the resurrection. Wives and husbands are second priorities, not first. Christ is first. Marriage is for making much of him.

So that means if she is exquisitely desirable, beware of desiring her more than Christ. And if she is deeply disappointing, beware of being hurt too much. This is temporary—only a brief lifetime. Then comes the never-disappointing life that is life indeed.

So it is with voting. We should do it, but only as if we were not doing it. Its outcomes do not give us the greatest joy when they go our way, and they do not demoralize us when they don't. Political life is for making much of Christ, whether the world falls apart or holds together.

2. *"And those who mourn [do so] as though they were not mourning" (v. 30).*

Christians mourn with real, deep, painful mourning, especially over losses—loss of those we love, loss of health, loss of a dream. These losses hurt. We cry when we are hurt. But we cry as though not crying. We mourn knowing we have not lost something so valuable we cannot rejoice in our mourning. Our losses do not incapacitate us. They do not blind us to the possibility of a fruitful future serving Christ. The Lord gives and takes away, but he remains blessed (Job 1:21). And we remain hopeful in our mourning.

So it is with voting. There are losses. We mourn. But not as those who have no hope. We vote and we lose, or we vote and we win. In either case, we win or lose as if we were not winning or losing. Our expectations and frustrations are modest. The best this world can offer is short and small. The worst it can offer has been predicted in the book of Revelation. And no vote will hold it back. In the short run, Christians lose (Revelation 13:7). In the long run, we win (Revelation 21:4).

3. *"And those who rejoice [do so] as though they were not rejoicing"* (v. 30).

Christians rejoice in health (James 5:13) and in sickness (James 1:2). There are a thousand good things that come down from God that call forth the feeling of happiness. Beautiful weather. Good friends who want to spend time with us. Delicious food and someone to share it with. A successful plan. A person helped by our efforts.

But none of these good and beautiful things can satisfy our soul. Even the best cannot replace what we were made for, namely, the full experience of the risen Christ (John 17:24). Even fellowship with him here is not the final and best gift. There is more of him to have after we die (Philippians 1:21–23), and even more after the resurrection (2 Corinthians 5:1–5). The best experiences here are foretastes. The best sights of glory are through a mirror dimly. The joy that rises from these previews does not and should not rise to the level of the hope of glory. These pleasures will one day be as though they were not.

So we rejoice remembering this joy is a foretaste and will be replaced by a vastly better joy. Not less. And not less material. But better in the radically renewed material universe. God created matter and will not simply throw it away. He will not turn the whole universe into a spirit. But in that new material universe with a resurrected, material body, which Paul nevertheless called a "spiritual body" (1 Corinthians 15:44), our joy will be vastly superior to all we have known here.

So it is with voting. There are joys. The very act of voting is a joyful statement that we are not under a tyrant. And there may be happy victories. But the best government we get is a foreshadowing. Peace and justice are approximated now. They will be perfect when Christ comes. So our joy is modest. Our triumphs are short lived—and shot through with imperfection. So we vote as though not voting.

4. "And those who buy [do so] as though they had no goods" (v. 30).
Let Christians keep on buying while this age lasts. Christianity is not
withdrawal from business. We are involved but as though not involved.
Business simply does not have the weight in our hearts that it has for
many. All our getting and all our having in this world are getting and
having things that are not ultimately important. Our car, our house, our
books, our computers, our heirlooms—we possess them with a loose
grip. If they are taken away, we say that, in a sense, we did not have them.
We are not here to possess. We are here to lay up treasures in heaven
(Matthew 6:19–20).

This world matters, but it is not ultimate. It is the stage for living in
such a way as to show that this world is not our God but that Christ is
our God. It is the stage for using the world to show that Christ is more
precious than the world.

So it is with voting. We do not withdraw. We are involved, but as if
not involved. Politics does not have ultimate weight for us. It is one more
stage for acting out the truth that Christ, and not politics, is supreme.

*5. "And those who deal with the world [do so] as though they had no
dealings with it" (v. 31).*
Christians should deal with the world. This world is here to be used.
Dealt with. There is no avoiding it. Not to deal with it is to deal with it
that way. Not to weed your garden is to cultivate a weedy garden. Not to
wear a coat in Minnesota is to freeze, to deal with the cold that way. Not
to stop when the light is red is to spend your money on fines or hospital
bills or lawsuits or a funeral and deal with the world that way. We must
deal with the world.

But as we deal with it, we don't give it our fullest attention. We don't
ascribe to the world the greatest status. There are unseen things that are
vastly more precious than the world. We use the world without offering
it our whole soul. We may work with all our might when dealing with
the world, but the full passions of our heart will be attached to something

higher—Godward purposes. We use the world but not as an end in itself. It is a means. We deal with the world as a gratefully received gift *from* Christ and in order to make much *of* Christ.

So it is with voting. We deal with the system. We deal with the news. We deal with the candidates. We deal with the issues. But we deal with it all as if not dealing with it. It does not have our fullest attention. It is not the great thing in our lives. Christ is. And Christ will be ruling over his people with perfect supremacy, no matter who is elected and no matter what government stands or falls. So we vote as though not voting.

By all means vote. But remember, "The world is passing away along with its desires, but whoever does the will of God abides forever" (1 John 2:17).

13

Does God Lie?

Reflections on God's Truthfulness

and Sovereignty over Falsehood

Does God lie? The short answer is no. God never says anything like "I am not God." Or "You are not sinful." Or "Christ is not a great Savior." Or "If you believe in Christ, you will not be saved." Or "It is foolish to follow my counsel." Or "My word is unreliable."

But God does ordain that lying happens as part of his judgment on the guilty. That is why the question comes up.

- The prophet Micaiah stood against all the prophets of Ahab and said that the king would fall in battle. To explain why all the other prophets were saying the opposite, Micaiah said, "Now therefore behold, *the LORD has put a lying spirit in the mouth of all these your prophets;* the LORD has declared disaster for you" (1 Kings 22:23).

- Similarly, God said he will punish those who try to use prophets to buttress their sin. In that situation he said, "If the prophet is deceived and speaks a word, *I, the LORD, have deceived that prophet,* and I will stretch out my hand against him and will destroy him from the midst of my people Israel. And they shall bear their punishment—the punishment of the prophet and the punishment of the inquirer shall be alike" (Ezekiel 14:9–10).

- And at the end of this age, God will ordain a "strong delusion" as part of the punishment for those who "refused to love the truth":

The coming of the lawless one is by the activity of Satan with all power and false signs and wonders, and with all wicked deception for those who are perishing, because they refused to love the truth and so be saved. Therefore, *God sends them a strong delusion,* so that they may believe what is false, in order that all may be condemned who did not believe the truth but had pleasure in unrighteousness. (2 Thessalonians 2:9–12)

When we say that God never lies but ordains that lying happens, we do not mean that he approves of lying or that his law permits lying. We mean that God governs all things in the universe, including the sins of sinful men. Sin does not cease to be sin because God governs it and guides it for the good of his people and the glory of his name.

That is what he did in the sin of Joseph's brothers' deceptive sale of him into Egypt (Genesis 50:20) and Judas's deceptive kiss of betrayal (Luke 22:2–22; Acts 2:23). The one led to the greatest act of salvation in the Old Testament (the Exodus from Egypt), and the other led to the greatest act of salvation in history (the death of Christ for our sins).

When God said, "I, the LORD, have deceived that prophet" (Ezekiel 14:9), he meant that he can and does govern a sinful prophet's mind so that the prophet believes a lie. But God does it in such a way that he himself is not lying. God is able to superintend a thousand circumstances and influences so that a sinful prophet will think a lie, without God himself lying or in any way compromising his perfect truthfulness.

Let the Word of God about the word of God stand firm:

- "God is not man, that he should lie, or a son of man, that he should change his mind. Has he said, and will he not do it? Or has he spoken, and will he not fulfill it?" (Numbers 23:19).
- "The Glory of Israel will not lie" (1 Samuel 15:29).
- "The word of the LORD is upright, and all his work is done in faithfulness" (Psalm 33:4).

- "This God—his way is perfect; the word of the LORD proves true" (2 Samuel 22:31).
- "Every word of God proves true" (Proverbs 30:5).
- "The words of the LORD are pure words, like silver refined in a furnace on the ground, purified seven times" (Psalm 12:6).

God can be trusted. But do not play games with him. Do not begin to be careless with the truth. Do not take "pleasure in unrighteousness" and forsake the love of the truth. If you do, you may be abandoned to "a strong delusion" and never be able to see again (2 Thessalonians 2:10–12). God's elect will never be abandoned to apostasy, for he keeps his elect in the truth (Hebrews 13:21).

14

WHEN SATAN HURTS CHRIST'S PEOPLE

Reflections on Why Christians Suffer Losses

When huge pain comes into your life—such as divorce, or the loss of a precious family member, or the shattered dream of wholeness—it is good to have a few things settled with God ahead of time. The reason for this is not because it makes grieving easy, but because it gives focus and boundaries for the pain.

Being confident in God does not make the pain less deep but less broad. If some things are settled with God, there are boundaries around the field of pain. In fact, by being focused and bounded, the pain of loss may go deeper, as a river with banks runs deeper than a flood plain. But with God in his firm and proper place, the pain need not spread out into the endless spaces of ultimate meaning. This is a great blessing, though at the time it may simply feel no more tender than a brick wall. But what a precious wall it is!

As a father, I wanted to help our twelve-year-old daughter Talitha settle some things with God then, so that when little or big losses come—and I knew they would come, and will come—her pain would be bounded and would not carry her out like a riptide into the terrifying darkness of doubt about God. So as we would read God's Word together twice a day, I pointed out the mysterious ways of God.

So one day we read this from the lips of Jesus to the church at Smyrna:

> Do not fear what you are about to suffer. Behold, the devil is
> about to throw some of you into prison, that you may be tested,
> and for ten days you will have tribulation. Be faithful unto death,
> and I will give you the crown of life. (Revelation 2:10)

I asked Talitha, "Is Jesus stronger than the devil?"

"Yes," she said.

"Indeed," I added, "ten million times stronger. It's not even close. In fact, as Mark 1:27 says, 'He commands even the unclean spirits, and they obey him.' So all Jesus has to do is say to the devil, 'You shall not throw my loved ones into prison,' and the devil will not be able to do it. Right, Talitha?"

"Right," she said.

"So, Talitha, why does Jesus let the devil do this? Why does he let the devil throw his precious followers in jail and even kill some of them?" She shook her head. I said, "Well, let's read it again slowly, and you tell me the reason that the Bible gives. 'Behold the devil is about to throw some of you into prison...that...you...may...be...tested.' So why does Jesus let this happen, Talitha?"

"That they may be tested."

"That's right. And what does it mean to be tested? The answer is given in the way Jesus described what passing the test looks like. He said, 'Be faithful unto death, and I will give you the crown of life.' Faithfulness to Jesus is being tested. Will his loved ones keep trusting him? Will they keep believing that he has their best interest at heart? That he is wise? That he is good? That he is stronger than all?

"So, Talitha, there are a thousand things that God is doing every time something painful happens to you. Most of these you do not know or understand. Job, Joseph, and Esther didn't know what God was doing in their losses—not when the losses were happening. But there is always one thing you *can* know God is doing when pain comes into your life. This is something you can settle with God ahead of time. He is always testing you.

"If the test leads to your death, as it did for some of the Christians in Smyrna, Jesus wants you to know something ahead of time. You will receive 'the crown of life.' That means he will raise you from the dead and will crown you with the kind of everlasting joy in his presence that will make up for your losses ten thousandfold. *Crown* signifies 'majestic, royal restoration, and exaltation.'

"James says the same thing: 'Blessed is the man who remains steadfast under trial, for when he has stood the test he will receive the crown of life, which God has promised to those who love him' (James 1:12).

"Passing the test means loving God to the end. So settle it, Talitha. Loss and pain will come into your life. But Jesus is infinitely stronger than the devil. So even if the devil is causing it, as he did in Smyrna, Jesus is letting it happen. He's still in control. And he always has his reasons for what he permits—more reasons than we can know. One of those reasons is always testing, namely, the testing of our faith and our love for him."

We cannot answer every *why* question. But there is always this answer: my faith is being tested by the Lord who loves me and will help me. And our Lord never wastes his tests. Whether we believe this truth is, in fact, part of the test. In the mind of Jesus, the promise that he would give them the crown of life was enough to sustain the Christians in Smyrna. I praise God that this has been, and pray that it always will be enough for Talitha—and for you.

15

APOSTLE OF JESUS AND ABOLITIONIST WITH THE GOSPEL

How Paul Worked to Overcome Slavery

The historic and contemporary reality of slavery is never far away from how we think about the Bible. Instead of a frontal attack on the culturally pervasive institution of slavery in his day, Paul took another approach, for example, in his letter to Philemon.

Onesimus was a slave. His master, Philemon, was a Christian. Onesimus had evidently run away from Colossae (Colossians 4:9) to Rome where Paul, in prison, had led him to faith in Jesus—an amazing providence, since Paul evidently knew Onesimus's master. Now he was sending Onesimus back to Philemon. This letter tells Philemon how to receive Onesimus.

In the process, Paul did at least eleven things that work together to undermine slavery.

1. Paul drew attention to Philemon's love for all the saints: "I hear of your love and of the faith that you have toward the Lord Jesus and for all the saints" (Philemon 1:5). This puts Philemon's relation with Onesimus (now one of the saints) under the banner of love, not just commerce.

2. Paul modeled for Philemon the superiority of appeals over commands when it comes to relationships governed by love: "Accordingly, though I am bold enough in Christ to command you to do

what is required, yet for love's sake I prefer to appeal to you" (vv. 8–9). This points Philemon to the new dynamics that will hold sway between him and Onesimus. Acting out of freedom from a heart of love is the goal in the relationship.

3. Paul heightened the sense of Onesimus's being in the family of God by calling him his child: "I appeal to you for my child, Onesimus, whose father I became in my imprisonment" (v. 10). Remember, Philemon, however you deal with him, you are dealing with my child.

4. Paul raised the stakes again by saying that Onesimus had become woven into Paul's own deep affections: "I am sending him back to you, sending my very heart" (v. 12). The word for *heart* is "bowels." So he was saying, "I am deeply bound emotionally to this man, so treat him that way."

5. Paul again emphasized that he wanted to avoid force or coercion in his relationship with Philemon: "I would have been glad to keep him with me...but I preferred to do nothing without your *consent* in order that your goodness might not be by compulsion but of your own accord" (vv. 13–14). He was instructing Philemon how to deal with Onesimus so he too would act "of his own accord."

6. Paul raised the intensity of the relationship again with the word *forever* when he said, "This perhaps is why he was parted from you for a while, that you might have him back forever" (v. 15). In other words, Onesimus would not be coming back into any ordinary, secular relationship but a forever relationship.

7. Paul said that Philemon's relationship would no longer be the usual master-slave relationship: "[You have him back] *no longer as a slave* but more than a slave, as a beloved brother" (v. 16). Whether Philemon would let Onesimus go back as a free man to serve Paul or keep him in his service, things could not remain as

they were. "No longer as a slave" did not lose its force when Paul added "more than a slave."

8. In that same verse (v. 16), Paul referred to Onesimus as Philemon's "beloved brother." This is the relationship that takes the place of slave. "No longer as a slave but...as a beloved brother." Onesimus got the "holy kiss" (1 Thessalonians 5:26) from Philemon and would eat by his side at the Lord's Table.

9. Paul made clear that Onesimus was with Philemon in the Lord: "[He is] a beloved brother...in the Lord" (Philemon 1:16). Onesimus's identity was now the same as Philemon's. He was "in the Lord." Union with Christ is the great barrier-demolishing reality.

10. Paul told Philemon to receive Onesimus the way he would receive Paul: "So if you consider me your partner, receive him as you would receive me" (v. 17). This is perhaps as strong as anything he has said. In other words, "Philemon, how would you see me, treat me, relate to me, receive me? Treat your former slave and new brother that way."

11. Paul said to Philemon that he would cover all Onesimus's debts: "If he has wronged you at all, or owes you anything, charge that to my account" (v. 18). Philemon would, no doubt, be shamed by this if he had any thought of demanding repayment from his new brother, because Paul was in prison! Paul lived off the gifts of others. Philemon was the one who was to prepare a guest room for Paul, not the other way around (v. 22)!

The upshot of all this is that, without *explicitly* prohibiting slavery, Paul has pointed the church away from slavery because it is an institution that is incompatible with the way the gospel works in people's lives. Whether the slavery is economic, racial, sexual, mild, or brutal, Paul's way of dealing with Philemon worked to undermine the institution across its various manifestations. To walk "in step with the truth of the gospel" (Galatians 2:14) is to walk away from slavery.

16

THE SORROWS OF FATHERS AND SONS

Thoughts from the Lives of C. S. Lewis and Robert Louis Stevenson

R obert Louis Stevenson, the author of *Treasure Island,* was born in 1850 and raised in a Christian home in Scotland. His father was a civil engineer and brought up his only child to know and believe the Bible and *The Westminster Shorter Catechism.*

When Robert went to Edinburgh University, he left this childhood faith and never returned. He formed a club that had as one of its mottos, "Ignore everything that our parents taught us." His father found this written on a piece of paper and was informed by Robert that he no longer believed in the Christian faith.

The father, in an overstatement that carried the weight of sorrow, not the precision of truth, said, "You have rendered my whole life a failure."

Robert wrote to an unbelieving friend, "It was really pathetic to hear my father praying pointedly for me today at family worship, and to think the poor man's supplications were addressed to nothing better able to hear and answer than the chandelier."

The path would not be altered nor the father's sorrow—not in this life. In the end, Robert pursued a married woman, who divorced her husband to marry him. Depression was not cured by alcohol. They sailed to the Samoan Islands in the South Seas, where Robert died suddenly at age forty-four of a cerebral hemorrhage in 1894.

He wrote that "the sods cover us, and the worm that never dies, the conscience sleeps well at last, [and life is a] pilgrimage from nothing to nowhere."

A son is not a father's only life investment, but there is none like it, and when it fails, there is no sorrow like this sorrow.*

Four years after the death of Robert Louis Stevenson, another literary giant, C. S. Lewis, was born. His story of unbelief has a happier ending, but his relationship with his father was especially painful for his father, Albert.

His mother, Florence, had died of cancer when Lewis was nine. His father did not remarry. There were ample defects on both sides, father and son. But the wounding by the son was more conscious and almost brutal.

By the time Lewis was twenty, he was, to his father's dismay, an avowed atheist and probably in a sexual affair with a woman old enough to be his mother. He was also living off his father's money at Oxford University and lying to him about it all.

Albert wrote in his journal about the breakdown in his relationship with his younger son, and one explosive encounter in particular when he discovered that the young man had lied to him about his bank account:

He said he had no respect for me—nor confidence in me....
That all my love and devotion and self-sacrifice should have come to this—that he doesn't respect me. That he doesn't trust me.... I

---

* My biographical sources in this meditation are Iain Murray, *The Undercover Revolution: How Fiction Changed Britain* (Edinburgh: Banner of Truth, 2009), and Alan Jacobs, *The Narnian: The Life and Imagination of C. S. Lewis* (New York: HarperCollins, 2006).

have during the past four weeks passed through one of the most miserable periods of my life—in many respects the most miserable.... The loss of Jack's affection, if it be permanent, is irreparable and leaves me very miserable and heart sore.

Albert dared mention this pain a few months later in a letter to his son and received back a remorseless response in which the son explained how his previous bluntness was beneficial:

As regards the other matter of which you spoke in your letters.... I am sure you will agree with me that the confidence and affection which we both desire are more likely to be restored by honest effort on both sides and toleration—such as is always necessary between imperfect human creatures—than by any answer of mine which was not perfectly sincere.

We see some truth there but no contrition.

Amazingly, both Stevenson's and Lewis's fathers kept on sending stipends to their sons through the years of rejection. In spite of words like "I am simply incapable of cohabiting any house with my father" (Stevenson) and "I really can't face him" (Lewis), the fathers kept supporting their sons.

Six years after his father's death, Lewis wrote to a friend to catch him up on the last decade: "My father is dead.... I have deep regrets about all my relations with my father (but thank God they were best at the end). I am going bald. I am a Christian."

Perhaps sending money through the broken years was the right thing to do. Perhaps not. What it shows is not approval nor that the sorrow had disappeared. Rather, it reveals a kind of bond between fathers and sons that is the foundation of pain, not its removal.

17

If You Can Be Godly and Wrong, Does Truth Matter?

Reflections on Right Doctrine and Right Doing

Since there are some Arminians who are more godly than some Calvinists and some Calvinists who are more godly than some Arminians, what is the correlation between true knowledge of God and godliness? The same could be asked of different groups representing other doctrinal differences.

The best of both groups have historically admired the godliness of those in the other group. Whitefield, the Calvinist, said of Wesley, the Arminian, "Mr. Wesley, I think, is wrong in some things; yet I believe...Mr. Wesley, and others, with whom we do not agree in all things, will shine bright in glory."*

But the sad thing about our day, unlike the days of Whitefield and Wesley, is that many infer from this that knowing God with greater truth and fullness is not important, since it doesn't appear to be decisive in what produces godliness. But those who know what the Bible says will be protected from that mistake.

Paul correlates knowing and doing in a way that shows that knowing profoundly influences doing. Fourteen times Paul implies that our sinful behavior would be different if we knew the truth more fully. For example:

---

* Iain Murray, *Wesley and the Men Who Followed* (Edinburgh: Banner of Truth, 2003), 71.

- "You yourselves wrong and defraud—even your own brothers! *Or do you not know* that the unrighteous will not inherit the kingdom of God?" (1 Corinthians 6:8–9).
- "Flee from sexual immorality.… *Or do you not know* that your body is a temple of the Holy Spirit?" (1 Corinthians 6:18–19).
- "Each one of you [should] know how to control his own body in holiness and honor, not in the passion of lust like the Gentiles *who do not know God*" (1 Thessalonians 4:4–5).

All godliness is owing to truth, that is, to God as he is truly known. Truth, known with the mind and loved with the heart, is the way God produces all godliness. "You will know the truth, and the truth will set you free" (John 8:32).

When a godlier person believes something erroneous about God, among other true things, it is not the error that God uses to produce the godliness. And when a less godly person believes something true about God, among other false things, it is not the truth that his sin uses to produce the ungodliness.

There are various reasons why a person with a more true view of God may be less godly, and the person with a less true view of God may be more godly:

1. The person with a less true view of God may nevertheless be more submissive and more powerfully influenced by the smaller amount of truth that he has, and the person with more truth may be less submissive and less influenced by the truth he has. The Holy Spirit (the Spirit of truth) always makes truth an instrument in his sanctifying influences, but he does not always do it in proportion to the amount of truth present in the mind.

   God's revealed will is that we grow in the knowledge of Christ (2 Peter 3:18), because in that way the Spirit can make our holiness the manifest fruit of what we know of Christ, so that Christ is more clearly honored (John 16:14). But the Spirit is free to make little knowledge produce much holiness, lest those with much knowledge be proud.

2. Two persons with radically different personalities and backgrounds may have more or fewer obstacles to overcome in the process of sanctification. Therefore, the one with fewer obstacles may respond in godly ways to less truth, while the one with more obstacles may struggle more, even though he has more truth.

3. A person with much truth may lag behind in godliness because there are hindrances that arise between the truth in the mind and the response of the heart to that truth. These hindrances may include loss of memory; ease of distraction; blind spots that keep a person from seeing how a truth applies to a long-held pattern of behavior; mental disorders (mild or profound) that create disconnects between thoughts and volitions; confusion and ignorance about the way sanctification is meant to work; or hidden rebellion of the heart that covers itself with a veneer of orthodoxy.

Therefore, let us humble ourselves. There are clouded views that are so obscured by error that the God on the other side of the unclear glass is not the true God. So the measure of truth in our views matters infinitely. But also, there is no guarantee that right thinking will produce right living. There is more to godliness than having clear views of God. Trusting him and loving him through those views matters decisively.

18

WHEN DOES GOD BECOME 100 PERCENT FOR US?

Were the Elect Ever Children of Wrath?

What the Bible teaches is that God becomes 100 percent irrevocably for us at the moment of justification, that is, the moment when we see Christ as a beautiful Savior and receive him as our substitute punishment and our substitute perfection. All of God's wrath, all of the condemnation we deserve, was poured out on Jesus. All of God's demands for perfect righteousness were fulfilled by Christ. The moment we see (by grace!) this Treasure and receive him in this way, his death counts as our death and his condemnation as our condemnation and his righteousness as our righteousness, and God becomes 100 percent irrevocably for us forever in that instant.

The question this leaves unanswered is, "Doesn't the Bible teach that in eternity God set his favor on us in election?" In other words, thoughtful people ask, "Did God become 100 percent for us only in the moment of faith and union with Christ and justification? Did he not become 100 percent for us in the act of election before the foundation of the world?" For example, Paul said, "[God] chose us in [Jesus] before the foundation of the world, that we should be holy and blameless before him. In love he predestined us for adoption as sons through Jesus Christ" (Ephesians 1:4–5).

Is God, then, not 100 percent for the elect from eternity? The answer hangs on the meaning of "100 percent." With the term "100 percent," I am trying to preserve a biblical truth found in several passages of Scripture. For example, in Ephesians 2:3, Paul said that Christians were "children of wrath" before they were made alive in Christ Jesus. "We all once lived [among the sons of disobedience] in the passions of our flesh, carrying out the desires of the body and the mind, and were by nature children of wrath, like the rest of mankind."

So Paul is saying that before regeneration God's wrath was on us. The elect were under wrath. This changed when God made us alive in Christ Jesus and awakened us to see the truth and beauty of Christ so that we received him as the One who died for us and as the One whose righteousness is counted as ours because of our union with Jesus. Before this happened to us, we were under God's wrath. Then, because of faith in Christ and union with him, all God's wrath was removed and he then became, in that sense, 100 percent for us.

Similarly in Romans 8:1, there is the crucial word *now*. "There is therefore *now* no condemnation for those who are in Christ Jesus." The implication of "now" is that there was once condemnation over us and now there is not. A real change in God's disposition toward us happened in the moment of our regeneration and faith and union with Christ and justification.

Notice the phrase "in Christ" at the end of this passage: "There is therefore now no condemnation for those who are *in Christ Jesus*" (Romans 8:1). This is why God's disposition toward us is different when we believe in Christ. When we believe in Christ, we are united to him— that is, we are "in Christ." This means that his death counts as our death and his righteousness counts as our righteousness. This is why there is *now* no condemnation, whereas before there was. Before Christ bore the curse of the law and we were united to him by faith, we were under the curse of the law. "Christ redeemed us from the curse of the law by becoming a curse for us" (Galatians 3:13).

When Paul used the language of God being "for us," it was in the context of what Christ has done for us in history. For example, Romans 8:31–32 says, "If God is for us, who can be against us? He who did not spare his own Son but gave him up for us all, how will he not also with him graciously give us all things?" Not sparing his Son is the act that secures God's being 100 percent for us forever.

So was God 100 percent for us from eternity because we were elect? Consider this analogy. Before justification, the elect were under the "sentence" of God's wrath but not the actual experience of its outpouring. For the elect to be born "children of wrath" (Ephesians 2:3) and to be "condemned already" (John 3:18) prior to conversion does not mean that the elect were enduring the *actual* wrath of God that is equivalent to what the nonelect experience in hell. It means that the *sentence* of God's wrath still hung over them.

So there is a real sense we can indeed say that God was 100 percent for the elect before we were justified. He was 100 percent certain that the sentence that hung over us would not be executed. He was 100 percent certain that he would bring us to faith and save us.

But when I ask, when did God become 100 percent for us? I mean more than, when did it become 100 percent certain that God would save us? I mean, when did it happen that God was for us and *only* for us? That is, when did it happen that the only disposition of God toward us was mercy? Or, when did God become for us so fully that there was not any wrath or curse or condemnation on us, but only mercy?

The answer, I still say, is at the point when, by grace, we saw Christ as a supremely valuable Savior and received him as our substitute sacrifice and substitute righteousness. In other words, it happened at the point of justification. The implication of this is that all our works, all our perseverance, all our continuing faith and obedience does not cause God to be 100 percent for us, but is the *result* of his being 100 percent for us. This is a hugely important distinction for your own soul, and how you press on in the fight of faith. As Paul said, "I press on to make it my own, *because* Christ Jesus has made me his own" (Philippians 3:12)—100 percent his own.

Paul's logic in Romans 8:32 is that because God gave his Son to die for us, therefore he will give us all things with him. That is, God will see to it that we persevere to the end, not only because we are elect, but because Christ died for us and we are in Christ. That is the logic of 1 Corinthians 1:8–9: "[God] will sustain you to the end, guiltless in the day of our Lord Jesus Christ. God is faithful, *by whom you were called* into the fellowship of his Son, Jesus Christ our Lord." The call is mentioned as the ground of God's faithfulness to sustain us to the end.

Therefore, exult in the truth that God will keep you. He will get you to the end because in Christ he is 100 percent for you. And therefore, getting to the end does not make God to be 100 percent for you. It is the effect of the fact that he is already totally for you.

19

FEEDING MY SOUL IN FOUR PARTS OF THE BIBLE

A Glimpse of My Morning Strolls in God's Garden

I hope you are reading your Bible steadily throughout the year. I hope you don't miss a day. The blessed person whose life is like a tree planted by streams of water savors the Word of God every day. "On his law he meditates day and night" (Psalm 1:2). I pray that there are times when it tastes so good, you slow down and steep your heart in it. Here is what often happens when you set your face like flint to see and savor God in his Word every day.

I was reading in four parts of the Bible, not for any ministry preparation but just to feed my soul. In every text, another text came to mind that made each clearer. And that blew some fog away so I could see and enjoy God more fully. So this meditation is not unified by a theme. It's a glimpse of what happens often in my morning stroll through the beautiful and nourishing garden of God's Word. Come with me to four very different parts of the garden.

1. Why did Saul die?

- "Saul took his own sword and fell upon it" (1 Chronicles 10:4).
- "So Saul died for his breach of faith. He broke faith with the LORD in that he did not keep the command of the LORD, and also consulted a medium" (1 Chronicles 10:13).
- "The LORD put him to death" (1 Chronicles 10:14).

One reason Saul died is that he committed suicide. Another is that he broke faith with the Lord much earlier. Another is that God put him to death. None of these excludes the others. To say God is the decisive actor does not mean Saul did not act. To say there are physical causes for a death (suicide) does not mean there were not moral causes (unfaithfulness).

To say that Saul brought his demise on himself (by unfaithfulness and suicide) does not mean God did not bring it on him. We would be unfaithful to Scripture if all we said was that the reason Saul died was the natural consequence of his own behavior. We must also say, "The LORD put him to death."

There was real punishment, not just impersonal, natural consequences. God is personal. God put him to death. There was punishment by a judge and executioner. There was wrath. The Bible is designed to make sure we do not turn death and hell into impersonal consequences. "The LORD put him to death."

Therefore, I was sobered as I read. I trembled in my spirit. I bowed to God's right and authority to give and take life. I reverenced him. Blessed be the name of the Lord.

2. Who will benefit from promises made to David?

- "I will make a horn to sprout for David; I have prepared a lamp for my anointed. His enemies I will clothe with shame, but on him his crown will shine" (Psalm 132:17–18).
- "Come, everyone who thirsts, come to the waters; and he who has no money, come, buy and eat!… And I will make with you an everlasting covenant, my steadfast, sure love for David" (Isaiah 55:1, 3).

Whoever comes to God through Jesus Christ, his Son, thirsting for what he is, rather than depending on who we are or what we do, God will make with that one a covenant.

What covenant? A covenant defined and secured by God's "sure love for David." I take that to mean that I am included in the Davidic covenant. What David gets I will get in Christ Jesus.

And what does that include? A horn will sprout for me. That is, great strength will fight for me and protect me. There will be a God-prepared lamp for me. So light will surround me and darkness will not overcome me. There will be a crown for me—I will reign with the Son of David and sit with him on his throne. "The one who conquers, I will grant him to sit with me on my throne" (Revelation 3:21).

It is an astonishing thing that I will benefit from the promises made to David. God means for me to be astonished. He means for me to leave my devotions astonished at the power and authority and surety with which I am loved by God.

3. Do everything in the name of Jesus.
- "Whatever you do, in word or deed, do everything in the name of the Lord Jesus" (Colossians 3:17).
- "The seventy-two returned with joy, saying, 'Lord, even the demons are subject to us in your name!'" (Luke 10:17).

Do everything with a sense of dependence on the power and authority of the Lord Jesus. Do everything with a view to Jesus being honored in it. Do everything with a view to others being helped by Jesus in it. These two passages speak of the pervasiveness (everything, Colossians 3:17) and the power (subjected demons, Luke 10:17) of the name of Jesus in the life of an obedient Christian. Let it be that pervasive, and let it bring that much power.

4. Who forgives whom first?
- "Forgive us our sins, for we ourselves forgive everyone who is indebted to us" (Luke 11:4).
- "As the Lord has forgiven you, so you also must forgive" (Colossians 3:13).

When Jesus teaches us to pray that God forgive us "for we ourselves forgive," he is not saying that the first move in forgiveness is our move. Rather it goes like this: God forgave us when we believed in Christ (Acts 10:43). Then, from this broken, joyful, grateful, hopeful, experience of being forgiven, we offer forgiveness to others. This signifies that we have been "savingly" forgiven. That is, our forgiving others shows that we have faith; we are united to Christ; we are indwelt by the Spirit.

But we still sin (1 John 1:8, 10). So we still turn to God for fresh applications of the work of Christ on our behalf, fresh applications of forgiveness. We cannot do this with any confidence if we are harboring an unforgiving spirit (Matthew, 18:23–35). That's why Jesus says we ask for forgiveness because we are forgiving. This is like saying: "Father, continue to extend to me the mercies purchased by Christ because by these mercies I forsake vengeance and extend to others what you have extended to me."

Oh, how sweet is the Word of God! I looked out my window into the bright morning and said, *"I love you, God. I love you, Lord Jesus. I love your Word. Oh, what a privilege to know you and to have your Word. Please keep me faithful to it. In Jesus' name. Amen."*

20

GLEANING TRUTH FROM
G. K. CHESTERTON

How a Roman Catholic Can Serve
Today's Happy Calvinists

G. K. Chesterton was a British journalist and a brilliant writer. Nobody exploits the power of paradox like Chesterton. I heartily recommend his book *Orthodoxy*.

The title gives scarcely a clue as to what you will find inside. It had a huge influence on me forty years ago in ways that would have exasperated Chesterton. He did all he could to keep me from becoming a Calvinist, and instead made me a romantic one—a happy one.

If I thought his broadsides against predestination really hit home and undid true biblical doctrine, I would keep my mouth shut or change my worldview. But his celebration of poetry and paradox undermines his own abomination of the greatest truth-and-mystery-lovers around today, the happy Calvinists.

Nothing in this Calvinism-abominating book came close to keeping me from embracing the glorious sovereignty of God. On the contrary, the poetic brightness of the book, along with the works of C. S. Lewis, awakened in me an exuberance about the strangeness of all things, which in the end made me able to embrace the imponderable paradoxes of God's decisive control of all things and the total justice of his holding us accountable.

One of the reasons that Calvinism is stirring today is that it takes both truth and mystery seriously. It's a singing, poetry-writing, running-through-the-fields Calvinism.

It's the Arminians who are the rationalists. Arminianism trumps biblical sentences with metaphysics: God can't control all things and hold us responsible. God can't choose some and love all. Why? Metaphysics. Out with mystery! It just can't be!

So Chesterton's anti-Calvinist shotgun sprays all around today's poet-Calvinist and misses the mark.

Read *Orthodoxy.*

A few of you may be swept away into the folly of Roman Catholic sacramentalism. A few others may be confirmed in your tiff with joyless Calvinists. But for many readers, especially the Bible-saturated ones, this book will awaken such a sense of wonder in you that you will not feel at home again until you enter the new world of the wide-eyed children called the happy Reformed.

Here is a flavor of what to expect in *Orthodoxy:**

- "[This book] recounts my elephantine adventures in pursuit of the obvious." (12)
- "It is one thing to describe an interview with a…creature that does not exist. It is another thing to discover that the rhinoceros does exist and then take pleasure in the fact that he looks as if he didn't." (11)
- "Exactly what does breed insanity is reason. Poets do not go mad; but chess-players do. Mathematicians go mad, and cashiers; but creative artists very seldom." (17)
- "Only one great English poet went mad, Cowper. And he was definitely driven mad by logic, by the ugly and alien logic of predestination. Poetry was not the disease but the medicine.… He was damned by John Calvin." (17)

---

* Page numbers are from my 1959 edition by Doubleday and Co., Garden City, New York.

- "The poet only desires exaltation and expansion, a world to stretch himself in. The poet only asks to get his head into the heavens. It is the logician who seeks to get the heavens into his head. And it is his head that splits." (17)
- "The madman is not the man who has lost his reason. The madman is the man who has lost everything but his reason." (19)
- "Mysticism keeps men sane. As long as you have mystery you have health. When you destroy mystery you create morbidity." (28)
- "The ordinary man...has always cared more for truth than for consistency. If he saw two truths that seemed to contradict each other, he would take the two truths and the contradictions along with them." (28)
- "When we are very young children we do not need fairy tales: we only need tales. Mere life is interesting enough. A child of seven is excited by being told that Tommy opened the door and saw a dragon. But a child of three is excited by being told that Tommy opened a door." (54)
- "Man is more himself, man is more manlike, when joy is the fundamental thing in him, and grief the superficial. Melancholy should be an innocent interlude, a tender and fugitive frame of mind; praise should be the permanent pulsation of the soul. Pessimism is at best an emotional half-holiday; joy is the uproarious labor by which all things live." (159)
- "Tradition means giving votes to the most obscure of all classes, our ancestors. It is the democracy of the dead. Tradition refuses to submit to the small and arrogant oligarchy of those who merely happen to be walking about." (48)

How can I not give thanks for this jolly Catholic whose only cranky side seemed to be his clouded views of happy Calvinists!

21

WHAT'S THE PLACE OF
CONFRONTATION IN MARRIAGE?

Guidance from Ephesians 5:25–27

Sometimes I finish sermons in articles and books. This is one of those finishings. I preached a sermon originally titled "Marriage: Confronting, Forgiving, Forbearing." In the end, I struck the word confronting—not because it shouldn't happen, but because I had no time. So this is what I would have said if there had been time.

Focusing on forgiving and forbearing might give the impression that none of our sinful traits or annoying idiosyncrasies ever changes. All you do is forgive and forbear. But that's not true. God gives grace, not only to forgive and to forbear, but also to change, so that less forgiving and forbearing are needed. That too is a gift of grace. Grace is not just power to return good for evil but also power to do less evil—even power to be less bothersome.

But I have approached this by putting the emphasis on forgiveness and forbearance first, not on change. The reason is because gracious forgiveness and forbearance are the rock-solid foundation on which the call for change can be heard with hope and security rather than fear and a sense of being threatened. Only when a wife or husband feels that the other is totally committed—even if he or she doesn't change—can the call for change feel like grace rather than an ultimatum.

So a message on forgiveness and forbearance came first. But now I am emphasizing that marriage should not be—and, God willing, need not be—a static stretch of time inhabited by changeless personalities in persistent conflict. Even that is better than divorce in God's eyes and has a glory of its own. But it is not the best picture of Christ and the church. The durability of the relationship, in spite of conflict, tells the truth about Christ and the church. The unwillingness to change does not.

In Christ's relationship to the church, he is clearly seeking the transformation of his bride into something morally and spiritually beautiful. This is plain in Ephesians 5:25–27.

> Husbands, love your wives, as Christ loved the church and gave
> himself up for her, that he might sanctify her, having cleansed her
> by the washing of water with the word, so that he might present
> the church to himself in splendor, without spot or wrinkle or any
> such thing, that she might be holy and without blemish.

This implies that the husband, who is to love like Christ, bears a unique responsibility for the moral and spiritual growth of his wife, which means that over time she will change.

If a husband is loving and wise, this will feel, to a humble wife, like she is being served, not humiliated. Christ died to purify his bride. Moreover, Christ not only died to sanctify his bride, he goes on speaking to her in his Word with a view to applying his sacrifice to her for her transformation. Similarly, the wise and loving husband seeks to speak in a way that brings his wife more and more into conformity to Christ.

Submission does not mean that a wife cannot seek the transformation of her husband, even while respecting him as her head: her leader, protector, and provider. There are several reasons I say this. One is that prayer is something that the church does toward God through Christ with a view to asking him to do things a certain way. If we are sick, we ask him for healing. If we are hungry, we ask for our daily bread. If we are lost, we ask for direction. And so on. Since we believe in the absolute sovereignty of Christ to govern all things, this means that we look at the present situation that he has ordained, and we ask him to change it. That's what prayer is. And it's not inconsistent with Christ's sovereignty.

Prayer is only an analogy to what the wife does toward her husband. We never "confront" Jesus with his imperfection and seek his change. He has no imperfections. But we do seek from him changes in the situation he has brought about, because it may well be his will to change them. That is what petitionary prayer is. So wives, in this analogy, will ask their husbands that some things be changed in the way he is doing things.

But the main reason we can say that wives should seek their husbands' transformation is that husbands are only similar to Christ in the relationship with their wives. They are not Christ. And one of the main differences is that husbands need to change and Christ doesn't. When Paul said, "The husband is the head of the wife even *as* Christ is the head of the church" (Ephesians 5:23), the word *as* does not mean that husbands are identical to Christ in authority or perfection or wisdom or grace or in any other way. They are not "equal to" Christ; they are "as" Christ. They are, unlike Christ, sinful and finite and fallible. They need to change.

Wives are not only submissive wives; they are also loving sisters. There is a unique way for a submissive wife to be a caring sister toward her imperfect brother-husband. She will, from time to time, follow Galatians 6:1 in his case: "If anyone is caught in any transgression, you who are spiritual should restore him in a spirit of gentleness." She will do that for him.

Both of them will obey Matthew 18:15 as necessary and will do so in the unique demeanor and context called for by headship and submission: "If your brother sins against you, go and tell him his fault, between you and him alone."

So from these and other observations that could be made from the New Testament, I hope it is clear that a faithful, covenant-keeping marriage is not merely forgiving and forbearing. It is also confronting—in loving and wise ways formed by the calling of headship and submission. To see how I worked all this out more fully, the sermon series actually made its way into a book called *This Momentary Marriage: A Parable of Permanence.*

22

CHANGED LIVES IN JESUS' NEW LIFE

Radical Effects of the Resurrection

> *If in Christ we have hope in this life only, we are of all people most to be pitied.... Why are we in danger every hour?*
>
> —1 CORINTHIANS 15:19, 30

> *I protest, brothers, by my pride in you, which I have in Christ Jesus our Lord, I die every day! What do I gain if, humanly speaking, I fought with beasts at Ephesus? If the dead are not raised, "Let us eat and drink, for tomorrow we die."*
>
> —1 CORINTHIANS 15:31–32

> *But in fact Christ has been raised from the dead, the firstfruits of those who have fallen asleep.*
>
> —1 CORINTHIANS 15:20

Paul pondered how he would assess his lifestyle if there were no resurrection from the dead. He said it would be ridiculous—pitiable (1 Corinthians 15:19). The resurrection guided and empowered him to do things that would be ludicrous without the hope of resurrection.

For example, Paul looked at all the dangers he willingly faced. He said they come "every hour" (v. 30).

On frequent journeys, in *danger* from rivers, *danger* from robbers, *danger* from my own people, *danger* from Gentiles, *danger* in the city, *danger* in the wilderness, *danger* at sea, *danger* from false brothers. (2 Corinthians 11:26)

Then he considered the extent of his self-denial and said, "I die every day!" (1 Corinthians 15:31). This is Paul's experience of what Jesus said in Luke 9:23, "If anyone would come after me, let him deny himself and take up his cross daily and follow me." I take this to mean that there was something pleasant that Paul had to put to death every day. No day was without the death of some desire.

With far greater labors, far more imprisonments, with countless beatings, and often near death. Five times I received at the hands of the Jews the forty lashes less one. Three times I was beaten with rods. Once I was stoned. Three times I was shipwrecked; a night and a day I was adrift at sea;... in toil and hardship, through many a sleepless night, in hunger and thirst, often without food, in cold and exposure. And, apart from other things, there is the daily pressure on me of my anxiety for all the churches. (2 Corinthians 11:23–28)

Then he recalled that he "fought with beasts at Ephesus" (1 Corinthians 15:32). We don't know what he is referring to. A certain kind of opponent to the gospel is called a beast in 2 Peter 2:12 and Jude 10. In any case, it was utterly disheartening. "We do not want you to be unaware, brothers, of the affliction we experienced in Asia. For we were so utterly burdened beyond our strength that we despaired of life itself" (2 Corinthians 1:8).

So Paul concluded from his hourly danger and his daily dying and his fighting with beasts that the life he had chosen in following Jesus was foolish and pitiable if he would not be raised from the dead: "If in

Christ we have hope in this life only, we are of all people most to be pitied" (1 Corinthians 15:19). In other words, only the resurrection with Christ and the joys of eternity can make sense out of this voluntary suffering.

If death were the end of the matter, he said, "Let us eat and drink, for tomorrow we die" (1 Corinthians 15:32). This doesn't mean let's all become gluttons and drunkards. They are pitiable too, with or without the resurrection. He means if there is no resurrection, what makes sense is middle-class moderation to maximize earthly pleasures.

But that is not what Paul chose. He chose suffering, because he chose obedience. When Ananias came to him at his conversion with the words from the Lord Jesus, "I will show him how much he must suffer for the sake of my name" (Acts 9:16), Paul accepted this as part of his calling. Suffer he must.

How could Paul do it? What was the source of this radical obedience? The answer is this: "In fact Christ has been raised from the dead, the firstfruits of those who have fallen asleep" (1 Corinthians 15:20). In other words, Christ was raised, and Paul will be raised with him. Therefore, nothing suffered for Jesus is in vain (1 Corinthians 15:58).

The hope of the resurrection radically changed the way Paul lived. It freed him from materialism and consumerism. It gave him the power to go without things that many people feel they must have in this life. For example, though he had the right to marry (1 Corinthians 9:5), he renounced that pleasure because he was called to bear so much suffering. This he did because of the resurrection.

This is the way Jesus said the hope of the resurrection is supposed to change our behavior. For example, he told us to invite to our homes people who cannot pay us back in this life. How are we to be motivated to do this? Jesus said, "You will be repaid at the resurrection of the just" (Luke 14:14).

This is a radical call for us to look hard at our present lives to see if they are shaped by the hope of the resurrection. Do we make decisions on the basis of gain in this world or gain in the next? Do we take risks for love's sake that can only be explained as wise if there is a resurrection?

Do we lose heart when our bodies give way to the aging process and we have to admit that we will never do certain things again? Or do we look to the resurrection and take heart?

> We do not lose heart. Though our outer self is wasting away, our inner self is being renewed day by day. For this light momentary affliction is preparing for us an eternal weight of glory beyond all comparison. (2 Corinthians 4:16–17)

May God give us the grace to rededicate ourselves to a lifetime of letting the resurrection have its radical effects.

23

How God Teaches the Deep Things of His Word

A Meditation on Psalm 119:65–72

> You have dealt well with your servant,
>> O LORD, according to your word.
> Teach me good judgment and knowledge,
>> for I believe in your commandments.
> Before I was afflicted I went astray,
>> but now I keep your word.
> You are good and do good;
>> teach me your statutes.
> The insolent smear me with lies,
>> but with my whole heart I keep your precepts;
> their heart is unfeeling like fat,
>> but I delight in your law.
> It is good for me that I was afflicted,
>> that I might learn your statutes.
> The law of your mouth is better to me
>> than thousands of gold and silver pieces.
>
> —PSALM 119:65–72

The reason Psalm 119 has 176 verses is that the Hebrew alphabet has twenty-two letters. The psalmist exults in the multifaceted preciousness of God's Word by taking each letter of the alphabet and writing eight verses of exultation, each verse beginning with that letter. It's like saying: "The Word of God is precious in every way from A to Z—beyond perfection." Eight is one more than seven, the number of completeness and perfection.

Ordinarily, in each group of eight verses, the psalmist uses mostly different words that start with the letter for that section of the acrostic. For example, the verses beginning with the letter *heth* (vv. 57–64) use eight different words beginning with that letter. But verses 65–72, which start with the Hebrew letter *teth,* stand out, because they begin with the same word five times—the word *good (tov).* This makes us sit up and take notice.

Something really good is being emphasized. What is the good the psalmist wants us to see?

Here is my translation in awkward English that lets you see the prominence of the word *good.*

Verse 65: Good *(tov)* you did, Yahweh, with your servant according to your word.

Verse 66: Good *(tov)* discernment and knowledge teach me, because in your commandments I trust.

Verse 67: Before I was afflicted I erred, but now I keep your word.

Verse 68: Good *(tov)* you are, and you cause good to happen. Teach me your statutes.

Verse 69: Smear upon me lies—so do the proud—but I, with all my heart, watch your precepts.

Verse 70: Gross like fat is their heart. I delight in your instruction.

Verse 71: Good for me *(tov li)*. I was afflicted so that I might learn your statutes.

Verse 72: Good for me *(tov li)* is the instruction of your mouth, more than thousands of gold and silver pieces.

These are not random comments about what is good. They are connected, and a specific good is in mind.

Verse 65 says that God did something good: Good you did, Yahweh, with your servant according to your word. The good he did accords with his word. That means God's Word is designed for our good and that what God does to help us go deep with his Word is good. What did he do that makes the psalmist write this?

In verse 66 the psalmist prays that God would give him good discernment *because he trusts in God's commandments.* That means God does not bless with discernment a negative attitude toward his word. If we trust that his words are the best counsel in the world, he will give us discernment when we ask.

So the psalmist pleads for a mind and heart that penetrates deep into the Word of God and becomes spiritually discerning for all the hundreds of situations that are not addressed directly by the Bible. So he prays—and we should pray—*God, do whatever you must do to teach me your Word.*

Verse 67 tells us what God did to answer this prayer for biblical discernment: "Before I was afflicted I went astray, but now I keep your word." God sent affliction. And this affliction was a profound teacher. It moved the psalmist into deeper obedience: Now—after the affliction—"I keep your word." We see not only obedience but also understanding.

Verse 71: Good it was for me that I was afflicted, so that I might learn your statutes. Affliction brought learning. This is the discernment he had prayed for.

So the good that God did (v. 65) was Bible-illuming, discernment-giving, obedience-producing affliction. What was the affliction? It was slander from spiritually hardened adversaries.

Verse 69: The proud smear me with lies, but I with all my heart watch your precepts.

This is the good the psalmist wants us to see.

Verse 68: Good you are, and you cause good to happen. The good is the affliction that brings about understanding, discernment, and obedience. Good it was for me that I was afflicted, so that I might learn your statutes (v. 71).

How can he call affliction *good*? It's because in his value-scheme, penetrating insight into God's Word is more valuable than thousands of gold and silver pieces—or freedom from affliction.

Verse 72: Good to me is the instruction of your mouth, more than thousands of gold and silver pieces. If God and his word are your highest values—your greatest desires—then whatever helps you know them and experience them deeply will be good—not easy, and maybe not even morally right (like slander from your adversaries), but good in the sense that God ordains it to give you what is absolutely best—the illumining effect of God's infinitely valuable word.

In Martin Luther's meditation on these verses he said that trials (*Anfechtungen*) were one of his best teachers:

> I want you to know how to study theology in the right way. I
> have practiced this method myself.... Here you will find three
> rules. They are frequently proposed throughout Psalm [119]
> and run thus: *Oratio, meditatio, tentatio* (Prayer, meditation,
> trial).... [Trials] teach you not only to know and understand
> but also to experience how right, how true, how sweet, how
> lovely, how mighty, how comforting God's word is: it is wisdom
> supreme.
>
> As soon as God's word becomes known through you, the
> devil will afflict you...and will teach you by his temptations to
> seek and to love God's word. For I myself...owe my papists many
> thanks for so beating, pressing, and frightening me through the
> devil's raging that they have turned me into a fairly good theolo-
> gian, driving me to a goal I should never have reached.*

---

* Martin Luther, *What Luther Says: An Anthology*, compiler Ewald M. Plass (St. Louis: Concordia, 1986) 1359–60.

Lord, incline our hearts to your Word and not to gold and silver. Make us cherish your Word so much that we embrace whatever it takes to give us understanding and good discernment and faithful obedience.

And when it comes, give us the grace to say, "Good you are, and you cause good to happen."

24

How Shall We Love Our Muslim Neighbor?

Winning Them to Jesus by Echoing His Love

There are as many answers to the question, "How shall we love our Muslim neighbor?" as there are ways to do good and not wrong. "Love does no wrong to a neighbor" (Romans 13:10). "Love bears all things, believes all things, hopes all things, endures all things" (1 Corinthians 13:7). Below I give nine ways of loving Muslims that I think need to be emphasized in our day.

No human beings are excluded from the love of Christians—not the closest friend and not the worst enemy. "Love your enemies and pray for those who persecute you" (Matthew 5:44). The mention of loving our enemies is not meant to imply that all Muslims feel or act with enmity toward Christians. They don't. They are often hospitable and kind and caring. The point is, even when someone treats us with enmity (of whatever religion or nonreligion), we should continue loving. So when I refer to loving our enemies in the points below, keep in mind that I do so not to imply all Muslims are our enemies but to make sure that none is excluded.

Another clarification is needed in our contemporary context. When I say in what follows that love calls us to do good in practical ways that meet physical needs, I do not mean that this help is offered contingent on Muslims becoming Christians. To be sure, every act of love, no matter how practical, longs for the eternal good of the one being loved. We always aim for the salvation of the people we love, no matter what we are doing for them. But we don't stop loving if they are unresponsive. Practical love is a witness to the love of Christ. Witness is not withheld where it is needed most. Conversions coerced by force or finances contradict the very nature of saving faith. Saving faith is a free embrace of Jesus as our Savior, Lord, and highest Treasure. He is not a mere means to treasure. He is the Treasure.

Here is how we can extend ourselves in love toward Muslim people.

1. Pray the fullest blessing of Christ on them whether they love you or not.

- "Bless those who curse you, pray for those who abuse you" (Luke 6:28).
- "Bless those who persecute you; bless and do not curse them" (Romans 12:14).
- "When reviled, we bless" (1 Corinthians 4:12).

2. Do good to them in practical ways that meet their physical needs.

- "Love your enemies, do good to those who hate you" (Luke 6:27).
- "As you wish that others would do to you, do so to them" (Luke 6:31).
- "See that no one repays anyone evil for evil, but always seek to do good to one another and to everyone" (1 Thessalonians 5:15).
- "If your enemy is hungry, feed him; if he is thirsty, give him something to drink; for by so doing you will heap burning coals on his head" (Romans 12:20).

3. Do not retaliate when you're personally wronged.

- "Do not repay evil for evil or reviling for reviling, but on the contrary, bless, for to this you were called, that you may obtain a blessing" (1 Peter 3:9).
- "Repay no one evil for evil.... Beloved, never avenge yourselves, but leave it to the wrath of God, for it is written, 'Vengeance is mine, I will repay, says the Lord'" (Romans 12:17, 19).

4. Live peaceably with them as much as it depends on you.

- "If possible, so far as it depends on you, live peaceably with all" (Romans 12:18).

5. Pursue their joyful freedom from sin and from condemnation by telling them the truth of Christ.

- "Jesus said to the Jews who had believed him, 'If you abide in my word, you are truly my disciples, and you will know the truth, and the truth will set you free'" (John 8:31–32).

6. Earnestly desire that they join you in heaven with the Father by showing them the way, Jesus Christ.

- "Brothers, my heart's desire…for them is that they may be saved" (Romans 10:1).
- "Jesus said to him, 'I am the way, and the truth, and the life. No one comes to the Father except through me'" (John 14:6).
- "Whoever believes in him should not perish but have eternal life" (John 3:16).

7. Seek to comprehend the meaning of what they say, so that your affirmations or criticisms are based on true understanding, not distortion or caricature.

- "[Love] does not rejoice at wrongdoing, but rejoices with the truth" (1 Corinthians 13:6).

8. Warn them with tears that those who do not receive Jesus Christ as the crucified and risen Savior, who takes away the sins of the world, will perish under the wrath of God.

- "To all who did receive him, who believed in his name, he gave the right to become children of God" (John 1:12).
- "If you confess with your mouth that Jesus is Lord and believe in your heart that God raised him from the dead, you will be saved" (Romans 10:9).
- "For many, of whom I have often told you and now tell you even with tears, walk as enemies of the cross of Christ" (Philippians 3:18).

9. Don't mislead them or give them false hope by saying, "Muslims worship the true God."

This statement communicates to almost everybody a positive picture of the Muslim heart knowing, loving, and honoring the true God. But Jesus makes a person's response to himself the litmus test of the authenticity of a person's response to God. And he is explicit that if a person rejects him as the Divine One who gave his life as a ransom for sins and rose again—that person does not know, love, or honor the true God.

- "They said to [Jesus] therefore, 'Where is your Father?' Jesus answered, 'You know neither me nor my Father. If you knew me, you would know my Father also'" (John 8:19).
- "Whoever does not honor the Son does not honor the Father who sent him" (John 5:23).
- "[Jesus said,] 'I know that you do not have the love of God within you. I have come in my Father's name, and you do not receive me'" (John 5:42–43).

We do not mislead Muslims, or those who care about Muslims, by saying that they "know" or "honor" and "love" the true God when they do not receive Jesus for who he really is. We cannot see people's hearts. How do we know if they know and honor and love the true God? We lay down our lives to offer them Jesus. If they receive him, they know and love and honor God. If they don't, they don't. Jesus is the test.

That was Jesus' point when he said, "The one who rejects me rejects him who sent me" (Luke 10:16). And, "Whoever receives me receives him who sent me" (Matthew 10:40). And, "If you believed Moses, you would believe me" (John 5:46).

The most loving thing we can do for Muslims, or anyone else, is to tell them the whole truth about Jesus Christ, in the context of sacrificial care for them and willingness to suffer for them rather than abandon them. And then plead with them to turn away from vain worship (Mark 7:7) and receive Christ as the crucified and risen Savior for the forgiveness of their sins and the hope of eternal life. Our great joy would be to have brothers and sisters from all the Muslim peoples of the world.

25

WHAT LOVE DOES AND DOES NOT DO

An Anniversary Meditation on

1 Corinthians 13:4–7

> *Love is patient and kind; love does not envy or boast; it is*
> *not arrogant or rude. It does not insist on its own way; it is*
> *not irritable or resentful; it does not rejoice at wrongdoing,*
> *but rejoices with the truth. Love bears all things, believes all*
> *things, hopes all things, endures all things.*
>
> —1 CORINTHIANS 13:4–7

Noël and I pondered and prayed over 1 Corinthians 13 on our recent wedding anniversary. As a tradition we pick a portion of Scripture and pray our way through it on our anniversary. We turn it into thanks and praises and requests for ourselves and our family and the church and the world. Mainly, we focus on our own shortcomings with a view to improvement. We seek God's grace and power to turn biblical truth into real life. So this time we focused on 1 Corinthians 13, especially verses 4–7.

What is Paul doing here? He says fifteen things about what love does and does not do. When you ponder the list, it is peculiar. If you come expecting a definition of love, it doesn't work very well. Crucial things seem to be missing. Think about other places where the core of love is defined: John 15:13, "Greater love has no one than this, that someone lay down his life for his friends." First John 4:10, "In this is love...that he loved us and sent his Son to be the propitiation for our sins." Romans 5:8, "God shows his love for us in that while we were still sinners, Christ died for us." At the core of love is a self-sacrificing pursuit of the beloved's greatest good. Love saves. Love rescues. Love helps. And it does so, if necessary, at cost to the lover.

But this core element of helping another person is not the stress in 1 Corinthians 13:4–7. When you try to group the fifteen elements into categories, there are two big ones: (1) statements about how love is durable and doesn't give up, and (2) statements about how love is not proud. Thirteen of the fifteen elements seem to fit into these two categories. Of the remaining two elements, one comes close to the proactive helpfulness (as opposed to reactive patience), namely, "love is kind." The other stresses that love rejoices when truth holds sway. So here is one way to categorize what love is and is not:

Enduring (Not Fragile)
- is patient (long-suffering)
- bears all things
- believes all things
- hopes all things
- endures all things

Humble (Not Proud)
- isn't envious or jealous
- isn't boastful or proud
- isn't arrogant or puffed up
- isn't rude or offensive
- doesn't insist on own way or seek its own
- isn't irritable or easily peeved

- isn't resentful or keep an account of wrongs
- doesn't rejoice at wrongdoing or boast of licentious freedom

Pro-kindness and Truth
- is kind
- rejoices with the truth and glad for the truth to advance

What I conclude from this is that Paul was not trying to define *love* in the abstract. He was laying love as a grid over the messed-up Corinthian church, where he saw all these pride-based negative behaviors and said their attitudes and behaviors were *not* how love acts or feels. They were boasting in men (3:21). They were puffed up, even in wrongdoing (5:1–2). They were unwilling to suffer long and bear all things and so were taking each other to court (6:1–8). They were insisting on their own way in eating meat that caused others to stumble (8:11–12). They were acting in rude or unseemly ways, not wearing the customary head coverings (11:1–16). They were insisting on their own way as they ate their own meal at the Lord's Supper without any regard to others (11:21–22). They were jealous and envious as they compared their spiritual gifts and thought that some were needed and others were not (12:21–22).

In other words, Paul is not defining love. He is applying love to the Corinthians' situation and using it as the criterion for why some of their attitudes and behaviors are unacceptable.

But this is not less useful for us. Noël and I saw immediately how relevant these categories were for us. The first category (endurance) says that wherever there is love there is pain—love *suffers* long *(makrothumia)*, *endures* all things, *bears* all things. This is realism and therefore comforting. If two people, or two thousand people, are in a relationship of love, all will be hurt sooner or later. And all will need to "suffer long" and endure and bear. It struck us as amazing that this was so prominent in Paul's treatment of love. So we prayed hard that we would be good lovers in this way (giving less offense and taking less offense).

Then even more penetrating is the major emphasis on pride. Is it not surprising that the opposite of love in 1 Corinthians 13 is not hate but pride? The main category of what love does not do is "arrogance" (boasting, seeking its own way). So we set ourselves to self-examination and prayer again: *O Lord, reveal and destroy the pride in our lives.*

And of course, even though they are in a small category, the other two elements of love are huge: Be kind. And be happy about the prevailing of truth. So that too is our prayer for our marriage.

I offer Noël and me simply as an example. This is all for your sake. Married or single, you can apply the patterns of love in 1 Corinthians 13 to your situation. May I even be so bold as to ask that you pray for us. As I write this, we have been married for almost forty-five years.

Verses 4–7 of this beautiful love chapter would be a great prayer list for any couple. I am praying for you as I close this chapter. Oh, that we all might never stop growing "in the grace [love!] and knowledge of our Lord and Savior Jesus Christ" (2 Peter 3:18).

26

PUTTING MY DAUGHTER TO BED AFTER THE BRIDGE COLLAPSED

What Do Tragedies Like This Mean for Us?

A t about 6 p.m. on August 1, 2007, the I-35W highway bridge over the Mississippi River in Minneapolis collapsed. The bridge was located within sight of our church. Most of us who ministered at the church crossed this bridge several times a week. Some who were heading home that day had been on the bridge fifteen minutes before it collapsed. Thirteen people died in the collapse. Writing from this distance today, that seems miraculous. It was rush hour and the bridge was full of cars. But that first night we knew little and expected much loss of life.

For our family devotions that evening our appointed reading was Luke 13:1–9. It was not my choice. This is surely no coincidence. I thought, *Oh that all of the Twin Cities, in shock at this major calamity, would hear what Jesus has to say about it from Luke's passage.* People came to Jesus with heart-wrenching news about the slaughter of worshipers by Pilate. Here is what he said:

> There were some present at that very time who told him about
> the Galileans whose blood Pilate had mingled with their sacri-
> fices. And he answered them, "Do you think that these Galileans
> were worse sinners than all the other Galileans, because they suf-
> fered in this way? No, I tell you; but unless you repent, you will

all likewise perish. Or those eighteen on whom the tower in Siloam fell and killed them: do you think that they were worse offenders than all the others who lived in Jerusalem? No, I tell you; but unless you repent, you will all likewise perish." (Luke 13:1–5)

Jesus implied that those who brought him this news thought he would say that those who died deserved to die and that those who didn't die did not deserve to die. That is not what he said. He said everyone deserves to die. And if you and I don't repent, we too will perish. This is a stunning response. It only makes sense from a view of reality that is radically oriented on God.

All of us have sinned against God, not just against man. This is an outrage ten thousand times worse than the collapse of the I-35W bridge. That any human is breathing at this minute on this planet is sheer mercy from God. God makes the sun rise and the rain fall on those who do not treasure him above all else. He causes the heart to beat and the lungs to work for millions of people who deserve his wrath. This is a view of reality that desperately needs to be taught in our churches so that we are prepared for the calamities of the world.

The meaning of that bridge's collapse was that John Piper is a sinner and should repent or forfeit his life forever. That means I should turn from the silly preoccupations of my life and focus my mind's attention and my heart's affection on God and embrace Jesus Christ as my only hope for the forgiveness of my sins and for the hope of eternal life. That is God's message in the collapse of that bridge. This is his most merciful message: there is still time to turn from sin and unbelief and destruction for those of us who live. If we could see the eternal calamity he is offering escape from, we would hear this as the most precious message in the world.

Not long after we saw the news about the bridge, we prayed during our family devotions. Talitha (eleven years old), Noël, and I prayed earnestly for the families affected by the calamity and for the others in our city. Talitha prayed, "Please don't let anyone blame God for this but give thanks that they were saved."

When I sat on her bed and tucked her in and blessed her and sang over her, I said, "You know, Talitha, that was a good prayer, because when people blame God for something, they are angry with him, and they are saying that he has done something wrong. That's what *blame* means: to accuse somebody of wrongdoing. But you and I know that God did not do anything wrong. God always does what is wise. And you and I know that God could have held up that bridge with one hand." Talitha said, "With his pinky." "Yes," I said, "with his pinky, which means that God had a purpose for not holding up that bridge, knowing all that would happen, and he is infinitely wise in all that he wills."

Talitha said, "Maybe he let it fall because he wanted all the people of Minneapolis to fear him." "Yes, Talitha," I said, "I am sure that is one of the reasons God let the bridge fall."

I sang to her the song I always sing:

Come rest your head and nestle gently
And do not fear the dark of night.
Almighty God keeps watch intently,
And guards your life with all his might.
Doubt not his love, nor power to keep,
He never fails, nor does he sleep.

I said, "You know, Talitha, that is true whether you die in a bridge collapse or in a car accident or from cancer or terrorism or old age. God always keeps you, even when you die. So you don't need to be afraid, do you?" "No," she shook her head. I leaned down and kissed her. "Good night. I love you."

That night across the Twin Cities, families were wondering if they would ever kiss a loved one good night again. Some would not. I prayed that they would find Jesus Christ to be their Rock and Refuge in those agonizing hours of uncertainty and loss.

The word *bridge* does not occur in the Bible. There may be two reasons. One is that God doesn't build bridges; he divides seas. The other is that usually his people must pass through the deadly currents of suffering and death, not simply ride over them. "When you pass through the waters, I will be with you; and through the rivers, they shall not overwhelm you" (Isaiah 43:2). They may drown you. But he will be with you in life and death.

> Who shall separate us from the love of Christ? Shall tribulation, or distress, or persecution, or famine, or nakedness, or danger, or sword? As it is written, "For your sake we are being killed all the day long; we are regarded as sheep to be slaughtered." No, in all these things we are more than conquerors through him who loved us. For I am sure that neither death nor life...will be able to separate us from the love of God in Christ Jesus our Lord. (Romans 8:35–39)

Killed all day long. But not separated from Christ. We go through the river, not over it. He went before us, crucified. He came out on the other side. He knows the way through. With him we will make it. That is the message we had that night, and still have, for the precious sinners in the Twin Cities. He died for your sins. He rose again. He saves all who trust him. We die, but because of him, we do not die.

Jesus said, "I am the resurrection and the life. Whoever believes in me, though he die, yet shall he live, and everyone who lives and believes in me shall never die" (John 11:25–26).

Talitha slept peacefully. I looked down on her with great love and thankfulness. But one day she will die. I teach her this. I will not always be there to bless her. But Jesus is alive and is the same yesterday, today, and forever. He will be with her because she trusts him. And she will make it through the river. And you will too, if you trust him. "When you pass through the waters, I will be with you; and through the rivers, they shall not overwhelm you" (Isaiah 43:2).

27

HOW THE CROSS CONQUERS
SATAN'S WORK

*God's Deliverance from God as the Foundation
of God's Deliverance from Satan*

S atan's work is not the chief peril dealt with in the death of Christ. God's wrath is. God is opposed to us in his righteous wrath, and he is for us in his love. Therefore, in his great love, he sends his Son to endure his own wrath against us. In this way, his righteousness is upheld and his love is expressed. His wrath and curse and condemnation of our sin are endured for us by another—a substitute, Jesus Christ. Here are some of the texts that teach this:

- "Whoever believes in the Son has eternal life; whoever does not obey the Son shall not see life, but the *wrath of God* remains on him" (John 3:36).
- "Since...we have now been justified by his blood, much more shall we be saved by him from the *wrath of God*" (Romans 5:9).
- "[We] were by nature *children of wrath....* But God...made us alive together with Christ" (Ephesians 2:3–5).
- "God has not destined us *for wrath,* but to obtain salvation through our Lord Jesus Christ who died for us" (1 Thessalonians 5:9–10).

- "Christ redeemed us from *the curse* of the law [which is an expression of his wrath] by becoming a curse for us [so that we do not bear God's wrath]" (Galatians 3:13).
- "By sending his own Son in the likeness of sinful flesh and for sin, [God] *condemned* sin in the flesh [thus, his wrathful condemnation of sin is expended on his Son's flesh, not ours]" (Romans 8:3).

Nevertheless, in dealing with God's wrath in this way, the double work of Satan is itself overcome. It is crucial that we see this wrath-bearing work of Christ as foundational to our deliverance from Satan's work. To say it more provocatively, it is crucial that we see our deliverance from God as foundational to our deliverance from Satan.

The double work of Satan is his work of *accusation* and his work of *temptation*. His name, Satan, means "accuser." And John described him that way, "The accuser of our brothers has been thrown down, who accuses them day and night before our God" (Revelation 12:10). And both Matthew and Paul called him "the tempter" (Matthew 4:3; 1 Thessalonians 3:5). Consider then how Christ's deliverance from the wrath of God is the foundation of his deliverance from both these works of Satan.

When Satan accuses us before God, what he accuses us with is sin. The only reason this accusation has a significance is that it is true. Both Satan and God know that we have sinned. And they both know that "the wages of sin is [eternal] death" (Romans 6:23). That is, God's appointed punishment for sin is eternal torment (Matthew 25:41, 46; Revelation 14:11). Sin deserves and receives God's wrath. "On account of these [sins] *the wrath of God* is coming" (Colossians 3:6). So Satan is laying claim to humans and saying that on God's own terms they must be damned like he is for his sin.

But at this point in Satan's accusation, Jesus Christ stands forth as our Advocate and intercedes for us. God designed this, desires this, and delights in this. "If anyone does sin, we have an advocate with the Father,

Jesus Christ the righteous. He is the propitiation for our sins" (1 John 2:1–2). Christ's advocacy is based on his propitiation—his infallible securing of the removal of God's wrath for all who are in him. So Satan's accusations fall to the ground because our Advocate pleads his own blood and righteousness on our behalf. "Who is to condemn? Christ Jesus is the one who died—more than that, who was raised—who is at the right hand of God, who indeed is interceding for us" (Romans 8:34). Christ's advocacy and intercession for us nullify Satan's accusations against us. This advocacy and intercession are based on his death for us. By this death for us, Christ endured God's wrath against us. Therefore, Christ's deliverance from God's wrath is the foundation of his deliverance of us from Satan's accusations.

This is also true of our deliverance from Satan's temptations. Christ's propitiating work to deliver us from God's wrath is not only the foundation of our deliverance from Satan's accusations but also from his temptations. Many Christians fail to see this. That is why the gospel (the news of Christ's wrath-enduring, guilt-removing death and resurrection) is so often associated with starting the Christian life but not living the Christian life.

There are at least two ways that the New Testament shows how Christ's deliverance from God's wrath is the foundation for our deliverance from Satan's temptations. One is that our victory over Satan's temptations assumes God's merciful help by his Spirit. "Put on the whole armor of God, that you may be able to stand against the schemes of the devil" (Ephesians 6:11). "God may perhaps grant them repentance…and they may…escape from the snare of the devil" (2 Timothy 2:25–26). "By the Spirit you put to death the deeds of the body" (Romans 8:13).

Without the merciful gift of God's Spirit and the gift of God's armor and the gift of repentance, we cannot defeat the temptations of the devil. But the only reason God's full sanctifying mercy is flowing to us (through his Spirit and armor and repentance) is because his wrath isn't. And the reason his wrath isn't is because Christ endured it for us on the cross.

The Satisfied Soul

Therefore, our deliverance from Satan's temptations is based on our deliverance from God's wrath.

One other way that the New Testament shows this is by teaching us that when Christ died for us, we died with him. And because we died with him, we can reckon ourselves dead to Satan's temptations to sin. "We have been united with [Christ] in a death like his.… Our old self was crucified with him in order that the body of sin might be brought to nothing, so that we would no longer be enslaved to sin" (Romans 6:5–6; see also Galatians 2:20). "One has died for all, therefore all have died" (2 Corinthians 5:14). Therefore, one of the ways we fight Satan's temptations to sin is to reckon ourselves dead to sin: "So you also must consider yourselves dead to sin and alive to God in Christ Jesus" (Romans 6:11). We can do this because when Christ died for us, we died in him.

But why did he have to die for us? Why did we have to die in him? Because the wages of sin is death. God's righteous wrath sooner or later falls on all sin (Colossians 3:6). Therefore, the death of Christ, by which we die to sin, is the same death that endures the wrath of God for us. The death that we die in Christ is both our punishment *for* sin and our death *to* sin. They are inseparable. That is why Christ's work to deliver us from the wrath of God is not only his deliverance from the accusations of the devil but also from the temptations of the devil.

Summarizing, Christ's wrath-enduring, propitiating work on the cross is the foundation of our justification *and* our sanctification. This justifying work of God corresponds to and conquers Satan's work of accusation. And this sanctifying work of God corresponds to and conquers Satan's work of temptation. In our justification, Satan's accusations lose their condemning power, and in our sanctification, Satan's temptations lose their corrupting power. And both—our deliverance from his accusations and our deliverance from his temptations—are based on our deliverance from God's wrath by the cross of Christ (that is, by his propitiation).

Therefore, in the defense of the gospel, let us never surrender the wrath-enduring substitution of Christ on our behalf. It is foundational to everything that matters in our lives. And in the radical living of the gospel for the glory of Christ and the good of the world, let us never get beyond the gospel of Christ crucified in our place. May it be our daily bread. May we live by its Satan-defeating power.

28

HOW DO YOU "GIVE" GOD STRENGTH?

A Meditation on Psalm 96:7

Ponder with me the meaning of Psalm 96:7. All the modern versions translate it "Ascribe to the LORD...strength" (ESV, NIV, NASB). Only the King James Version renders it with the literal "Give unto the LORD...strength." The translation "ascribe" is surely legitimate. But we will go deeper on the way to that legitimacy if we ponder how one "gives" power to God.

There's nothing unusual about this Hebrew word *yahab*, or "give." It's used in the ordinary way the word *give* would be used. "*Give* your advice and counsel here" (Judges 20:7). "Oh *grant* us help against the foe" (Psalm 108:12). "The leech has two daughters: *Give* and *Give*" (Proverbs 30:15). "*Give* me my wife that I may go in to her" (Genesis 29:21).

"Ascribe" in Psalm 96:7 is an interpretation. It's a paraphrase. It's a good interpretation, I think, but, as with all paraphrases, it short-circuits our reflection. But for me, full-circuited reflection is where my soul gets its best food.

I start with the obvious. God is infinitely strong and cannot get stronger by my service. "[He is not] served by human hands, as though he needed anything" (Acts 17:25). So giving God strength stands for something different from adding to his strength. What then would be included in a full experience of what the psalmist means by "Give unto the LORD…strength."

First, by God's grace, we give attention to God and see that he is strong. We give heed to his strength. Then we give our approval to the greatness of his strength. We give due regard to its worth.

We find his strength to be wonderful. But what makes this wonder a "giving" kind of wonder is that we are especially glad that the greatness of the strength is his and not ours. We feel a profound fitness in the fact that he is infinitely strong and we are not. We love the fact that this is so. We do not envy God for his strength. We are not covetous of his power. We are full of joy that all strength is his. We are happy to *give* him all the credit for his power.

Everything in us rejoices to go out to behold this power, as if we had arrived at the celebration of the victory of a distance runner who had beaten us in the race, and we found our greatest joy in admiring his strength, rather than resenting our loss.

We find the deepest meaning in life when our hearts freely go out to admire God's power, rather than turning inward to boast of our own— or even think about our own. We discover something overwhelming: It is profoundly satisfying not to be God and to give up all thoughts or desires to be God.

In our giving heed to God's power there rises up in us a realization that God created the universe for this, so that we could have the supremely satisfying experience of not being God but admiring the *Godness* of God, the strength of God. There settles over us a peaceful realization that *admiration of the Infinite* is the final end of all things.

We tremble at the slightest temptation to claim any power as coming from us. God has made us weak to protect us from this: "We have this treasure in jars of clay, to show that the surpassing power belongs to God and not to us" (2 Corinthians 4:7).

Oh, what love this is, that God would protect us from replacing the everlasting heights of admiring his power with the futile attempt to boast in our own.

God have mercy on me. Protect me from the suicidal desires for power. Awaken in me daily and ever more deeply the lowly will to give the gladdest and greatest assessment to your immeasurable strength. Forbid that I would sell the endless satisfaction of admiration for the mirage of my own strength.

In this sense, Lord, I give you strength. In this sense, I join the twenty-four elders in heaven and say, "Worthy are you, our Lord and God, to receive…power" (Revelation 4:11). *Amen.*

29

"He Will Rejoice over You with Gladness"

Why God Tells His Children That
He Delights in Them

The question is not whether the triune God delights in his children. He does. The question is twofold: (1) What is it about us that he delights in? and (2) Why does he tell us this? What effect does he want it to have?

First, notice some of the texts that speak of God's delight in his people and his praise of them:

- "The LORD your God is in your midst, a mighty one who will save; *he will rejoice over you with gladness*" (Zephaniah 3:17).
- "*The Lord takes pleasure* in those who fear him, in those who hope in his steadfast love" (Psalm 147:11).
- "In this [salvation] you rejoice, though now for a little while, if necessary, you have been grieved by various trials, so that the tested genuineness of your faith—more precious than gold that perishes though it is tested by fire—may be found to result in *praise and glory and honor* at the revelation of Jesus Christ" (1 Peter 1:6-7).
- "A Jew is one inwardly, and circumcision is a matter of the heart, by the Spirit, not by the letter. His *praise* is not from man but from God" (Romans 2:29).

- "Therefore do not pronounce judgment before the time, before the Lord comes, who will bring to light the things now hidden in darkness and will disclose the purposes of the heart. Then each one will receive his *commendation from God*" (1 Corinthians 4:5).

To answer the two questions we asked at the beginning, we also need to see the truth that God commands us to delight in him:

- "*Delight yourself in the LORD,* and he will give you the desires of your heart" (Psalm 37:4).
- "Then I will go to the altar of God, to *God my exceeding joy*" (Psalm 43:4).
- "Because your steadfast love is better than life, my lips will praise you" (Psalm 63:3).
- "May all who seek you *rejoice and be glad in you!* May those who love your salvation say evermore, 'God is great!'" (Psalm 70:4).
- "Through him we have also obtained access by faith into this grace in which we stand, and we *rejoice in hope of the glory of God*" (Romans 5:2).
- "*Rejoice in the Lord always;* again I will say, rejoice" (Philippians 4:4).

Notice that the Psalm 63 and 70 texts show something crucial. One says that when you love God's salvation you don't mainly say, "God's *salvation* is great!" You say, "*God* is great!" And when you experience the steadfast love of the Lord, you don't mainly say, "My lips will praise *your steadfast love.*" You mainly say, "My lips will praise *you!*"

In other words, in all these texts the command is to delight in God himself, and all other blessings we enjoy should lead us to God himself as our final and fullest satisfaction. Therefore, in answer to our first question, What is it about us that he delights in?, my answer is: *At root, what God delights in about us is that we delight in him.*

One way to get at this and show why it is true is to say the obvious: God approves of what is *right.* He rejoices in our thinking and feeling and doing what is right. But that leads to a crucial question: What is right, ultimately? What makes something right?

My answer is, rightness. That is, *thinking and feeling and acting in a way that expresses in true proportion the value of what is most valuable.* It seems manifestly wrong to ascribe highest value to what is not of highest value. And it seems manifestly right to ascribe highest value to what has highest value.

To put it more precisely: Rightness is thinking, feeling, and doing what flows from a true perception of the supreme value of God. It is seeing truly, savoring duly, and showing consistently in action the infinite worth of God. Therefore, we are doing what is right when we are *understanding* the truth of God's value for what it is, *feeling* it proportionately to his universal supremacy, and *acting* in ways that express God's supreme value. That is what "right" means.

Therefore, when we say God rejoices in our thinking and feeling and doing what is right, we mean that he delights in our seeing, savoring, and showing *his* own supreme value. God values our valuing him. That brings us back to our original suggestion: God delights in our delighting in him. God too must do what is right. His worth defines it.

Now the second question we asked is, Why does he tell us this? Should we be glad to hear it? Yes, we should be glad to hear it. But why? What is the bottom of our joy in hearing it? It is possible to hear it, and be glad to hear it, in a way that is devastating.

The proper reason to be glad that God delights in our delight in him is because *it confirms that our delight is truly in God.* This fixes our gaze more steadfastly on him and deepens our joy in his beauty.

But there is a devastating way to respond to God's commendation of us. What if we hear God's praise and are drawn away from delighting in God to delighting in God's delighting in us? What if we hear his praise as a tickler of what we really enjoy, namely, being made much of? What if the bottom line of what makes us happy is not God himself but God's attention, God's praise?

If that is the bottom line, then we are not delighting in God but only using delight in God to get commendations. That would be devastating. When God's delight in us lures us to delight in being delighted in, we are ceasing to do the very thing God delights in.

The teaching that God delights in us is inescapably dangerous. The teaching is true. And the teaching is dangerous. The reason it is dangerous is that we are fallen, and the chief pleasure of our fallen nature is not sex but self-exaltation. Our sinful nature loves to be praised for what we are and what we have done.

The remedy for this is not to make God the praiser and think all is well. All may not be well but deadly. God's praises of us will do us good if we hear them as confirming that we are truly delighting in him. God's praise of our delight in God is meant to help us keep on delighting in God and not be distracted by anything. God forbid that his praise of our delight in him would lead us away from delighting in him to delighting in being praised by him.

Hear me well. We *do* delight in being praised by God. But not the way a carnal mind would. God's praise of us is not the *bottom* of our joy. We should not let his praise distract us from the very thing he is praising—namely, our delight in him. *We delight in being praised by God because it confirms and increases our focus on him,* rather than distracting us from him. Even his merciful approval of our imperfect delight in him makes him more beautiful in himself. May those who hear the words, "Well done, good and faithful servant," say, "How great and merciful is our God!"

The relationship between what I have said here and the doctrine of justification by faith is that God looks upon his children through the lens of Christ's imputed righteousness. That means two things: (1) God counts us perfect in Christ, and (2) he can still see us becoming *in practice* what we are *positionally* in Christ.

The lens of imputation secures our invincible right standing with God. It also warrants God's delight in our imperfect delight in him. That is, even though we are counted perfectly righteous in Christ, God can still see our actual sinning mingled with the fruit of the Spirit in our life. That is why he can be delighted in us to greater or lesser degrees. We know this because he both reckons us as perfectly righteous (Romans 4:4–6) and disciplines us for sin in our life (1 Corinthians 11:32). Therefore, God's delight in our delight in him varies in proportion to the affections of our heart, but it is possible only because God imputes to us Christ's perfect righteousness.

The upshot of all this is *Know your God.* Know his unsearchable excellence and supremacy. Savor what you know with all your heart. Admire fully the fully admirable. Enjoy deeply the infinitely enjoyable. Marvel that he looks on your happy heart and delights in you. Give praise to Christ for making all this possible by becoming your perfection.

30

CARING ENOUGH TO TAKE THE RISK

What to Say to the Depressed, Doubting, Skeptical, Confused, Angry

I f you care about people and risk talking to the depressed, the doubting, the skeptical, the confused, and the angry, you will soon run into a person who says to your counsel: "I've tried that." Whatever you say, they will minimize it and say it doesn't work. Do not be surprised at this response. This is what it means to be depressed, doubting, skeptical, confused, angry. It means that whatever they hear sounds useless.

So I want to offer some suggestions for what you say in a conversation that is about to be cut off like that.

1. Don't be offended.

First, resist the temptation to be offended. Don't pout or take your ball and go home. That's what you may feel like. They wanted to talk, and here they are throwing my suggestions back in my face with a dismissive attitude. Don't leave. Not yet. "Love is patient" (1 Corinthians 13:4).

2. Listen.

Next, listen to their responses. Part of your power is not only what you say but how they feel about the way you listen. If your truth produces empathetic ears, it will feel more compelling. This listening will be a witness. In 2 Timothy 2:24–26, Paul described the kind of engagement that may set people free from sin and error. One feature is "patiently enduring evil."

3. End with hope.

When you have spoken all the experiential counsel you can think of and they seem to have demeaned it all, don't let them have the last word of despair. You leave the last word of hope. The point is not to imitate these words but that you put hope-giving truth into their minds from God's Word, whether they think it is helpful or not. You might say something like this:

> I know you don't feel very helped by what I have said. I think I understand some of what that's like. I don't mean to be offering a quick fix, as though your problems or doubts can be turned around that easily. But I have more hope than you do at the moment that God's truth is powerful and will have its good effect in due time. May I share one more thing before you go?
>
> I simply want to make sure you hear the best news in the world. Jesus explained that the reason he spoke was so that we would have peace (John 16:33). And Paul said that faith comes by hearing the word of Christ (Romans 10:17). You don't feel this right now. But God says peace and faith come from hearing.
>
> Something happens. At one moment, you are not seeing Christ as beautiful and satisfying and compelling. Then in the next moment, you are. You don't see how this could happen. But it does.
>
> In the moments leading up to this experience, listening to God's Word seems empty and futile. That doesn't put me off. If you doubt what I am saying, you are the very person who needs to hear what I am saying. It's the Word that does the work, not you.
>
> *So let me tell you some spectacular news.* This comes from

Colossians: "You, who were dead in your trespasses and the uncircumcision of your flesh, God made alive together with him, having forgiven us all our trespasses, by canceling the record of debt that stood against us with its legal demands. This he set aside, nailing it to the cross. He disarmed the rulers and authorities and put them to open shame, by triumphing over them in him" (Colossians 2:13–15).

There are five mind-blowing things here for you as God's child:

1. God makes you spiritually alive.
2. God forgives all your sins.
3. He does this because he canceled the record of debts that stood against you. You owed God what you could never pay because of all your sins. And he canceled the debt.
4. How could he do that? He set it aside by nailing it to the cross. But the nails that went into the cross didn't go through parchment. They went through Jesus' hands and feet. That's the heart of everything I have to say to you. Christ became our substitute and bore our debt.
5. When that happened, the devil was disarmed. Why? Because the weapon of accusation was taken out of his hand. He always waved that record of debt in our face and God's court. But now that's canceled. The devil is disarmed. He can huff and puff, but he cannot damn you.

I leave you with this news. I will pray that the obstacles to peace-filled faith in your mind will be overcome by these truths. Jesus said, "You will know the truth, and the truth will set you free" (John 8:32). Meditate on these verses. Remember it is the Word that does the work, not you.

Then pray out loud with and for them. *Lord of mercy and great patience, do your wonderful awakening, life-giving, hope-giving work by your Word. In Jesus' name. Amen.*

31

Hero Worship and Holy Emulation

Navigating the New World of Media-Driven Celebrity

I have unanswered questions about how to navigate the new world of media-driven celebrity attention to pastors. When I say media-driven attention, I am not mainly thinking about radio, TV, and newspapers. They are almost irrelevant. I mean Internet media. Most churches have websites. Sermons and articles and books are available. Often there's audio and video. And there's Facebook and Twitter. And by the time this book is in your hands, there will probably be some remarkable new development for putting your thoughts and your face before millions.

What happens then is that anywhere in the world people can read, watch, or listen. If they are helped, they can click and share it immediately with others anywhere in the world, who, in turn, share it again.

Tens of thousands of linkings may take place almost instantly— through blogs, Twitter, texting, Facebook, and a dozen other sharing tools. This means that what a pastor does or says may be known in hours by hundreds of thousands of people around the world. This can contribute to media-driven celebrity status.

Then stir into the mix that some pastors write books. There is a popular mystique about authors. *Author* connotes authority or creativity or wisdom. Authors are generally thought to be interesting people. I think very often these conceptions are not true. But for some, the fact *that* an author writes is more significant than *what* he writes.

What is the meaning of the attention given to well-known pastors? What does the desire for autographs and photographs mean? The negative meaning would be something akin to name-dropping. Our egos are massaged if we can say we know someone famous. You see this on blogs with statements like "my friend Barack" and the like. And I presume that, for some, an autograph or a photo has the same ego boost.

However, I don't assume the worst of people. There are other possible motives. We will see this below. But it is good to emphasize that all of this is more dangerous to our souls than bullets and bombs. Pride is more fatal than death.

When I say "our souls" I mean all of us—the autograph seeker, the autograph giver, and the cynic who condemns it all. There is no escaping this new world of media technology. The question is, How do we navigate it for the glory of Christ—the crucifixion of self, the spreading of truth, the deepening of faith, and the empowering of sacrificial love?

Here is one small contribution. In spite of all the legitimate warnings against hero worship, I want to risk waving a flag for holy emulation, which includes realistic admiration. Hero worship means admiring someone for unholy reasons and seeing all he does as admirable (whether it's sin or not). Holy emulation, on the other hand, sees evidences of God's grace, and admires them for Christ's sake, and wants to learn from them and grow in them.

This theme is strong in the New Testament:
- "Be imitators of me, as I am of Christ" (1 Corinthians 11:1).
- "Brothers, join in imitating me, and keep your eyes on those who walk according to the example you have in us" (Philippians 3:17).
- "What you have learned and received and heard and seen in me—practice these things, and the God of peace will be with you" (Philippians 4:9).

- "And you became imitators of us and of the Lord" (1 Thessalonians 1:6).
- "You, however, have followed my teaching, my conduct, my aim in life, my faith, my patience, my love, my steadfastness" (2 Timothy 3:10).
- "Continue in what you have learned and have firmly believed, knowing from whom you learned it" (2 Timothy 3:14).
- "Show yourself in all respects to be a model of good works, and in your teaching show integrity, dignity" (Titus 2:7).
- "[Do] not be sluggish, but imitators of those who through faith and patience inherit the promises" (Hebrews 6:12).

The old Puritan Thomas Brooks commented on holy emulation in his book *The Secret Key to Heaven:*

> Bad men are wonderfully in love with bad examples.... Oh, that we were as much in love with the examples of good men as others are in love with the examples of bad men.
>
> Shall we love to look upon the pictures of our friends; and shall we not love to look upon the pious examples of those that are the lively and lovely picture of Christ? The pious examples of others should be the mirrors by which we should dress ourselves.
>
> He is the best and wisest Christian...that imitates those Christians that are most eminent in grace.... It is noble to live by the examples of the most eminent saints.*

It is right and risky to aim at being worthy of emulation. It is more foundationally right to aim at being helpful. It is essential in both that we be amazed that we are forgiven through Christ and that we serve rather than seek to be served.

---

* Thomas Brooks, *The Secret Key to Heaven* (Edinburgh: Banner of Truth, 2006), 12–13.

32

BLESS THE MOTHER OF JESUS—
BUT MAINLY BE THE MOTHER
OF JESUS

Admiring the Imitable Mary

The veneration given to Mary in the Roman Catholic Church is beyond what is warranted by the New Testament. In fact, it is astonishing how little we see of Mary in the New Testament. Let us honor her unique motherhood. Let us count her blessed as the mother of our incarnate Lord. But let us not put her on a pedestal that neither she nor Jesus would have approved of.

After she turns up with the disciples praying in the upper room in Acts 1:14, she is never mentioned again in the New Testament. This is astonishing to anyone who thinks that the veneration of Mary was an essential part of early church life. It was not important enough to be mentioned in any of the New Testament books after Acts.

In fact, in the one place where Paul came close to mentioning Mary, he chose not to, and simply used the generic "woman": "When the fullness of time had come, God sent forth his Son, born of woman" (Galatians 4:4).

And when she is mentioned in Acts 1:14, she is "Mary the mother of Jesus, and his brothers." This inclusion of the brothers has the effect of minimizing any emerging elevation of Mary as having significance only in being the mother of Jesus, rather than the mother of his brothers as well.

Mary is unique among all women in being a virgin when she gave birth to her firstborn son. "Behold, the virgin shall conceive and bear a son" (Matthew 1:23). When she asked the angel how that could be, he answered, "The Holy Spirit will come upon you, and the power of the Most High will overshadow you; therefore the child to be born will be called holy—the Son of God" (Luke 1:35).

Yet amazingly, the virgin birth of Jesus by Mary is never mentioned again in the New Testament. That doesn't mean it is untrue or unimportant. It simply means that it was not prominent in the life of the church. Celebrating it was not an essential part of the worship of the New Testament church. Otherwise, it would have been mentioned somewhere in the letters to those churches.

When Mary is referred to during the adult life of Jesus in the Gospels, she is not treated in a way that sets her apart in any unusual way. At the cross, for example, Matthew referred to her without even mentioning that she was Jesus' mother: "There were also many women there, looking on from a distance, who had followed Jesus from Galilee, ministering to him, among whom were Mary Magdalene and Mary the mother of James and Joseph and the mother of the sons of Zebedee" (Matthew 27:55–56).

Calling Jesus' mother "the mother of James and Joseph" is striking. We know that this is Jesus' mother because of Matthew 13:55: "Is not his mother called Mary? And are not his brothers James and Joseph and Simon and Judas?" "James and Joseph" are the sons in both Matthew 27:56 and 13:55. So Matthew referred to Mary without calling her the mother of Jesus, and a few verses later he simply referred to her as "the other Mary" (27:61).

Most striking of all is the way Jesus intentionally deflected a certain kind of honor from his mother. Once a woman in the crowd "raised her voice and said to him, 'Blessed is the womb that bore you, and the breasts at which you nursed!'" But Jesus replied, "Blessed rather are those who hear the word of God and keep it!" (Luke 11:27–28). Jesus ranks obedience to the Word of God above the special veneration of his mother.

Similarly, Jesus was once told, "Your mother and your brothers are standing outside, desiring to see you." But Jesus answered, "My mother and my brothers are those who hear the word of God and do it" (Luke 8:20–21). Again Jesus ranks obedience above the standing of his mother.

Mary was a magnificent person.

- Her humility shone: "He has looked on the humble estate of his servant" (Luke 1:48).

- Her faith was profound: "Blessed is she who believed that there would be a fulfillment of what was spoken to her from the Lord" (Luke 1:45).

- Her suffering was deep: "A sword will pierce through your own soul" (Luke 2:35).

- Her God was sovereign: "He has shown strength with his arm; he has scattered the proud in the thoughts of their hearts; he has brought down the mighty from their thrones" (Luke 1:51–52).

- And her meditations were full of truth: "Mary treasured up all these things, pondering them in her heart" (Luke 2:19).

Therefore, remember her. Admire her. Bless her. Be inspired by her. But do not go beyond what the New Testament portrays. Our calling is to *be* the mother of Jesus more than to venerate her. "My mother is the one who hears the word of God and does it" (Luke 8:21).

33

How the Lord of Life Gives Life

A Meditation on Acts 16:14

I t seems that everywhere Paul preached, some believed and some did not. How are we to understand why some of those who are "dead in trespasses and sins" (Ephesians 2:1) believed and some did not?

One answer why some did not believe is that they "thrust it aside" (Acts 13:46) because the message of the gospel was "folly to [them], and [they were] not able to understand" (1 Corinthians 2:14). The mind of the flesh "is hostile to God, for it does not submit to God's law; indeed, it cannot" (Romans 8:7). Those who hear and reject the gospel "[hate] the light" and do not come to the light lest their deeds should be exposed (John 3:20). They remain "darkened in their understanding...because of the ignorance that is in them, due to their hardness of heart" (Ephesians 4:18). It is a guilty ignorance. The truth is available. But "by their unrighteousness [they] suppress the truth" (Romans 1:18).

But why then do some believe, since all are in this condition of rebellious hardness of heart, dead in our trespasses? The book of Acts gives the answer in at least three different ways. One is that they are appointed to believe. When Paul preached in Antioch of Pisidia, the Gentiles rejoiced and "as many as were appointed to eternal life believed" (Acts 13:48).

Another way of answering why some believe is that God granted repentance. When the saints in Jerusalem heard that Gentiles were responding to the gospel and not just Jews, they said, "Then to the Gentiles also God has granted repentance that leads to life" (Acts 11:18).

But the clearest answer in Acts to the question why a person believes the gospel is that God opens the heart. Lydia is the best example. Why did she believe? Acts 16:14 says, "The Lord opened her heart to pay attention to what was said by Paul." Notice four aspects of this conversion—four things necessary for a person to believe and be saved.

1. **"What was said by Paul."** First, someone must speak the gospel. God does not open the eyes of the heart to see nothing. He opens them to see the glory of Christ in the truth of the gospel (2 Corinthians 4:4–6). Therefore, we must speak the gospel. We don't make the new birth happen when we do. But we fit into God's way of doing it. The point of the new birth is to grant spiritual sight. The point of speaking the gospel is so that an unbeliever has something to see when God opens the eyes. New birth—the miracle that enables faith (1 John 5:1)—is for the glory of Christ. Therefore, God causes it to happen when Christ is lifted up.

2. **"The Lord."** Next, the speaker of the gospel relies upon the Lord. Prayer is not mentioned here. But that is what we do when we realize that it is the Lord who is the decisive actor, not us. We have a significant role in speaking the gospel, but it is the Lord himself who does the decisive work.

3. **"Opened her heart."** Since the key problem in not believing the gospel is the hardness, or the *closedness,* of the heart, this is where the Lord does his decisive work. He *opens the heart* of Lydia. This means he takes out the heart of stone and puts in the heart of flesh (Ezekiel 36:26). God says with sovereign authority, "Let there be light," and "[shines] in our hearts to give the light of the knowledge of the glory of God in the face of Jesus Christ" (2 Corinthians 4:6). So the darkness flies away and the light of truth reveals the beauty of Christ in the gospel as irresistibly compelling.

4. **"To pay attention to what was said by Paul."** The effect of the Lord's opening Lydia's heart is a true spiritual hearing of the gospel. "Pay

attention to" is a weak translation of the Greek *prosechein*. It is stronger than that in this context. In this verse, it is a hearing with attachment. The work of the Lord does not just help Lydia focus. It brings about faith. She was granted repentance (2 Timothy 2:25) and faith (Philippians 1:29).

Or, in the terms of John 6, she was given by the Father to the Son (v. 37), and was drawn by the Father to the Son (v. 44), and was granted by the Father to come to the Son (v. 65). She was made alive (Ephesians 2:5) and was born again (John 3:3, 7).

This is what we should pray for. When God does this for many at the same time in the same area, we have historically called it "revival." It is the great need of our day, as every day. As the old gospel song says, "Mercy drops around us are falling, but for the showers we plead"— showers of the kind of spiritual awakening Lydia received.

34

AWAKENED BY SUFFERING AND PAIN

Abraham Lincoln's Path to Divine Providence

Into his forties, Abraham Lincoln remained skeptical, and at times even cynical, about religion. But it is remarkable how, as time went by, personal and national suffering drew Lincoln into the reality of God, rather than pushing him away.

In 1862, when Lincoln was fifty-three years old, his eleven-year-old son, Willie, died. Lincoln's wife tried to deal with her grief by searching out New Age mediums. Lincoln turned to Phineas Gurley, pastor of the New York Avenue Presbyterian Church in Washington, DC. Several long talks led to what Gurley described as "a conversion to Christ." Lincoln confided that he was "driven many times upon my knees by the overwhelming conviction that I have nowhere else to go."

Similarly, the horrors of the dead and wounded soldiers assaulted him daily. There were fifty hospitals for the wounded in Washington. The rotunda of the Capitol held 2,000 cots for wounded soldiers. Typically, fifty soldiers a day died in these temporary hospitals. All of this drove Lincoln deeper into the providence of God. "We cannot but believe, that He who made the world still governs it."

His most famous statement about the providence of God in relation to the Civil War was in his second inaugural address, given a month before he was assassinated. It is remarkable for his not making God a simple supporter for the Union or Confederate cause. God has his own purposes and does not excuse sin on either side:

> Fondly do we hope—fervently do we pray—that this mighty scourge of war might speedily pass away.... Yet if God wills that it continue, until all the wealth piled by the bond-man's two hundred years of unrequited toil shall be sunk, and until every drop of blood drawn with the lash, shall be paid with another drawn with the sword, as was said three thousand years ago so still it must be said, "the judgments of the Lord, are true and righteous altogether."

The paradoxical words of Alexander Solzhenitsyn eighty years later, whose imprisonment in Joseph Stalin's "corrective labor camps" led not to despair but to the discovery of goodness, would have resonated with Lincoln:

> It was granted to me to carry away from my prison years on my bent back, which nearly broke beneath its load, this essential experience: how a human being becomes evil and how good. In the intoxication of youthful successes I had felt myself to be infallible, and I was therefore cruel. In the surfeit of power I was a murderer and an oppressor. In my most evil moments I was convinced that I was doing good, and I was well supplied with systematic arguments. It was only when I lay there on rotting prison straw that I sensed within myself the first stirrings of good. Gradually it was disclosed to me that the line separating good and evil passes not through states, nor between classes, nor between political parties either—but right through every human heart—and through all human hearts.... That is why I turn back to the years of my imprisonment and say, sometimes to the astonishment of

those about me: *"Bless you, prison!"* I…have served enough time there. I nourished my soul there, and I say without hesitation: *"Bless you, prison,* for having been in my life!"*

As I write this, I am praying for you, the reader—you, who sooner or later will suffer loss and injury and great sorrow. I pray that it will awaken for you, as it did for Lincoln and Solzhenitsyn not an empty nihilism, but a deeper reliance on the infinite wisdom and love of God's inscrutable providence. "Oh, the depth of the riches and wisdom and knowledge of God! How unsearchable are his judgments and how inscrutable his ways!" (Romans 11:33).

---

* Alexander Solzhenitsyn, *The Gulag Archipelago: 1918–1956,* (New York: Harper & Row, 1974), 615–17.

35

THE STRANGE TASK OF
WITNESSING ABOUT LIGHT

A Meditation on John 1:7

Witnessing about light is a strange task if your aim is for people to see the light and believe in the light. Light illumines by itself. When you want someone to see a light, do you talk about the light? You hold up the light. If you have a torch in your hand, and you want someone to see the torch, you don't say, "This is a torch." You hold up the torch.

But John 1:7 says that John the Baptist "came as a witness, to bear witness about the light." So as strange as this task is, that was John's mission. And it is ours too. So then, what do we learn about our task when it is described as witnessing to the light?

1. We learn that Christ, the Light of the world (John 8:12), shines not like a physical torch before the physical eye but like a spiritual glory before the spiritual eye. This is why Jesus said, "Seeing they do not see" (Matthew 13:13). And it is why Paul prayed that you would have "the eyes of your hearts enlightened, that you may know what is the hope to which he has called you" (Ephesians 1:18). There is a seeing that we do with "the eyes of [the] heart," not merely with the eyes of the head.

2. We learn that the light of Christ, this spiritual glory which we see with the eyes of the heart, shines mainly through a message—the gospel. That is, it shines mainly through the witness of human beings, about what Jesus accomplished when he died and rose again. This is strange—strange and wonderful. Light shines through words. Yes, it does. Paul said:

> The god of this world has blinded the minds of the unbelievers, to keep them from seeing *the light of the gospel of the glory of Christ,* who is the image of God.... God, who said, "Let light shine out of darkness," has shone in our hearts to give *the light of the knowledge of the glory of God in the face of Jesus Christ.* (2 Corinthians 4:4–6)

The glory of Christ is his light. This glory, Paul said, shines as "the light of the gospel." That means it shines through a *witness.* When we witness to what Christ achieved for us in dying, we are *witnessing about the light.* That is how the light of Christ shines in this world. Deeds of love are crucial in this shining (Matthew 5:14–16). But deeds alone cannot witness effectually to the greatest glory of Christ, namely, his achievement on the cross. That light shines through the gospel in the mouths of witnesses.

3. We learn that people need to have the eyes of their hearts opened to see the light of Christ in the gospel. Jesus said to Paul when he sent him to witness to the light, "I am sending you to *open their eyes,* so that they may turn from darkness to light and from the power of Satan to God, that they may receive forgiveness of sins" (Acts 26:17–18).

God does this eye-opening work through human witnesses. The book of Luke tells us that the way Lydia saw the light was that "the Lord opened her heart to pay attention to what was said by Paul" (Acts 16:14). Paul witnessed to the light. God opened her heart to see the light. So Paul prays that this would happen: "I do not cease to give thanks for you, remembering you in my prayers, that...[you would have] the eyes of your hearts enlightened" (Ephesians 1:16–18). God's answer to that prayer is described in 2 Corinthians 4:6: "[God] has shone in our hearts to give the light of the knowledge of the glory of God in the face of Jesus Christ."

So we witness about the light, even though we know that people are blind to this light. But that does not daunt us, because we know that God's eye-opening power accompanies the witness about his Son. This is why the Holy Spirit was given. As Jesus said, "He will glorify me" (John 16:14).

4. We learn that the miracle of spiritual sight through the gospel happens when witnesses tell blind people to look at Christ and then describe what they will see when they look there. There is a mental analogy to this spiritual reality. Consider a typical optical illusion like this one:

Suppose someone only sees one picture in this illustration. They are "blind" to the other. Then you "witness" to them: "Look at this. There are two pictures: a girl's face and a man playing a saxophone." That very witness opens their eyes to both pictures.

It's only an analogy, because in the spiritual realm the process is not merely mental or natural. It is spiritual and supernatural. But we can get some idea of how it is possible to be spiritually blind and yet God can use a witness to open our eyes.

Therefore, don't let the strangeness of witnessing about light stop you. It is gloriously strange. It is strange in a way that gives us hope that we really can help the blind to see. It is strange in a way that will get all the glory for God—*both* in the gospel itself and in the way people see the glory of Christ in it.

36

SUBMISSION AND HEADSHIP IN THE HOME WHERE I GREW UP

Female Competency and Biblical Complementarity

My mother and father were unusually clear examples of headship and submission in its happiest, healthiest form. What made it so illuminating in retrospect was that my mother's submissive role in relation to my father's was not owing to lesser competencies. Nor was it demanded, coerced, or abused by my father. It was owing to the God-given nature of manhood and womanhood and how they are designed in marriage to display the covenant relationship between Christ and the church.

I grew up in a home where my father was away for about two-thirds of each year. He was an evangelist. He held about twenty-five evangelistic crusades each year, ranging in length from one to three weeks. He would leave on Saturday, be gone for one to three weeks, and come home on a Monday afternoon. In my eighteen years growing up in this home, I went to the Greenville airport hundreds of times. And some of the sweetest memories of my childhood include the smile on my father's face as he came out of the plane and down the steps and almost ran across the runway to hug and kiss me (no jetways in those days).

This meant that my sister and I were reared and trained mostly by my mother. She taught me almost everything practical that I know. She taught me how to cut the grass (overlap enough so you don't miss any), how to keep a checkbook and ride a bike, how to drive a car, make notes for a speech, set the table with the fork in the right place, and make pancakes (notice when the bubbles form on the edges). She paid the bills, handled repairs, cleaned house, cooked meals, helped me with my homework, took us to church, led us in devotions. She was superintendent of the intermediate youth department at church, head of the community garden club, and tireless doer of good for others.

She was incredibly strong in her loneliness. The early sixties were the days in Greenville, South Carolina, when civil rights were in the air. The church took a vote one Wednesday night on a resolution to not allow black people to worship in our church. When the vote was taken, she stood, as I recall, entirely alone in opposition. And when my sister was married in the church in 1963 and one of the ushers tried to seat some black friends of our family all alone in the balcony, my mother indignantly marched out of the sanctuary and seated them herself on the main floor with everyone else.

I have never known anyone quite like Ruth Piper. She seemed to me to be omnicompetent and overflowing with love and energy.

But here is my point. When my father came home, my mother had the extraordinary ability and biblical wisdom and humility to honor him as the head of our home. She was, in the best sense of the word, submissive to him. In fact, it was manifest even to a child that she loved the homecoming of my father and the relief of his leadership. This was not a sacrifice for her to submit to his leading. It was a burden lifted. It was an amazing thing to watch week after week as my father came and went. He went, and my mother ruled the whole house with a firm and competent and loving hand. And he came home, and my mother deferred to his leadership.

Once he was home, he was the one who prayed at the meals. It was he who led in devotions. It was he who drove us to worship, watched over us in the pew, and answered our questions. My fear of disobedience shifted from my mother's wrath to my father's, for there too he took the lead. Their preciousness and the overwhelming dominance of their happy smiles made their disapproval all the worse.

I never heard my father attack my mother or put her down in any way. They sang together and laughed together and put their heads together to bring each other up to date on the state of the family. The happy complementarity of Ruth and Bill Piper was a gift of God that I could never begin to repay or earn.

And here is what I learned: a biblical truth before I knew it was in the Bible. There is no correlation between submission and incompetence. There is such a thing as masculine leadership that does not demean a wife. There is such a thing as submission that is not weak or mindless or manipulative.

It never entered my mind until I began to hear feminist rhetoric in the late sixties that this beautiful design in my home was somehow owing to anyone's inferiority. It wasn't. It was owing to this: My mother and my father put their hope in God and believed that obedience to his Word would create the best of all possible families. I am thankful. And I exhort you with all my heart to consider these things with great seriousness, and do not let the world squeeze you into its mold.

37

WHEN SIGNS AND WONDERS GO BAD

Reflections on Heresy, Deception, and Love for God

Does God have designs for deceptive signs and wonders? Does he have purposes for heresies?

From the time of Moses to the end of history, this has been and will be an issue. Jesus promised that "false christs and false prophets will arise and perform *great signs and wonders,* so as to lead astray, if possible, even the elect" (Matthew 24:24). These are not little tricks. They are *great* signs and wonders. Great. But aimed to deceive.

Paul said that "the coming of the lawless one is by the activity of Satan with all power and *false signs and wonders,* and with all wicked deception for those who are perishing, because they refused to love the truth and so be saved" (2 Thessalonians 2:9–10). "False signs and wonders" is a literal translation to show that the falseness of the signs and wonders is not that they aren't real miracles, but that they lie about reality. They are real miracles, and they lead away from Christ.

Similarly, to the end of history—*especially* at the end of history— false teaching and heresies will dog the church. "The time is coming when people will not endure sound teaching, but having itching ears they will accumulate for themselves teachers to suit their own passions, and will turn away from listening to the truth and wander off into myths" (2 Timothy 4:3–4).

At the other end of history, things have been this way from the time of Moses. And it is Moses who answers our two questions: Does God have designs for deceptive signs and wonders? Does he have purposes for heresies? He does. Here's the key passage:

> If a prophet or a dreamer of dreams arises among you and gives you a sign or a wonder, and the sign or wonder that he tells you comes to pass, and if he says, "Let us go after other gods," which you have not known, "and let us serve them," you shall not listen to the words of that prophet or that dreamer of dreams. For the LORD your God is testing you, to know whether you love the LORD your God with all your heart and with all your soul. (Deuteronomy 13:1–3)

Notice five things:

First, Moses tells us that signs and wonders in the service of heresy really happen. They are not tricks. "If a prophet…gives you a sign or a wonder, and the sign or wonder that he tells you comes to pass…" (v. 1). They really do come to pass. It is not smoke and mirrors. These are supernatural but not in the service of truth.

Second, some miracle workers aim to draw believers away from the true God. "If he says, 'Let us go after other gods…' you shall not listen to the words of that prophet" (vv. 2–3). In other words, some heresies ("let us go after other gods") are endorsed with miraculous signs and wonders.

Third, God has a design in these deceptive signs and wonders, and he has purposes for the heresies they support. He mentions one of these designs and purposes: "For the LORD your God is testing you, to know whether you love the LORD your God with all your heart and with all your soul" (v. 3). When temptation happens from man, a test is happening from God. This is God's design in the deceptive signs and heresies.

Fourth, your love for God is what God is testing. "Your God is testing you, to know whether you love the LORD your God with all your heart and with all your soul" (v. 3).

Fifth, I conclude from this that the heart that loves God sees through miraculous deception. It is not deluded. Love for God is not based mainly on miraculous power. It is based on seeing through miraculous power to true divine beauty. Therefore, love for God is a powerful protection against heresy, even when it comes with miraculous confirmation.

Understanding these five things from Deuteronomy 13:1–3 helps protect us from deceptive signs and wonders and from heresies. But understanding is not enough. Love for God is both the aim of God's testing and the means by which his tests are passed. Understanding awakens us to our need to love him. But love for God sees through deceptive signs and wonders to the falsehood they support and flees to Christ. Love for God sees through the heresy and holds fast to him.

Recall 2 Thessalonians 2:10 from above. People are swept into the satanic delusion "because they refused to *love* the truth." It isn't just *knowing* truth that protects us; it's *loving* it. Because *it* reveals *him*—our God, our all-surpassing Treasure and Refuge.

May God deepen our love for him so that it has this kind of penetrating, protecting power.

38

COED COMBAT AND CULTURAL COWARDICE

Why Women Suffer as Chivalry Collapses

If I were the last man on the planet to think so, I would want the honor of saying that no woman should go before me into combat to defend my country. A man who endorses women in combat is not pro-woman; he's acting like a wimp. He should be ashamed. For most of history, in most cultures, he would have been utterly scorned as a coward to promote such an idea. Part of the meaning of manhood as God created us is the sense of responsibility for the safety and welfare of our women.

Back in the seventies, when I taught in college, feminism was new and cool. So my ideas on manhood were viewed as the social construct of a dying chauvinistic era. I had not yet been enlightened that competencies, not divine wiring, governed the roles we assume. Unfazed, I said no. I still say no.

Suppose I said to a class one day, a couple of you students, Jason and Sarah, were walking to McDonald's after dark. And suppose a man with a knife jumped out of the bushes and threatened you. And suppose Jason knows that Sarah has a black belt in karate and could probably disarm the assailant better than he could. Should he step back and hope she would do it? No. He should step in front of her and be ready to lay down his life to protect her, irrespective of competency. It is written on his soul. That is what manhood does.

And collectively that is what society does, unless the men have all been emasculated by the self-destructive songs of egalitarian folly. God created man first in order to say that man bears a primary burden for protection, provision, and leadership. And when man and woman rebelled against God's ways, God came to the garden and said, "Adam, where are you?" (Genesis 3:9), not "Eve, where are you?" And when the apostle described the implications of being created male and female, the pattern he celebrates is: Save her, nourish her, cherish her, give her life (Ephesians 5:25–29).

God wrote manhood and womanhood on our hearts. Sin ruins the imprint without totally defacing it. It tells men to be heavy-handed oafs or passive wimps. It tells women to be coquettes or controllers. That is not God's imprint. Deeper down, men and women know it.

When God is not in the picture, the truth crops up in strange forms. For example, Kingsley Browne, law professor at Wayne State University in Michigan, wrote a book called *Co-ed Combat: The New Evidence That Women Shouldn't Fight the Nation's Wars*. In an interview with *Newsweek* he said, "The evidence comes from the field of evolutionary psychology.... Men don't say, 'This is a person I would follow through the gates of hell.' Men aren't hard-wired to follow women into danger."*

If you leave God out, the perceived hard-wiring appears to be evolutionary psychology. If God is in the picture, it has other names. We call it "the work of the law...written on their hearts" (Romans 2:15). We call it true manhood as God meant it to be.

As usual, the truth that comes in the alien form of evolutionary psychology gets distorted. It is true that "men aren't hard-wired to follow women into danger." But that's misleading. The issue is not that women are leading men into danger. The issue is, they are leading men. Men aren't hard-wired to follow women, period. They are hard-wired to get in

---

* Martha Brant, "The Case Against Women in Combat," *Newsweek,* October 23, 2007, www.newsweek.com/id/61568.

front of their women—between them and the bullets. They are hard-wired to lead their women out of danger and into safety. And women, at their deepest and most honest selves, give profound assent to this noble impulse in good men. That is why coed combat situations compromise men and women at their core and corrupt even further the foolhardy culture that put them there.

Consider where we have come. One promotion for Browne's book states, "More than 155,000 female troops have been deployed to Iraq and Afghanistan since 2002. And more than seventy of those women have died.... Those deaths exceed the number of military women who died in Korea, Vietnam, and the Gulf War combined."

What cowardly men do we thank for this collapse of chivalry? Browne suggests, "There are a lot of military people who think women in combat is a horrible idea, but it's career suicide to say it." In other words, let the women die; I'll keep my career. May God restore sanity and courage once again to our leading national defenders. And may he give you a voice.

39

WHY REQUIRE UNREGENERATE CHILDREN TO ACT LIKE THEY'RE GOOD?

Three Reasons for Parenting by God's Revealed Will

If mere external conformity to God's commands (like don't lie, don't steal, don't kill) is hypocritical and spiritually defective, then why should parents require obedience from their unregenerate children? Won't this simply confirm them in unspiritual religious conformity, hypocritical patterns of life, and legalistic moralism?

Here are at least three reasons why Christian parents should require their small children (regenerate or unregenerate) to behave in ways that conform externally to God's revealed will.

I say "small children" because as a child gets older, there are certain external conformities to God's revealed will that should be required and others that should not. It seems to me, for example, while parents should require drug-free, respectful decency from a fifteen-year-old, it would do little good to require an unbelieving, indifferent, angry fifteen-year-old to read his Bible every day. But it would be wise to require that of a six-year-old, while doing all they can to help him enjoy it and see the benefit in it. Where to draw this line is a matter of wisdom.

So the following points are reasons why we should require younger children to behave in ways that conform, at least externally, to God's Word.

1. For children, external, unspiritual conformity to God's commanded patterns of behavior is better than external, unspiritual nonconformity to those patterns of behavior.

A respectful and mannerly five-year-old unbeliever is better for the world than a more authentic defiant, disrespectful, ill-mannered, unbelieving bully. The family, the friendships, the church, and the world in general will be thankful for parents who restrain the egocentric impulses of their children and confirm in them every impulse toward courtesy and kindness and respect.

2. Requiring obedience from children in conformity with God's will confronts them with the meaning of sin in relation to God, the nature of their own depravity, and their need for inner transformation by the power of grace through the gospel of Christ.

There comes a point where the "law" dawns on the child. That is, he realizes that God (not just his parents) requires a certain way of life from him and that he does not like some of it and that he cannot do all of it.

At this crisis moment, the good news of Christ's dying for our sins becomes all important. Will the child settle into a moralistic effort the rest of his life, trying to win the acceptance and love of God? Or will he hear and believe that God's acceptance and forgiveness and love are free gifts, and then receive this God in Christ as the supreme Treasure of his life?

The child will have a hard time grasping the meaning of the Cross if parents have not required of him behaviors, some of which he dislikes, and none of which he can do perfectly.

Christ lived and died to provide for us the righteousness we need (but cannot perform) and to endure for us the punishment we deserve (but cannot endure). If parents do not require external righteousness and apply measures of punishment, the categories of the Cross will be difficult for a child to grasp.

3. The marks of devotion, civility, and manners ("please," "thank you," and good eye contact) are habits that, God willing, are filled later with grace and become more helpful ways of blessing others and expressing a humble heart.

No parents have the luxury of teaching their child nothing while they wait for his regeneration. If we are not requiring obedience, we are confirming defiance. If we are not inculcating manners, we are training in boorishness. If we are not developing the disciplines of prayer and Bible-listening, we are solidifying the sense that prayerlessness and Biblelessness are normal.

Inculcated good habits may later become formalistic legalism. Inculcated insolence, rudeness, and irreligion will likely become worldly decadence. But by God's grace, and saturated with parental prayer, good habits may be filled with the life of the Spirit by faith. But the patterns of insolence and rudeness and irreligion will be hard to undo.

Caution: Here we are only answering one question. Why should parents require submissive behaviors of children when they may be unregenerate rebels at heart? Of course, that is not all Christian parents should do.

- Let us spontaneously celebrate verbally every hopeful sign of life and goodness in our children.
- Let us express forgiveness often and be long-suffering.
- Let us apologize often when we fall short of our own Father's requirements.
- Let us serve them and not use them.
- Let us lavish them with joyful participation in their interests.
- Let us model for them the joy of knowing and submitting to the Lord Jesus.
- Let us pray for them without ceasing.

- Let us saturate them with the Word of God from the moment they are in the womb (the uterus is not soundproof).
- Let us involve them in happy ministry experiences and show them it is more blessed to give than to receive.
- Let them see us sing to the King.
- Let us teach them relentlessly the meaning of the gospel in the hope that God will open their eyes and make them alive. It happens through the gospel (1 Peter 1:22–25).

Each of those points deserves a chapter. But the point here is narrower: When children are small, they are being taught by us, even if we do nothing (which we never do). We should not fear requiring of them external behaviors in accord with God's Word from the time they can process any command. We are not making hypocrites out of them; we are preparing them for the gospel and for a fruitful life.

40

"Do Good to Everyone"

If God Wills Disease, Why Should
We Try to Eradicate It?

The question arises from biblical teaching, are all things ultimately under God's control? Scripture answers it this way: "My counsel shall stand, and I will accomplish all my purpose" (Isaiah 46:10). "Whatever the Lord pleases, he does, in heaven and on earth, in the seas and all deeps" (Psalm 135:6). "He does according to his will among the host of heaven and among the inhabitants of the earth; and none can stay his hand or say to him, 'What have you done?'" (Daniel 4:35). "[He] works all things according to the counsel of his will" (Ephesians 1:11).

This means that God governs all calamity and all disease. Satan is real and has a hand in it, but he is not ultimate and can do nothing but what God permits (Job 1:12–2:10). And God does not permit things willy-nilly. He permits things for a reason. There is infinite wisdom in all he does and all he permits. So what he permits is part of his plan just as much as what he does more directly.

Therefore, this raises the question, if God wills disease, why should we try to eradicate it? This is a crucial question for me because I have heard Christians say that believing in the sovereignty of God hinders Christians from working hard to eradicate diseases like malaria and tuberculosis and cancer and AIDS.

They think the logic goes like this: If God sovereignly wills all things, including malaria, then we would be striving against God to invest millions of dollars to find a way to wipe it out.

That is not the logic the Bible teaches. And it is not what lovers of God's sovereignty have historically believed. In fact, lovers of God's sovereignty have been among the most aggressive scientists who have helped subdue creation and bring it under the dominion of man for his good, just as Psalm 8:6 says, "You have given [man] dominion over the works of your hands; you have put all things under his feet."

The logic of the Bible says to act according to God's "will of command," not according to his "will of decree." God's will of decree is whatever comes to pass. "If the Lord wills, we will live and do this or that" (James 4:15). God's "will of decree" ordained that his Son be betrayed (Luke 22:22), ridiculed (Isaiah 53:3), mocked (Luke 18:32), flogged (Matthew 20:19), forsaken (Matthew 26:31), pierced (John 19:37), and killed (Mark 9:31). But the Bible teaches us plainly that we *should not* betray, ridicule, mock, flog, forsake, pierce, or kill innocent people. That is God's will of command. We do not look at the death of Jesus, clearly willed by God, and conclude that killing Jesus is good and that we should join the mockers.

In the same way, we do not look at the devastation of malaria or AIDS and conclude that we should join the ranks of the indifferent. No. "Love your neighbor" is God's will of command (Matthew 22:39). "Do to others as you would have them do to you" is God's will of command (Matthew 7:12, NIV). "If your enemy is hungry, feed him" is God's will of command (Romans 12:20). The disasters that God ordains are not aimed at paralyzing his people with indifference but mobilizing them with compassion.

When Paul taught that "the creation was subjected to futility," he also taught that this subjection was "in hope that the creation itself will be set free from its bondage to corruption and obtain the freedom of the glory of the children of God" (Romans 8:20–21). There is no reason that

Christians should not embrace this futility-lifting calling now. God will complete it in the age to come. But it is a good thing to conquer as much disease and suffering now, in the name of Christ, as we can.

In fact, I would wave the banner right now and call some of you who are reading this to enter vocations of research that may be the means of undoing some of the great diseases of the world. This is not fighting against God. God is as much in charge of the research as he is of the disease. You can be an instrument in his hand.

This may be the time appointed for the triumph that he wills over the disease that he ordained. Don't try to read the mind of God from his mysterious decrees of calamity. Do what he says: "Do good to everyone" (Galatians 6:10).

41

DOES ANYONE STANDING BY THE LAKE OF FIRE JUMP IN?

Reflections on How Willingly Sinners Enter Hell

C. S. Lewis is one of the top five dead people who have shaped the way I see and respond to the world. But he is not a reliable guide on a number of important theological matters. Hell is one of them.

His relentless stress was that people are not "sent" to hell but become their own hell. His emphasis was that we should think of "a bad man's perdition not as a sentence imposed on him but as the mere fact of being what he is."*

This inclines him to say, "All that are in hell choose it." And this leads some who follow Lewis in this emphasis to say things like, "All God does in the end with people is give them what they most want."

I come from the words of Jesus to this way of talking and find myself in a different world of discourse and sentiment. I think it is misleading to say that hell is giving people what they most want. I'm not saying you can't find a meaning for that statement that's true, perhaps in Romans 1:24–28. I'm saying that it's not a meaning that most people would give to it in light of what hell really is. I'm saying that the way Lewis dealt with

---

* For all the relevant quotes, see Wayne Martindale and Jerry Root, eds., *The Quotable Lewis* (Carol Stream, IL: Tyndale, 1990), 288–95.

hell and the way Jesus dealt with it are very different. And we would do well to follow Jesus.

The misery of hell will be so great that no one will want to be there. They will be weeping and gnashing their teeth (Matthew 8:12). Between their sobs, they will not speak the words, "I want this." They will not be able to say amid the flames of the lake of fire (Revelation 20:14), "I want this." "The smoke of their torment goes up forever and ever, and they have no rest, day or night" (Revelation 14:11). No one wants this.

When there are only two choices, and you choose against one, it does not mean that you want the other, if you are ignorant of the outcome of both. Unbelieving people know neither God nor hell. This ignorance is not innocent. Apart from regenerating grace, all people "by their unrighteousness suppress the truth" (Romans 1:18).

The person who rejects God does not know the real horrors of hell. This may be because he does not believe hell exists, or it may be because he convinces himself that it would be tolerably preferable to heaven.

But whatever he believes or does not believe, when he chooses against God, he is wrong about God and about hell. He is not, at that point, preferring the real hell over the real God. He is blind to both. He does not perceive the true glories of God, and he does not perceive the true horrors of hell.

So when a person chooses against God and, therefore, de facto chooses hell—or when he jokes about preferring hell with his friends over heaven with boring religious people—he does not know what he is doing. What he rejects is not the real heaven (nobody will be boring in heaven), and what he wants is not the real hell but the tolerable hell of his imagination.

When he dies, he will be shocked beyond words. The miseries are so great he would do anything in his power to escape. That it is not in his power to repent does not mean he wants to be there. Esau wept bitterly that he could not repent (Hebrews 12:17). The hell he was entering into he found to be totally miserable, and he wanted out. The meaning of hell is the scream, "I hate this, and I want out."

What sinners want is not hell but sin. That hell is the inevitable consequence of unforgiven sin does not mean people who choose sin want hell. It is not what people want—certainly not what they most want. Wanting sin is no more equal to wanting hell than wanting chocolate is equal to wanting obesity. Or wanting cigarettes is equal to wanting cancer.

Beneath this misleading emphasis on hell being what people "most want" is the notion that God does not "send" people to hell. But this is simply unbiblical. God certainly does send people to hell. He does pass sentence, and he executes it. Indeed, worse than that. God does not just *send*, he *throws*. "If anyone's name was not found written in the book of life, he was thrown (Greek, *eblethe*) into the lake of fire" (Revelation 20:15; see also Matthew 13:42; 25:30; Mark 9:47).

The reason the Bible speaks of people being "thrown" into hell is that no one will willingly go there, once they see what it really is. No one standing on the shore of the lake of fire jumps in. They do not choose it, and they will not want it. They have chosen sin. They have wanted sin. They do not want the punishment. When they come to the shore of this fiery lake, they must be thrown in.

When someone says that no one is in hell who doesn't want to be there, they give the false impression that hell is within the limits of what humans can tolerate. It inevitably gives the impression that hell is less horrible than Jesus says it is.

We should ask, How did Jesus expect his audience to think and feel about the way he spoke of hell? The words he chose were not chosen to soften the horror by being accommodating to cultural sensibilities. He spoke of a "fiery furnace" (Matthew 13:42) and "weeping and gnashing of teeth" (Luke 13:28) and "outer darkness" (Matthew 25:30) and "their worm [that] does not die" (Mark 9:48) and "eternal punishment"

(Matthew 25:46) and "unquenchable fire" (Mark 9:43) and being "cut…in pieces" (Matthew 24:51).

These words are chosen to portray hell as an eternal, conscious experience that no one would or could ever want if they knew what they were choosing. Therefore, if someone is going to emphasize that people freely choose hell or that no one is there who doesn't want to be there, surely he should make every effort to clarify that, when they get there, they will *not* want this.

Surely the pattern of Jesus, who used blazing words to blast the hell-bent blindness out of everyone, should be followed. Surely, we will grope for words that show no one, no one, *no one* will *want* to be in hell when they experience what it really is. Surely everyone who desires to save people from hell will not mainly stress that it is "wantable" or "choosable," but that it is horrible beyond description: weeping, gnashing teeth, darkness, worm-eaten, fiery, furnacelike, dismembering, eternal, punishment, "an abhorrence to all flesh" (Isaiah 66:24).

As a hell-deserving sinner, I thank God for Jesus Christ my Savior, who became a curse for me and suffered hellish pain that he might deliver me from the wrath to come. While there is time, he will do that for anyone who turns from sin and treasures him and his work above all.

42

Stereotypes and Racism

Checking Ethnocentrism in Our Statistical Generalizations

One of the serious challenges to freeing ourselves from ethnocentrism, or racism, is discerning when using a generalization is, in fact, the use of a stereotype. There is a difference. Life can't be lived without generalizations, as we will see, but they can be misused with great harm. Christians should want to get their cues on these things from God's Word, not the surrounding culture. In trying to think through these things, I came to three exhortations.

Exhortation #1: *Christians should not simply reflect the morality of their era but the morality of the Bible.*
The Bible says, "Do not be conformed to this world, but be transformed by the renewal of your mind" (Romans 12:2), and "Take no part in the unfruitful works of darkness, but instead expose them" (Ephesians 5:11).

Consider this quote from Shelby Steele's *White Guilt: How Blacks and Whites Together Destroyed the Promise of the Civil Rights Era.* As you read, ask, How many Christians simply fit into the moral laxity of Eisenhower in his day and of Clinton in his day? Reflecting on the Clinton-Lewinsky sexual scandal compared to Dwight Eisenhower's reputed use of the N-word, Steele wrote:

I wondered if President Clinton would be defended with relativism if he had done what, according to gossip, Eisenhower was said to have done. Suppose that in a light moment he had slipped into a parody of an old Arkansas buddy from childhood and, to get the voice right, used the word "nigger" a few times. Suppose further that a tape of this came to light so that all day long in the media—from the unctuous morning shows to the freewheeling late-night shows to the news every half hour on radio—we would hear the unmistakable presidential voice saying, "Take your average nigger.…"

A contribution of the civil rights movement was to establish the point that a multiracial society cannot be truly democratic unless social equality itself becomes a matter of *personal* morality. So a president's "immorality" in this area would pretty much cancel his legitimacy as a democratic leader.

The point is that President Clinton survived what would certainly have destroyed President Eisenhower, and Eisenhower could easily have survived what would almost certainly have destroyed Clinton. Each man, finally, was no more than indiscreet within the moral landscape of his era (again, Eisenhower's indiscretion is hypothetical here for purposes of discussion). Neither racism in the fifties nor womanizing in the nineties was a profound enough sin to undermine completely the moral authority of a president. So it was the good luck of each president to sin into the moral relativism of his era rather than into its Puritanism. And, interestingly, the moral relativism of one era was the Puritanism of the other. Race simply replaced sex as the primary focus of America's moral seriousness.*

---

* Shelby Steele, *White Guilt: How Blacks and Whites Together Destroyed the Promise of the Civil Rights Era* (New York: Harper, 2007), 5–6.

The Satisfied Soul

This is the implication for Christians: Let the Bible, and not the era, govern our moral seriousness.

Exhortation #2: *Christians should not be guilty of stereotyping groups, recognizing that stereotyping is different from the just and loving use of generalization.*
The Bible says, "Do not judge by appearances, but judge with right judgment" (John 7:24).

In our ordinary use of language today, a stereotype is a generalization that is *not* built on what Jesus calls "right judgment." Merriam-Webster defines *stereotype* as a "standardized mental picture that is held in common by members of a group and that represents an *oversimplified* opinion, *prejudiced* attitude, or *uncritical* judgment."

This is the implication for Christians: Beware of forming stereotypes, or unjustified generalizations. Not only do they tend to hurt people (or unduly puff up the pride of others), but they are also unreliable guides in life.

Exhortation #3: *Christians should use generalizations justly and lovingly to form true and helpful judgments about people and life.*
The Bible says, "So whatever you wish that others would do to you, do also to them, for this is the Law and the Prophets" (Matthew 7:12).

What is a generalization? A *generalization* is a general statement, law, principle, or proposition about a situation or a thing or a person or a group based on what we have generally observed from similar situations, things, persons, groups. Without them wise living is impossible.

- Many mushrooms are poisonous, and in general they have a certain spongy appearance. This generalization will keep you from experimenting with them in the woods when you are hungry and may save your life.

- Thin boards generally will not hold up a heavy man when stretched over wide spaces. This generalization will keep you from falling in the river.
- Generally, people in America stop when the light is red for them and green for you. You count on this and thus the traffic can keep flowing.

So the tough question is, When is a generalization about a group racist? I am using the word *racist* as something sinful, and the following answers move toward a definition. The following way of using a generalization would be wrong (racist):

- Using a generalization is wrong when you want a person to fit a negative generalization that you have formed about a group (even if the generalization statistically is true).
- Using a generalization is wrong when you assume that a statistically true negative generalization is true of a particular person in the face of individual evidence to the contrary.
- Using a generalization is wrong when you treat all the members of a group as if all must be characterized by a negative generalization.
- Using a generalization is wrong when you speak disparagingly of an entire group on the basis of a negative generalization without any regard for those in the group who don't fit the generalization. Or when you speak negatively of a group based on a generalization without giving any evidence that you acknowledge and appreciate the exceptions. (I assume that Jesus' generalizations about the Pharisees in Matthew 23 and Paul's generalization about the Cretans in Titus 1:12 are not sinful because they did have such regard and did appreciate the exceptions.)

This is the implication for Christians: While realizing that life is not livable without generalizations, be careful not to let your pride lead you to use statistical generalizations in unloving ways.

43

THE UNBELIEVING POET CATCHES A GLIMPSE OF TRUTH

When Beauty Becomes Irresistible

Since all humans are created in the image of God (Genesis 1:27), and the work of God's law is written on every heart (Romans 2:15), and the heavens are telling the glory of God to everyone who can see (Psalm 19:1), and God has put eternity in man's heart (Ecclesiastes 3:11), and by God's providence every person is set to grope for God (Acts 17:27), and in God we all live and move and have our being (Acts 17:28), it is not surprising that even people without eyes to see the glory of Christ nevertheless have glimpses into the way the world really is, and then they don't know what to do with them.

Stephen Dunn is a Pulitzer Prize–winning poet and not a Christian. "I think of God as a metaphor. God is a metaphor for the origins and mysteries of the world.... I think of beliefs as provisional. They're not things that constitute anything fixed."

In an interview for *Books & Culture*, Aaron Rench asked him about his book *The Insistence of Beauty*.

RENCH: What is this notion that beauty has a demanding, compelling quality to it? Why is beauty that way?

DUNN: I just think beauty is irresistible. It disarms us. Takes away our arguments. And then if you expand the notion of

beauty—that there is beauty in the tawdry, beauty in ugliness—
things get complicated. But I think that beauty, which is more
related in my mind to the sublime, is what we cannot resist.*

Yes, and this is how we all were converted to Christ. The eyes of our
hearts were enlightened to see the beauty of Christ, and in that moment
he became irresistible. This is the way divine, spiritual beauty works. It
authenticates itself. It "takes away our arguments." Or better, it replaces
all our false arguments with one grand, true argument that cannot be
resisted.

This is the point Paul made: "The god of this world has blinded the
minds of the unbelievers, to keep them from seeing the light of the gospel
of the glory of Christ, who is the image of God" (2 Corinthians 4:4).

The "glory of Christ" is the beauty of Christ. It is the radiance of the
fullness of his person—the impact of all his perfections. The reason
people do not believe in Christ is that they do not see what is really there.
That is what it means to be blind. Beauty is really there to be seen, but
we are blind to it.

If we see it, we believe. "Beauty is irresistible." If you resist, you have
not seen Christ as beautiful as he is (1 John 3:6). So the way we are converted to Christ is by having this blindness taken away. Scripture says,
"[God] has shone in our hearts to give the light of the knowledge of the
glory of God in the face of Jesus Christ" (2 Corinthians 4:6). God
replaces blindness with light. The light is specifically "the glory of God
in the face of Christ." It's the beauty of Christ.

That is all it takes. There is no coercion after that revelation. The
light—the beauty—compels. We don't behold it and then ponder
whether to believe. If we are still pondering, we have not yet seen.

Poet Stephen Dunn, groping toward God, says that beauty "is
related…to the sublime." It is "what we cannot resist." Yes, the sublime

---

* March/April, 2008, 26–27.

is summed up in Jesus Christ. And it is his glory that is supremely irresistible.

Let this be your life: Ponder him; be pervaded with him; point to him. The more you know of him and the more you admire the fullness of his beauty, the more you will reflect him. Oh, that there would be thousands of irresistible reflections of the beauty of Jesus. May it be said of such reflections, "It disarms us. It takes away our arguments."

44

THE DECEITFUL AND DEADLY HEALTH-AND-WEALTH TEACHING

Seven Pleas to Prosperity Preachers

When I read about prosperity-preaching churches, my response is, if I were not on the inside of Christianity, I would not want in. In other words, if this is the message of Jesus, no thank you.

Luring people to Christ to get rich is both deceitful and deadly. It's deceitful because when Jesus himself called us, he said things like, "Any one of you who does not renounce all that he has cannot be my disciple" (Luke 14:33). And it's deadly because the desire to be rich plunges "people into ruin and destruction" (1 Timothy 6:9). So here is my plea to preachers of the gospel.

1. Don't develop a philosophy of ministry that makes it harder for people to get into heaven.

Jesus said, "How difficult it will be for those who have wealth to enter the kingdom of God!" His disciples were astonished, as many in the "prosperity" movement should be. So Jesus went on to raise their astonishment even higher by saying, "It is easier for a camel to go through the eye of a needle than for a rich person to enter the kingdom of God." They responded in disbelief, "Then who can be saved?" Jesus said, "With man it is impossible, but not with God. For all things are possible with God" (Mark 10:23–27).

My question for prosperity preachers is, why would you want to develop a ministry focus that makes it harder for people to enter heaven?

2. Don't develop a philosophy of ministry that kindles suicidal desires in people.

Paul said, "Godliness with contentment is great gain, for we brought nothing into the world, and we cannot take anything out of the world. But if we have food and clothing, with these we will be content" (1 Timothy 6:6–8). But then he warned against the desire to be rich. And by implication, he warned against preachers who stir up the desire to be rich instead of helping people get rid of it. He warned, "Those who desire to be rich fall into temptation, into a snare, into many senseless and harmful desires that plunge people into ruin and destruction. For the love of money is a root of all kinds of evils. It is through this craving that some have wandered away from the faith and pierced themselves with many pangs" (1 Timothy 6:9–10).

So my question for prosperity preachers is, why would you want to develop a ministry that encourages people to pierce themselves with many pangs and plunge themselves into ruin and destruction?

3. Don't develop a philosophy of ministry that encourages vulnerability to moth and rust.

Jesus warned against the effort to lay up treasures on earth: "Do not lay up for yourselves treasures on earth, where moth and rust destroy and where thieves break in and steal, but lay up for yourselves treasures in heaven, where neither moth nor rust destroys and where thieves do not break in and steal" (Matthew 6:19–20). That is, we must be givers, not keepers.

Yes, we all keep something. But given the built-in tendency toward greed in all of us, why would we take the focus off Jesus and turn it upside down?

4. Don't develop a philosophy of ministry that makes hard work a means of amassing wealth.

Paul said we should not steal. The alternative is hard work with our own hands. But the main purpose is not merely to hoard or even to have. The purpose is to have to *give:* "Let him labor, doing honest work with his own hands, so that he may have something to share with anyone in need" (Ephesians 4:28). This is not a justification for being rich in order to give more. It is a call to make more and keep less so we can give more. There is no reason why a person who makes $200,000 should live any differently from the way a person who makes $80,000. Find a wartime lifestyle, cap your expenditures, and then give the rest away. It's not that simple. But that is the principle.

Why would you want to encourage people to think they should possess wealth in order to be a lavish giver? Why not encourage them to keep their lives more simple and be an even more lavish giver? Would that not add to their generosity a strong testimony that Christ, and not possessions, is their treasure?

5. Don't develop a philosophy of ministry that promotes less faith in the promises of God.

The reason the writer to the Hebrews tells us to be content with what we have is that being the opposite implies having less faith in the promises of God. He said, "Keep your life free from love of money, and be content with what you have, for he has said, 'I will never leave you nor forsake you.' So we can confidently say, 'The Lord is my helper; I will not fear; what can man do to me?'" (Hebrews 13:5–6).

If the Bible tells us that being content with what we have honors the promise of God never to forsake us, why would we want to teach people to want to be rich?

6. Don't develop a philosophy of ministry that contributes to your people being choked to death.

Jesus warned that the Word of God, which is meant to give us life, can be choked off from any effectiveness by riches. He said it is like a seed that grows up among thorns that choke it to death: "They are those who hear, but as they go on their way they are choked by the...riches...of life, and their fruit does not mature" (Luke 8:14).

Why would we want to encourage people to pursue the very thing that Jesus warned will choke us to death?

7. Don't develop a philosophy of ministry that takes the seasoning out of the salt and puts the light under a basket.

What is it about Christians that makes us the salt of the earth and the light of the world? It is not wealth. The desire for wealth and the pursuit of wealth tastes and looks just like the world. It does not offer the world anything different from what it already believes in. The great tragedy of prosperity preaching is that a person does not have to be spiritually awakened in order to embrace it; one needs only to be greedy. Getting rich in the name of Jesus is not the salt of the earth or the light of the world. In this, the world simply sees a reflection of itself. And if it works, they will buy it.

The context of Jesus' saying shows us what the salt and light are. They are the joyful willingness to suffer for Christ. Jesus said, "Blessed are you when others revile you and persecute you and utter all kinds of evil against you falsely on my account. Rejoice and be glad, for your reward is great in heaven, for so they persecuted the prophets who were before you. You are the salt of the earth.... You are the light of the world" (Matthew 5:11–14).

What will make the world taste (the salt) and see (the light) Christ in us is not that we love wealth the same way they do. Rather, it will be the willingness and the ability of Christians to love others through suffering, all the while rejoicing because their reward is in heaven with Jesus. This is inexplicable in human terms. This is supernatural. But to attract people with promises of prosperity is simply natural. It is not the message of Jesus. It is not what he died to achieve.

45

SHEEP, WOLVES, SNAKES, AND DOVES

Thoughts on Matthew 10:16

Jesus said, "Behold, I am sending you out as sheep in the midst of wolves, so be wise as serpents and innocent as doves" (Matthew 10:16).

When Jesus sends us to bear witness to him in the world, he does not send us out as dominant and strong but as weak and seemingly defenseless in ourselves. The only reason I say "seemingly" defenseless is that it is possible that, since all authority belongs to Jesus, he might intervene and shut the mouths of the wolves, as he did the mouths of the lions that surrounded Daniel.

But that does not appear to be his intention. The text goes on to say that the "wolves" will deliver the "sheep" to courts and flog them and drag them before governors and have parents and children put to death and hate them and persecute them from town to town and malign them and kill them (Matthew 10:17–31). So it is clear that when Jesus says he is sending us as sheep in the midst of wolves, he means that we will be treated the way wolves treat sheep.

But even though sheep are proverbially stupid—which, on the face of it, is what it looks like when they walk toward wolves and not away from them—Jesus countered that notion by saying "be wise as serpents." So vulnerability, not stupidity, is the point of calling us sheep. Be like snakes, not sheep, when it comes to being smart. I take that to mean that snakes are quick to get out of the way. They go under a rock.

So, yes, go among wolves and be vulnerable as you preach the gospel, but when they lunge at you, step aside. When they open their mouths, don't jump in. And not only that, be as innocent as doves. That is, don't give them any legitimate reason to accuse you of injustice or immorality. Keep your reputation as clean as you can.

So both the snakelike intelligence and the dovelike innocence are designed to keep the sheep out of trouble. Jesus does not mean for us to get ourselves into as much difficulty as possible. He means to risk your lives as vulnerable, noncombative, sheeplike, courageous witnesses, but try to find ways to give your witness in a way that does not bring down unnecessary persecution.

This brings us to the dilemma that has faced many faithful witnesses: When do you flee from danger, and when do you embrace it and witness through it? In 1684, John Bunyan published a book called *Seasonable Counsel or Advice to Sufferers*. In it, he addressed this question: When does a sufferer flee (from danger) and when does he stand (and suffer the danger)? Bunyan knew how to answer for himself. He had four children, one of them blind, and he chose to remain in prison for twelve years rather than promise not to preach the gospel. How does he answer the question for others? May we try to escape?

> Thou mayest do in this as it is in thy heart. If it is in thy heart
> to fly, fly; if it be in thy heart to stand, stand. Anything but a
> denial of the truth. He that flies, has warrant to do so; he that
> stands, has warrant to do so. Yea, the same man may both fly
> and stand, as the call and working of God with his heart may
> be. Moses fled, Exodus 2:15; Moses stood, Hebrews 11:27.
> David fled, 1 Samuel 19:12; David stood, 1 Samuel 24:8. Jere-
> miah fled, Jeremiah 37:11–12; Jeremiah stood, Jeremiah 38:17.
> Christ withdrew himself, Luke 9:10; Christ stood, John

18:1–8. Paul fled, 2 Corinthians 11:33; Paul stood, Acts 20:22–23....

There are few rules in this case. The man himself is best able to judge concerning his present strength, and what weight this or that argument has upon his heart to stand or fly.... Do not fly out of a slavish fear, but rather because flying is an ordinance of God, opening a door for the escape of some, which door is opened by God's providence, and the escape countenanced by God's word, Matthew 10:23....

If, therefore, when thou hast fled, thou art taken, be not offended at God or man: not at God, for thou art his servant, thy life and thy all are his; not at man, for he is but God's rod, and is ordained, in this, to do thee good. Hast thou escaped? Laugh. Art thou taken? Laugh. I mean, be pleased which [how]soever things shall go, for that the scales are still in God's hand.*

Let us be slow to judge the missionary who chooses death rather than escape. And let us be slow to judge the missionary who chooses escape. Rather, let us give ourselves daily to the disciplines of Word saturation and obedience, which transform us by the renewing of our minds that we may prove what is the will of God, what is good and acceptable and perfect in the moment of absolute urgency (Romans 12:2).

---

* John Bunyan, *Seasonable Counsels, or Advice to Sufferers,* in Works, Vol. 2, ed. George Offor (Edinburgh: The Banner of Truth Trust, 1991, reprinted from the 1854 edition published by W. G. Blackie and Son, Glasgow), 726.

46

ABOLITION AND THE ROOTS OF PUBLIC JUSTICE

The Public Power of Protestant Justification

One of the most important and least known facts about the battle to abolish the slave trade in Britain two hundred years ago is that it was sustained by a passion for the doctrine of justification by faith alone. William Wilberforce was a spiritually exuberant and doctrinally rigorous evangelical. He battled tirelessly in Parliament for the outlawing of the British slave trade. It was doctrine that nourished the joy that sustained the battle that ended the vicious trade.

The key to understanding Wilberforce is to read his own book, *A Practical View of Christianity*. It's the only book he wrote. There he argued that the fatal habit of his day was to separate Christian morals from Christian doctrines. His conviction was that there is "perfect harmony between the leading doctrines and the practical precepts of Christianity." He had seen the devastating effects of denying this: "The peculiar doctrines of Christianity went more and more out of sight, and…the moral system itself also began to wither and decay, being robbed of that which should have supplied it with life and nutriment." But Wilberforce knew that "the whole superstructure of Christian morals is grounded on their deep and ample basis."

This "ample basis" and these "peculiar doctrines" that sustained Wilberforce in the battle against the slave trade were the doctrines of human depravity, divine judgment, the substitutionary work of Christ on the cross, justification by faith alone, regeneration by the Holy Spirit, and the practical necessity of fruit in a life devoted to good deeds. Wilberforce was not a political pragmatist. He was a radically God-centered, Christian politician. And his zeal for Christ, rooted in these "peculiar doctrines," was the strength that sustained him in the battle.

At the center of these essential "gigantic truths" was (and is) justification by faith alone. The indomitable joy that perseveres in the battle for justice is grounded in the experience of Jesus Christ as our righteousness. "If we would...rejoice," Wilberforce said, "as triumphantly as the first Christians did; we must learn, like them to repose our entire trust in [Christ] and to adopt the language of the apostle, 'God forbid that I should glory, save in the cross of Jesus Christ,' 'who of God is made unto us wisdom and righteousness, and sanctification, and redemption.'"

In other words, the doctrine of justification is essential to right living—and that includes political living. Astonishingly, Wilberforce said that the spiritual and practical errors of his day that gave strength to the slave trade were owing to the failure to experience the truth of this doctrine:

> They consider not that Christianity is a scheme "for justifying the
> ungodly" by Christ's dying for them "when yet sinners"—a
> scheme "for reconciling us to God"—when enemies; and for
> making the fruits of holiness the effects, not the cause, of our
> being justified and reconciled.

This was why he wrote *A Practical View of Christianity*. The "bulk" of Christians in his day, he observed, were "nominal"—that is, they pursued morality without first relying utterly on the free gift of justification by grace alone through faith alone on the basis of Christ alone. They got things backward. First they strived for moral uplift, and then they appealed to God for approval. That is not the Christian gospel. And it will not transform a nation. It would not sustain a politician through eleven parliamentary defeats over twenty years of vitriolic opposition.

The battle for abolition was sustained by getting the gospel right: "The true Christian...knows...that this holiness is not to precede his reconciliation to God, and be its cause; but to follow it, and be its effect. That, in short, it is by faith in Christ only that he is to be justified in the sight of God." When Wilberforce put things in this order, he found invincible strength and courage to stand for the justice of abolition.

When we call to mind the abolition of the British slave trade, may Jesus Christ, the righteous One, receive the credit he is due in the life of William Wilberforce.

47

TOPPLE EVERY IDOL

Fighting Covetousness by Looking at Others

Achan stole and lied (Joshua 7:11). Jericho had fallen before Israel. The riches of the city were not to be taken, but Achan took garments and silver and gold. He hid them and tried to deceive the leaders.

Why did he do that? When he was caught, Achan gave the answer: "I *coveted* them and took them" (Joshua 7:21). Covetousness. He *desired* the silver, gold, and garments more than he desired fellowship with God.

There is no difference between the Hebrew word for "desire" and the Hebrew word for "covet." Coveting means "desiring something too much." And too much is measured by how that desiring compares to desiring God. If desiring leads you away from God rather than closer to God, it is covetousness. It is sin.

I suspect that the reason the Ten Commandments began with the commandment "You shall have no other gods before me" (Exodus 20:3) and ends with the commandment "You shall not covet" (Exodus 20:17) is that they are essentially the same commandment, one focusing on what we should desire (God) and one focusing on what we shouldn't (anything else more than God). They bracket the other eight commandments and reveal their source.

Not coveting means not desiring anything in a way that diminishes God as your supreme treasure. And not having any gods before God means the same thing: Don't treasure anything or anyone in a way that competes with God's supreme place in your life. Idolatry is what we call disobedience to the first commandment. And idolatry is what Paul called disobedience to the tenth commandment ("covetousness, which is idolatry," Colossians 3:5).

So Achan stole and lied because God was not his supreme treasure. He was not satisfied in all that God promised to be for him. That is probably why Joshua said to Achan when he was found out, "My son, give glory to the LORD God" (Joshua 7:19). It demeans the glory of God when we prefer anything above him. That was Achan's chief sin. Desiring gold more than God equals covetousness, which equals idolatry, which demeans God.

How can we keep our lives free from this dreadful condition—desiring other things more than God, coveting, being idolaters? One answer is the Word of God: "I have stored up your word in my heart, that I might not sin against you" (Psalm 119:11).

Another answer comes from Philippians. Paul described the condition we all want to be in. He said, "Whatever gain I had, I counted as loss for the sake of Christ. Indeed, I count everything as loss because of the surpassing worth of knowing Christ Jesus my Lord" (Philippians 3:7–8). That is exactly the opposite of covetousness. That is the opposite of idolatry. That is supreme satisfaction in Christ. That is freedom.

Does Paul have a practical suggestion that we can use to fight for this satisfaction in Christ? Yes, he does: "Brothers, join in imitating me, *and* keep your eyes on those who walk according to the example you have in us" (Philippians 3:17).

I have some amazingly practical help for us. Pick out some people whose lives show that they treasure Christ above other things. Then keep your eyes on them, as Paul said. Watch them. That is a good way to conquer covetousness.

There are some folks whose maturity and wisdom and spiritual fruitfulness in their marriages, for example, is so admirable that I look at them and think about them a lot. When I am struggling with what I should feel and do in my marriage, I think about what they would do. I think Paul meant something like that.

I would only add that it is good to have some dead saints to "keep your eyes on" as well. That's what Christian biographies are for.

So flee covetousness. Topple all your idols. "Count everything as loss because of the surpassing worth of knowing Christ." Be in the Word every day. But also find those who live this way and "keep your eyes on them." What you will see, if you look carefully, is the power and beauty of Christ. This sight will satisfy your soul. And your satisfied soul will keep you from coveting (and lying and stealing like Achan). And your life will make God look supremely valuable.

48

CREATING POINTERS TO THE
GREATNESS OF CHRIST

Why and How I Tweet

I see two kinds of responses to social media like blogging, Facebook, Twitter, and others.

One says: These media tend to shorten attention spans, weaken discursive reasoning, lure people away from Scripture and prayer, disembody relationships, feed the fires of narcissism, cater to the craving for attention, fill the world with drivel, shrink the soul's capacity for greatness, and make us second-handers who comment on life when we ought to be living it. So boycott them and write books (not blogs) about the problem.

The second response says: Yes, there is truth in all that, but instead of boycotting, try to fill these media with as much provocative, reasonable, Bible-saturated, prayerful, relational, Christ-exalting, truth-driven, serious, creative pointers to true greatness as you can.

I lean toward the second response. *Lean* is different from *leap*. We are aware that the medium tends to shape the message. This has been true, more or less, with every new medium that has come along—speech, drawing, handwriting, print, books, magazines, newspapers, tracts, 16mm home movies, flannelgraph, Cinerama, movies, Gospel Blimps, TV, radio, cassette tapes, 8-tracks, blackboards, whiteboards, overhead projection, PowerPoint, skits, drama, banners, CDs, MP3s, DVDs, skywriting, video, texting, blogging, tweeting, mynah bird training, etc.

Danger, danger everywhere. Yes. But it seems to us that aggressive efforts to saturate media with the supremacy of God, the truth of Scripture, the glory of Christ, the joy of the gospel, the insanity of sin, and the radical nature of Christian living is a good choice for some Christians. Not all. Everyone should abstain from some of these media. For example, the Pipers don't have a television.

That's my general disposition toward media.

Now what about Twitter? I find Twitter to be a kind of taunt: "Okay, truth-lover, see what you can do with 140 characters! You say your mission is to spread a passion for the supremacy of God in all things! Well, this is one of those 'all things.' Can you magnify Christ with this thimbleful of letters?"

To which I respond:

The sovereign Lord of the earth and sky
Puts camels through a needle's eye.
And if his wisdom judge it mete,
He will put worlds inside a tweet.

It also seems to be that the book of Proverbs is God's Twitter compilation for us. So when I think about my life goal and when I think about how God uses proverbs, I am not inclined to tweet that at 10 a.m. the cat pulled the curtains down. But I am inclined to tweet: "The Lion of Judah will roll up the sky like a scroll and put the sun out with his brighter glory" (128 characters). If God answers my prayer, that tweet might distract someone from pornography and make him look up to something greater.

In spite of all the dangers, Twitter seemed like a risk worth taking. "All things were created through [Christ] and for [Christ]" (Colossians 1:16). The world does not know it, but that is why Twitter exists and that's why I tweet.

49

WHAT WILL THE FINAL JUDGMENT MEAN FOR YOU?

Thoughts on the Book of Life and Union with Christ

I am writing this on New Year's Eve. The ending of another year moves my mind to other endings—like the final judgment. Ponder with me, if you wish, what it will be like to go through the last great judgment. It is good to settle in our minds what it will be like. If we could see it clearly now, it would make those who trust Christ the happiest and bravest people in the days ahead.

I do believe we will all face a final judgment with the rest of the world. "We will all stand before the judgment seat of God" (Romans 14:10; see also 2 Corinthians 5:10). When Jesus said, "Whoever hears my word and believes him who sent me has eternal life. *He does not come into judgment,* but has passed from death to life" (John 5:24), I take him to mean that we will not be condemned in the final judgment because our sentence has already been passed—not guilty. So why are we there at the last judgment?

John paints us a picture in Revelation:

I saw the dead, great and small, standing before the throne, and books were opened. Then another book was opened, which is the book of life. And the dead were judged by what was written in the books, according to what they had done. And the sea gave up the dead who were in it, Death and Hades gave up the dead who were in them, and they were judged, each one of them, according to what they had done. Then Death and Hades were thrown into the lake of fire. This is the second death, the lake of fire. And if anyone's name was not found written in the book of life, he was thrown into the lake of fire. (20:12–15)

There are books (v. 12), and there is a book (vv. 12, 15). The book is called "the book of life." The books record the deeds of all people (including ours). This is implied when John said, "The dead were judged by what was written in the *books, according to what they had done*...and they were judged, each one of them, *according to what they had done*" (vv. 12–13).

All the dead are judged in view of what is written in the books. This includes believers and unbelievers, elect and nonelect. This is a judgment of all people: "I saw the dead, great and small" (v. 12). "The dead were judged" (v. 12). "The sea gave up the dead who were in it, Death and Hades gave up the dead who were in them, and they were judged" (v. 13). So believers and unbelievers face what is written in the books. It matters. But how does it matter?

To answer that, we need to see what it means to have your name written in the book of life (vv. 12, 15). In Revelation 13:8, John said, "All who dwell on earth will worship [the beast], everyone whose name has not been written before the foundation of the world in the book of life of the Lamb who was slain." Two things are crucial here:

- The names have been in the book of life since before Creation. So this is a reference to the elect (Revelation 3:5)—those who would certainly believe on Christ and be saved through him.
- A name written in the book of life ensures that a person will not worship the beast. This is implied in saying everyone will worship the beast *except* those whose names are written in the book of life. If your name is in the book of life, you will not worship

the beast. That is not a coincidence. Being in the book means belonging to God, who keeps his elect from demon worship.

John said the same thing again in chapter 17: "The dwellers on earth whose names have not been written in the book of life from the foundation of the world will marvel to see the beast" (Revelation 17:8). Being in the book ensures that you will not marvel at the beast. It means God will keep you. You will persevere and be saved.

So we come back to the judgment in Revelation 20. "If anyone's name was not found written in the book of life, he was thrown into the lake of fire" (v. 15). This implies that being in the book of life ensures that one will not perish. Salvation is secured for all who are written in the book of life.

The reason that being written in the book of life secures our salvation is that the book is called "the book of life of the Lamb who was slain" (Revelation 13:8). The names in this book are not saved on the basis of their deeds. They are saved on the basis of Christ's being slain. He "loves us and has freed us from our sins by his blood" (Revelation 1:5). We have been ransomed by his blood (Revelation 5:9).

So how then does the record of our lives contained in "the books" have a part in our judgment? The answer is that the books contain enough evidence of our belonging to Christ that they function as a public confirmation of our faith and our union with him. Consider this passage: "Nothing unclean will ever enter [the New Jerusalem], nor anyone who does what is detestable or false, but only those who are written in the Lamb's book of life" (Revelation 21:27).

Here the result of "being written in the book of life" is not only not perishing but also not making a practice of detestable, sinful behaviors. In other words, just as in Revelation 13:8, where being in the book of life ensures that one will not worship the beast, so in Revelation 21:27, being in the book of life ensures that one will not make a practice of detestable deeds.

Therefore, our deeds confirm that our names are in the book and should be in the book—that is, they confirm that we trust Christ and are united with him. Our deeds are the fruit of our faith and union with Christ.

For example, consider the thief on the cross. Jesus said that he would enter paradise (Luke 23:43). But what will judgment be like for him when the books are opened? I believe 99.9 percent of his life will be sin, because whatever is not from faith is sin (Romans 14:23). Only the final minutes of his life on the cross will be the fruit of faith. I think God will open the book of life and show the name of the thief on the cross. His salvation will be secured by the blood of Christ. Then God will open the books and will use the record of sin to glorify his Son's supreme sacrifice, and then he will use the last page to show the change that was wrought in the thief's attitudes and words. That last page—the last hours on the cross—will be the public confirmation of the thief's faith and union with Christ.

Therefore, when I say that what is written in the books is a public confirmation of our faith and of union with Christ, I do not mean that the record will contain more good works than bad works. I mean that there will be recorded there the practical evidences that show the reality of faith—the reality of regeneration and union with Christ. There will be enough evidences of grace that God will be able to make a public display of what is in the books to verify the born-again reality of those written in the book of life.

No one is saved on the basis of his works. But everyone who is saved does new works. Not perfectly but with humble longing for more holiness. That is how I face today and tomorrow, confident that my condemnation is past (Romans 8:3), that my name is in the book of life, and that the One who began a good work in me will bring it to completion at the day of Christ. I pray for you, that you are with me in this confidence.

50

LET'S MAKE SOME RESOLUTIONS

Endeavoring Fresh Good for the Glory of God

God approves of New Year's resolutions. And midyear and three-quarters-year and monthly and weekly and daily resolutions. Any and all resolutions for good have God's approval—*if* we resolve by faith in Jesus.

I would like to encourage you to make some resolutions. Socrates said, "The unexamined life is not worth living." Well, the examined life is not worth living either if the examination produces no resolutions. What examination and experience teach us is that the unplanned life settles into fruitless routine. The drifting life—the coasting, *que sera sera* unreflective life—tends to be a wasted life.

The opposite of this is self-examination—life examination, routine examination, schedule examination, heart examination—followed by "resolves for good." That's what I encourage you to do. Here's why I think God will be pleased when you do this by faith in Jesus.

Paul said to the Thessalonians:

> To this end we always pray for you, that our God may make you worthy of his calling and may fulfill every resolve for good and every work of faith by his power, so that the name of our Lord Jesus may be glorified in you, and you in him, according to the grace of our God and the Lord Jesus Christ. (2 Thessalonians 1:11–12)

I find this extremely encouraging. Paul prays for us, and I pray for you even as I write this, that God will "fulfill every resolve for good" that we have. This means that it is good to have resolves. God approves of it. It also means that our resolving is important but that God's enabling us to fulfill the resolves is crucial. Paul wouldn't pray if God's help weren't needed. "The heart of man plans [resolves!] his way, but the LORD establishes [fulfills!] his steps" (Proverbs 16:9).

But it matters how we resolve. When Paul said, "Every resolve for good and every work of faith," he was not describing two different acts. He was describing one act in two ways. It is a "resolve for good" because we will it. It is a "work of faith" because we depend on Jesus to give us power to fulfill it. That's how we resolve. It's by faith in Jesus.

So Paul said that the fulfilling of the resolve is "by his power." That's what we are depending on. That's what we are looking for when we resolve. We are looking to Jesus, who promised to be with us and help us. "I know that through…the help of the Spirit of Jesus Christ this will turn out for my deliverance" (Philippians 1:19).

This explains the words "so that" in Paul's prayer: "*So that* the name of our Lord Jesus may be glorified in you" (2 Thessalonians 1:12). When you resolve something good and trust in the power of Jesus to help you do it, then "the name of our Lord Jesus is glorified." If you depend on *your* willpower, *your* name will be glorified. The giver gets the glory.

So Christian resolutions are different from the world's resolutions. We believe that by grace alone we have been called—that is, captured by the truth and beauty of Christ. We resolve things not to make God be for us, but because he is already for us—that's what his call makes plain. He opens our eyes to see and trust Christ. He shows us, in the cross, that he is totally for us. All our resolves are to walk more worthy of this calling, in ways more fitting for the beneficiaries of such free grace.

They are faith resolves—faith that we are loved and called and justified. And faith that, therefore, Jesus will help us do what we resolve to do. When we resolve like that, the name of our Lord Jesus is magnified.

So sometime soon, pause and examine your life. Examine what is missing that should be there. What is there that should be removed? What new dreams for ministry might you venture? What new habits do you want to build into your schedule?

Remember, God will be pleased with new resolves for good if you resolve *by faith in Jesus*. I am praying for you "that our God may make you worthy of his calling and may fulfill every resolve for good and every work of faith by his power" (2 Thessalonians 1:11).

51

DOES IT MATTER
WHAT OTHERS THINK?

Yes—What They Think about Christ!

L ife is too short to spend time and energy worrying about what others think of us. Or should we care about what others think precisely
because that really matters in this short life? Should we be radically free
from what others think, so that we don't fall into the indictment of being
a "second-hander" or "man-pleaser," a slave to expediency? Or should we
keep an eye out for what others think of what we do, so that we don't fall
into the indictment of being boorish and insensitive and offensive? The
answer is not simple. Some biblical texts seem to say it matters what others think. Others seem to say it doesn't.

For example, Jesus warned us: "Woe to you, when all people speak
well of you" (Luke 6:26). And his own enemies saw in him an indifference to what others thought: "Teacher, we know that you are true and
do not care about anyone's opinion. For you are not swayed by appearances, but truly teach the way of God" (Mark 12:14). Paul said that if he
tried to please men he would no longer be serving Christ: "Am I now
seeking the approval of man, or of God? Or am I trying to please man?
If I were still trying to please man, I would not be a servant of Christ"
(Galatians 1:10). "As we have been approved by God to be entrusted
with the gospel, so we speak, not to please man, but to please God who

tests our hearts" (1 Thessalonians 2:4). So it seems that Christians should not care much about what others think.

On the other hand, Proverbs 22:1 says, "A good name is to be chosen rather than great riches, and favor is better than silver or gold." This sounds like reputation matters. And Paul was vigilant that he not be discredited in his handling of the money he collected for the poor: "[We are] taking precaution so that no one will discredit us in our administration of this generous gift; for we have regard for what is honorable, not only in the sight of the Lord, but also in the sight of men" (2 Corinthians 8:20–21, NASB). It mattered what men thought.

Paul taught the Roman church, "Now we who are strong ought...not just please ourselves. Each of us is to please his neighbor for his good, to his edification" (Romans 15:1–2, NASB). And he taught that one of the qualifications for elders is that they must be "above reproach" (1 Timothy 3:2), including among unbelievers: "He must be well thought of by outsiders, so that he may not fall into disgrace, into a snare of the devil" (1 Timothy 3:7).

Similarly Peter charged us to care about what outsiders thought: "Keep your behavior excellent among the Gentiles, so that in the thing in which they slander you as evildoers, they may because of your good deeds, as they observe them, glorify God in the day of visitation" (1 Peter 2:12, NASB).

Question: How is the tension between these two groups of passages to be resolved?

Answer: By realizing that our aim in life is that "Christ will be magnified in my body, whether by life or by death" (Philippians 1:20, NKJV). In other words, with Paul, we do care—really care—about what others think *of Christ*. Their salvation hangs on what they think of Christ. And our lives are to display his truth and beauty. So we *must* care what others think of us *as representative of Christ*. Love demands it.

But we ought not to care much what others think of us for our own sake. Our concern is ultimately for Christ's reputation, not ours. The accent falls not on our value or excellence or virtue or power or wisdom. It falls on whether *Christ* is honored by the way people think of us. Does Christ get a good reputation because of the way we live? Is the excellence of Christ displayed in our lives? That should matter to us, not whether we ourselves are praised.

Again notice a crucial distinction: The litmus test of our faithfully displaying the truth and beauty of Christ in our lives is *not* in the opinion of others. We want them to see Christ in us and love him (and thus, very incidentally, to approve of us). When John the Baptist said, "He must increase, but I must decrease" (John 3:30), he spoke for every true Christian. We must insist on being less than Christ. I am vigilant, as far as it depends on me, to be less than Christ to others.

But we know others may be blind to spiritual reality and resistant to Christ. So they may think more of us than they thought of him. Or they may think less of us than they think of him, *not* because they think well of him, but, as Jesus said, "If they have called the master of the house Beelzebul, how much more will they malign those of his household" (Matthew 10:25). They may think he is a devil and we are worse. Jesus wanted men to admire him and trust him. That would have been their salvation. But he did not change who he was in order to win their approval. Nor can we change who he was, or who we are in him.

Yes, we want people to look on us with approval when we are displaying that Jesus is infinitely valuable to us. But we dare not make the opinion of others the measure of our faithfulness. They may be blind and resistant to truth. Then the reproach we bear is no sign of our unfaithfulness or lack of love.

52

THE TRANSFORMING POWER OF FEELING MERCY

Using Imagination and Revelation to Know Our Condition

What a difference it makes in everything, if we feel like we have just been rescued from torment and death! Picture your attitude on a Navy ship after being plucked from the ocean, where you spent weeks adrift on a life raft. Or picture yourself rescued from a deep, collapsing mine in Pennsylvania. Or think of a nine-month battle with malignant cancer, only to hear the doctor say, "I can't explain it, but it's gone." Think about your powers of patience and kindness and forgiveness in those early hours of relief and rejoicing.

Now add this to your imagination (though it shouldn't take imagination, only biblical revelation), that you don't deserve to be rescued. Let it sink in—pray right now that God would make it sink in—that you and I deserve nothing but trouble and persecution and sickness and death and hell. We are, the Bible says, "by nature children of wrath like the rest of mankind" (Ephesians 2:3). "All...are under sin...and every mouth [is] stopped, and the whole world...accountable to God" (Romans 3:9, 19). The "wages" of our sin is eternal death (Romans 6:23). We are under the curse of God's law, because "cursed be anyone who does not confirm the words of this law by doing them" (Deuteronomy 27:26). Our natural mind is "hostile to God" (Romans 8:7). We are "strangers to the covenants of promise, having no hope and without God in the world" (Ephesians 2:12). We are destined to be cast into "outer darkness" where there is "weeping and gnashing of teeth" (Matthew 8:12; 25:30). If something doesn't intervene, our lot will be in the lake of fire where "the smoke of their torment goes up forever and ever, and they have no rest" (Revelation 14:11).

Therefore, all you Christians—all you believers rescued by the blood of Christ, who has become a curse for us—add to the relief and happiness of your rescue the bewildering wonder and the brokenhearted joy that you deserve none of this, but are lavished with unceasing mercy.

Then look upon your afflictions in this light. Think with Jonathan Edwards on your condition:

> How far less [are] the greatest afflictions that we meet with in this world…than we have deserved…. The greatest outward troubles and calamities that we meet with…must needs appear very little things to the misery which we have deserved…. A man may meet with very great losses…his cattle may die, his corn may be blasted, his barn may be burnt down and all the goods consumed, and he may be brought from a comfortable living to a poor, low, stricken state. This is very hard to bear, but alas, how little reason have such to complain if they do but consider how little this is, compared with that eternal destruction that we have been informed of." (Jonathan Edwards, *The Works of Jonathan Edwards* [New Haven: Yale University Press, 1997], 321)

Is it any wonder that Paul said to such people, "Do all things without grumbling" (Philippians 2:14)? Ponder how you would react to things if you lived hour by hour in the heartfelt awareness that you are rescued from horrible death and eternal suffering, and that, in spite of deserving no help, you are lavished with mercy every day (even in the hard things) and will be made perfectly and eternally happy in the age to come.

Then add one more thing to your thinking. The one who rescued you had to die to do it, and he is the one Person in the universe who did NOT deserve to die. "Christ suffered once for sins, the righteous for the unrighteous, that he might bring us to God" (1 Peter 3:18).

Oh, Christian, know your condition—the misery and the mercy. And let the horror from which you have been rescued, and the mercy in which you live, and the price that Christ paid, make you humble and thankful and patient and kind and forgiving. You have never been treated by God worse than you deserve. And in Christ you are treated ten million times better. Feel this. Live this.

53

The Eye Is the Lamp of the Body

A Meditation on Matthew 6:19–24

Do not lay up for yourselves treasures on earth, where moth and rust destroy and where thieves break in and steal, but lay up for yourselves treasures in heaven, where neither moth nor rust destroys and where thieves do not break in and steal. For where your treasure is, there your heart will be also. The eye is the lamp of the body. So, if your eye is healthy, your whole body will be full of light, but if your eye is bad, your whole body will be full of darkness. If then the light in you is darkness, how great is the darkness! No one can serve two masters, for either he will hate the one and love the other, or he will be devoted to the one and despise the other. You cannot serve God and money.

Sandwiched between the command to lay up treasures in heaven (6:19–21) and the warning that you can't serve God and money (6:24) are the strange words about the eye being the lamp of the body. If the eye is good, or healthy (literally, "if the eye is single"), the whole body will be full of light. But if the eye is bad, the body will be full of darkness. In other words: How you see reality determines whether you are in the dark or not.

Now why is this saying about the good and bad eye sandwiched between two teachings on money? I think it's because the specific thing about seeing that shows the eye is good is how it sees God in relation to money and all it can buy. That's the issue on either side of the sandwich meat of Matthew 6:22–23. In Matthew 6:19–21 the issue is: You should desire heaven-reward not earth-reward. Which, in short, means: Desire God not money. In Matthew 6:24 the issue is whether you can serve two masters. Answer: You cannot serve God and money.

This is a double description of light! If you are laying up treasures in heaven, not earth, you are walking in the light. If you are serving God, not money, you are walking in the light.

Between these two descriptions of the light, Jesus says that the eye is the lamp of the body and that a good eye produces a fullness of this light. So what is the good eye that gives so much light and the bad eye that leaves us in the dark?

One clue is found in Matthew 20:15. Jesus has just said, in a parable, that men who worked one hour will be paid the same as those who worked all day, because the master is merciful, and besides, they all agreed to their wage. Those who worked all day grumbled that the men who worked one hour were paid too much. Jesus responded with the surprising words found here in Matthew 6:23, "Is your eye bad because I am good?" (ESV margin, a good, but perplexing, literal translation).

What is bad about their eye? What's bad is that their eye does not see the mercy of the master as beautiful. He gives generously to those who worked only an hour. The all-day workers see it as ugly. They don't see reality for what it is. They do not have an eye that can see mercy as more precious than money.

Now bring that understanding of the bad eye back to Matthew 6:23, and let it determine the meaning of the healthy eye.

The eye is the lamp of the body. So, if your eye is healthy, your whole body will be full of light, but if your eye is bad, your whole body will be full of darkness. If then the light in you is darkness, how great is the darkness!

What would the healthy eye be that fills us with light? It would be an eye that sees the Master's generosity as more precious than money. The healthy eye sees God and his ways as the great Treasure in life, not money.

You have a healthy eye if you look on heaven and love to maximize the reward of God's fellowship there. You have a healthy eye if you look at Master-money and Master-God and see Master-God as infinitely more valuable and desirable. In other words, a healthy eye is a valuing eye, a discerning eye, a treasuring eye. It doesn't just see facts about money and God. It doesn't just perceive what is true and false. It sees and assesses the true difference between beauty and ugliness, it senses value and worthlessness, it discerns what is really desirable and what is undesirable. The seeing of the healthy eye is not neutral. When it sees God, it sees God-as-beautiful. It sees God-as-desirable.

That is why the healthy eye leads to the path of light: laying up treasures in heaven and serving God, not money. The healthy eye is a single eye. It has one Treasure. God. When that happens in your life, you are full of light.

54

MY LIFE IS A VAPOR

A Meditation on James 4:13–16

Come now, you who say, "Today or tomorrow we will go into such and such a town and spend a year there and trade and make a profit"—yet you do not know what tomorrow will bring. What is your life? For you are a mist that appears for a little time and then vanishes. Instead you ought to say, "If the Lord wills, we will live and do this or that." As it is, you boast in your arrogance. All such boasting is evil.

When it comes to how we think and talk about our business plans, our mind-set and our mouth matter. According to Jesus' brother James, the person who says, "Tomorrow we will go to Denver and do business," is arrogant. He does not comprehend in his pride that his life is like a "mist" (or "vapor," NASB) and that God, not he, will decide if he lives and goes to Denver (or gets out of bed) tomorrow.

I can imagine some American pragmatist saying, "What practical difference would it make in my business planning whether I believe my life is a vapor? Do I stop planning because my life may be short or uncertain?" I think James would say, "No, you don't stop planning. You don't drop out of society. You don't become a hermit, waiting for your little vapor of life to disappear."

So what is the point? The point is that for James, and for God, it matters whether a true view of life informs and shapes the way you *think* and how you speak about your plans. Your mind-set matters. How you *talk* about your plans matters.

Ponder this. Believing that your life is a vapor may make no practical, bottom-line difference in whether you plan to do business in a place for one month or one year or ten years. But, in James's mind—and he speaks for God—it makes a difference how you think about it and talk about it. "Come now, you who *say*...." Saying the wrong thing about your plans matters.

Why? Why does that matter? Because God created us not just to do things and go places with our bodies, but to have certain attitudes and convictions and verbal descriptions that reflect a true view of life and God. God means for the truth about himself and about life to be known and felt and spoken as part of our reason for being. You weren't just created to go to Denver and do business; you were created to go to Denver with thoughts and attitudes and words that reflect a right view of God.

So James says in verse 14, in all your planning, keep in your mind, and express with your lips, this truth: "You are just a vapor that appears for a little while and then vanishes away" (NASB). That is, keep in mind that you have no firm substance on this earth. You are as fragile as a mist. Keep in mind that you have no durability on this earth, for you appear "for a little while"—just a little while. Your time is short. And keep in mind that you will disappear. You will be gone, and life will go on without you. It matters, he says, that you keep this view of life in mind.

Then verse 15 tells us the true view of God that we should have in our minds, and in our mouths, as we imagine our future—as we plot our investments and make our plans. Verse 13 began, "Come now, you who say, 'Today or tomorrow we will go into such and such a town and spend a year there and make a profit.'" Now he tells us what's wrong with that way of talking. He says in verse 15, "Instead you ought to say, '*If the Lord wills*, we will live and do this or that.'"

In other words, it not only matters that you have a right view of life when you make your plans (because you are like a vapor), but it also matters that you have a right view of God as you make your plans. And it matters that you give expression of this true view of God: "You ought to say"—say!—, "If the Lord wills, we will live and do this or that."

So what is the right view of God that he teaches us to have in verse 15? He tells us two very important things about God. One is contained in the words: "If the Lord wills, we will live." And the other is contained in the words, "If the Lord wills, we will...do this or that." How would you state the truth about God contained in each of those two sentences?

I will leave it for you to answer. But don't miss the obvious: Scripture puts a premium on how we think and how we talk. This is not surprising. Above all the animals, humans are created in the image of God with thought and language beyond all comparison. This gift is not gratuitous. It is meant to make the glory of God known. If he wills, we live. If he wills, we act. We have minds and tongues to speak this truly for all the world to hear.

55

GOD'S FAVORITE COLOR

Pondering Why Worry Doesn't Work

I remember walking to Oudall's Used Book Store with my colleague
Tom Steller. We were discussing Jesus' words about anxiety. As I
quoted the sentence, "Which of you by being anxious can add a single
cubit to his span of life?" I stepped onto Portland Avenue and almost got
run over.

Which, of course, set me to thinking: *Well, I suppose you really can
add a cubit to your span of life if you are anxious enough to watch the light.*
Now, of course, street-crossing was not so dangerous in Jesus' day. But
surely He would have agreed that you *can* add a cubit to your span of life
if you don't walk into the desert so far that you die of thirst trying to walk
out again. And if desert-phobia keeps you from doing that, then does not
anxiety add to your span of life?

No! It is not the anxiety which saves. It is reasonable precaution. The
desire not to die in the desert is not the same as anxiety about walking in
the desert. Anxiety is the twisty, tense, fearful feeling inside that may or
may not go with reasonable precaution, and it is the caution that can add
a cubit to your life, not bad feelings. Precautions have lengthened many
lives; anxiety has lengthened none and shortened many.

"Do not be anxious about your life" (Luke 12:22) does not mean
walk on red (at least not always). It means don't fantasize nervously about
getting pasted in the crosswalk. It means believe that, if you do get
pasted, God is still in control and you will be with him and he will take

care of your family. It means that if a carton of gold is across the street and the kingdom of God is on this side, don't cross even on green. It means that if a red light tries to stop you from giving generously and sacrificially to the poor and to missions this week, walk on red! Financial precautions are almost always too conservative. After blue, God's favorite color is green. Consider how the lilies grow.

56

KILL ANGER BEFORE IT KILLS YOU OR YOUR MARRIAGE

Weapons for the Battle

I n marriage, anger rivals lust as a killer. My guess is that anger is a worse enemy than lust. It also destroys other kinds of camaraderie. Some people have more anger than they think, because it has disguises. When willpower hinders rage, anger smolders beneath the surface, and the teeth of the soul grind with frustration.

It can come out in tears that look more like hurt. But the heart has learned that this may be the only way to hurt back. It may come out as silence because we have resolved not to fight. It may show up in picky criticism and relentless correction. It may strike out at persons that have nothing to do with its origin. It will often feel warranted by how wrongly it has been treated. After all, Jesus got angry (Mark 3:5), and Paul says, "Be angry and do not sin" (Ephesians 4:26).

However, good anger among fallen people is rare. That's why James says, "Be quick to hear, slow to speak, slow to anger; for the anger of man does not produce the righteousness of God" (James 1:19–20). And Paul says, "Men should pray, lifting holy hands without anger or quarreling" (1 Timothy 2:8). "Let all bitterness and wrath and anger and clamor and slander be put away from you" (Ephesians 4:31).

Therefore, one of the greatest battles of life is the battle to "put away anger," not just control its expressions. I invite you to join me in this battle by adding these nine biblical weapons to your arsenal.

1. *Ponder the right of Christ to be angry, but how he endured the cross, as an example of long-suffering.* "For to this you have been called, because Christ also suffered for you, leaving you an example, so that you might follow in his steps" (1 Peter 2:21).

2. *Ponder how much you have been forgiven, and how much mercy you have been shown.* "Be kind to one another, tenderhearted, forgiving one another, as God in Christ forgave you" (Ephesians 4:32).

3. *Ponder your own sinfulness and take the beam out of your own eye.* "Why do you see the speck that is in your brother's eye, but do not notice the log that is in your own eye? Or how can you say to your brother, 'Let me take the speck out of your eye,' when there is the log in your own eye? You hypocrite, first take the log out of your own eye, and then you will see clearly to take the speck out of your brother's eye" (Matthew 7:3–5).

4. *Ponder how harbored anger gives place to the devil.* You do not want to make room for him or invite him into your life. "Be angry and do not sin; do not let the sun go down on your anger, and give no opportunity to the devil" (Ephesians 4:26–27).

5. *Ponder the folly of your own self-immolation, that is, the numerous detrimental effects of anger to the one who is angry—some spiritual, some mental, some physical, and some relational.* "Be not wise in your own eyes; fear the LORD, and turn away from evil. It will be healing to your flesh and refreshment to your bones" (Proverbs 3:7–8).

6. *Confess your sin of anger to some trusted friend, and, if possible, to the offender.* This is a great healing act. "Therefore, confess your sins to one another and pray for one another, that you may be healed" (James 5:16).

7. *Let your anger be the key to unlock the dungeons of pride and self-pity in your heart and replace them with love.* "Love is patient and kind; love does not envy or boast; it is not arrogant or rude. It does not insist on its own way; it is not irritable or resentful; it does not rejoice at wrongdoing, but rejoices with the truth. Love bears all things, believes all things, hopes all things, endures all things" (1 Corinthians 13:4–7).

8. *Remember that God is going to work all your frustrating circumstances for your good as you trust in His future grace.* Your offender is even doing you good, if you will respond with love. "And we know that for those who love God all things work together for good, for those who are called according to his purpose" (Romans 8:28). "Count it all joy, my brothers, when you meet trials of various kinds, for you know that the testing of your faith produces steadfastness. And let steadfastness have its full effect, that you may be perfect and complete, lacking in nothing" (James 1:2–4).

9. *Remember that God will vindicate your just cause and settle all accounts better than you could.* Either your offender will pay in hell, or Christ has paid for him. Your payback would be either double jeopardy or an offense to the cross. "Beloved, never avenge yourselves, but leave it to the wrath of God, for it is written, 'Vengeance is mine, I will repay, says the Lord'" (Romans 12:19). "When he was reviled, he did not revile in return; when he suffered, he did not threaten, but continued entrusting [his cause] to him who judges justly" (1 Peter 2:23).

57

"LORD, COMMAND WHAT YOU WILL, AND GIVE WHAT YOU COMMAND"

Only God Can Do What Needs to Be Done

Augustine's prayer, "Lord, command what you will, and give what you command" (*Confessions,* X, 31), deeply offended Pelagius, his adversary. It implied that God not only told man what he must do, believe, and obey, but also that God gave the ability to do what He said we must do. This seemed to Pelagius to undermine human responsibility and lead straight to God's deciding ahead of time who would believe and who would not.

Second Chronicles 30:1–12 is a remarkable example of the kind of Scripture that formed Augustine's vision of God's way of working. Hezekiah has become king in the place of several very bad kings. He "did what was right in the eyes of the LORD" (2 Chronicles 29:2). One of the ways he does right is by reinstituting the Passover, which had not been heeded for a long time. So in chapter 30 he sends word to "all Israel and Judah," including Ephraim and Manasseh, that they should come to the house of the Lord to keep the Passover (v. 1).

In the letters that Hezekiah sends to the tribes, the blessing of God is made strictly conditional upon the response of the people. Here is what the letters say (vv. 6–9):

"O sons of Israel, return to the LORD God of Abraham, Isaac and Israel, *that* He may return to those of you who escaped and are left from the hand of the kings of Assyria. Do not be like your fathers and your brothers, who were unfaithful to the LORD God of their fathers, *so that* He made them a horror, as you see. Now do not stiffen your neck like your fathers, but yield to the LORD and enter His sanctuary which He has consecrated forever, and serve the LORD your God, *that* His burning anger may turn away from you. For *if* you return to the LORD, your brothers and your sons will find compassion before those who led them captive and will return to this land. For the LORD your God is gracious and compassionate, and will not turn His face away from you *if* you return to Him." (NASB)

Notice carefully how the italicized words in that passage make God's blessing contingent on the human response: "*If* you return to the LORD.... *If* you return." Many people read this kind of demand from the Lord and conclude that clearly God makes his blessing contingent on our ultimately self-determining response. Some will admit that God may give some assistance to encourage us to obey him—some measure of "prevenient grace" (grace that precedes our obedience), but they say, "These conditions in verse 9 (*"If* you return to the LORD.... *If* you return to Him....") cannot be real if God himself decisively causes the conditions to be fulfilled (some, like the open theists, would say the conditions are not real if God even *knows* what we will do ahead of time.)

This sounds reasonable to most people: When God says: "*If* you do this, *then* I will bless you," it seems reasonable that he is waiting to see what we will do by our own self-determining power, so that he can then make his move based not on what he does, but on what we do apart from his decisive control. But the problem with this apparent "reasonable" conclusion is that it contradicts the following verses.

When Hezekiah's letter arrives among the people of Israel and Judah, here is what happens (according to 2 Chronicles 30:10–12):

> So the couriers passed from city to city through the country of Ephraim and Manasseh, and as far as Zebulun, but they laughed them to scorn and mocked them. Nevertheless some men of Asher, Manasseh and Zebulun humbled themselves and came to Jerusalem. The hand of God was also on Judah to give them one heart to do what the king and the princes commanded by the word of the LORD. (NASB)

Verse 12 is stunning to the "reasonable" mind that concluded from verses 6–9 that the conditions given by God implied he would wait and see if people would meet them by their self-determining power. Verse 12 says that the hand of God was on Judah to give them a heart to do what king Hezekiah was commanding from the Lord. And the word "also" in the phrase "The hand of God was *also* on Judah," implies that the humble obedience of Asher, Manasseh, and Zebulun (not just Judah) was "also" caused by the hand of the Lord.

What is remarkable here is that the biblical writer does not feel any inconsistency or contradiction in saying that the obedience of the people is a condition they must meet *and* saying that this obedience is a work of God that he produced in their hearts.

This is the sort of thing that Augustine saw in many places in the Bible, which is why he prayed, "Lord, command what you will, and give what you command."

This implies that you simply cannot take all the conditions of the Bible and pile them up and use them as an argument that man has final self-determining power to give the final and ultimate veto to God's sovereign will. We must assert the conditions as strongly as the Bible does. (*If* you return to the Lord, *then* he will save you.) But we must also *not* follow the seemingly "reasonable" inference that therefore man has ultimate self-determination to meet the conditions. The Bible teaches two things: Many of the blessings of God are conditional upon our response of faith, *and* God himself ultimately enables that response of faith and obedience.

Therefore, we pray to God for the enablement of what he calls us to do and what he calls others to do. In fact, this is exactly why prayer is necessary. Only God can do what needs to be done. We are so sinful and so rebellious and so hard and resistant that if we are left to ourselves, we will carry on exactly as the people did in 2 Chronicles 30:10, with scorn and mockery.

Oh, how relevant and practical are the doctrines of God's sovereignty for our daily lives! If we did not know what Augustine knew, and what 2 Chronicles teaches us, how would we apply our wills and our assiduous efforts toward holiness and ministry without becoming self-reliant, self-exalting moralists? It is knowing that we must work out our salvation in such efforts, and that this effort is a gift of God's grace, that keeps us constant in our praying for enabling grace, and vigorous in our working (Philippians 2:12–13). How else could we say with the apostle Paul, "By the grace of God I am what I am, and his grace toward me was not in vain. On the contrary, I worked harder than any of them, though it was not I, but the grace of God that is with me"? (1 Corinthians 15:10). I worked hard, but it was not I. That is what 2 Chronicles and Augustine want us to learn.

58

ENDINGS ARE FOR GRATITUDE, BEGINNINGS ARE FOR FAITH

Seeing the World in a Biblical Way

The embrace may be only with the heart, or it may be with the arms, depending on proximity and the degree of the emotion. But in either case *gratitude* embraces a person with glad affections for *past* good-will aimed at helping us, and *faith* embraces a person with glad affections for *future* promises aimed at helping us.

Since every moment is the beginning of the rest of your life, and every moment is the end of the past, every moment should be governed by the glad affections of both gratitude and faith.

Of course this is only possible if you see the world a certain way. If you see it the way biologist Richard Dawkins claims to see it, you will not experience your moments this way. Dawkins sees the world as a naturalist, that is, without God: "Like successful Chicago gangsters our genes have survived...in a highly competitive world,... [and so] a predominant quality to be expected in a successful gene is ruthless selfishness.... We are survival machines—robot vehicles programmed to preserve the selfish molecules known as genes" (from his book *The Selfish Gene,* quoted in a review by Phillip Johnson, *First Things* 97 [November 1999]: 70).

If you see the world that way, there are no persons to embrace, but only biological machines; no personal affections to feel, but only genetic programming; no goodwill in the past and no promises for the future, but only ruthless, blind, genetic "selfishness," that is, mindless survival of superior might.

But if you see the world the way Gustav Oehler (German Lutheran professor of Old Testament at Tübingen, 1812–1872) sees it, you will experience your moments differently. Oehler said, "It is clear that the Old Testament teaches a providence which embraces everything.... No sphere of chance exists in the Old Testament.... Even what men call accidental death is under God's direction [Exodus 21:12–13]" (*Theology of the Old Testament* [Minneapolis, MN: Klock and Klock Christian Publishers, 1978], 122).

In this view of things, looking back is looking on the past providence of God: "As for you, you meant evil against me, but God meant it for good" (Genesis 50:20). And looking forward is looking on the future providence of God: "The heart of man plans his way, but the LORD establishes his steps" (Proverbs 16:9). "Are not two sparrows sold for a penny? And not one of them will fall to the ground apart from your Father" (Matthew 10:29). "Surely goodness and mercy shall follow me all the days of my life" (Psalm 23:6).

If you see the world in this biblical way—and if you stand inside that biblical world as your humbly-accepted world—then every moment will be a point of gratitude toward the past and faith toward the future. The practical implications of this are great. For example, gratitude is one of the humblest affections, and faith is one of the boldest. Just think what kind of people we would be in the next year for the cause of Christ if we were continually humbled by our backward look of gratitude and continually emboldened by our forward look of faith! No, don't just think about it. Pursue it—with all your mind and all your heart.

59

BOASTING IN MAN IS DOUBLY EXCLUDED

The Lord Alone Is to Be Exalted

God loves it when man boasts in God, and God hates it when man boasts in man. "Let the one who boasts, boast in the Lord" (2 Corinthians 10:17). "Far be it from me to boast except in the cross of our Lord Jesus Christ" (Galatians 6:14). "The haughty looks of man shall be brought low, and the lofty pride of men shall be humbled, and the Lord alone will be exalted in that day. For the Lord of hosts has a day against all that is proud and lofty, against all that is lifted up" (Isaiah 2:11–12).

There are two reasons (at least) why God hates for man to boast in man. One is that boasting in man deflects man's attention from the Fountain of his joy and so ruins his life. It tricks man into replacing Magnificence with a mirror. Man was not made to admire man. He was made to admire God. The joy of admiration is prostituted and ruined when man tries to find galaxy-size Glory in the glow of his own reflection. God does not like the human damage done by boasting in man.

The other reason God hates for man to boast in man is this: It conveys the conviction that man is more admirable than God. Now that is, of course, untrue. But we would miss the point if we said: "God hates lying, and therefore God hates boasting in man because it conveys a lie." No. That's not quite right. What God hates is the dishonoring of God.

Lying happens to be one way that he is dishonored as the God of truth. So the real problem with man's boasting in man is that it belittles God.

Boasting in God, on the other hand, does the double opposite: it honors God and gives man the joy for which he was made: admiring the infinitely admirable. Mercifully, therefore, God has doubly excluded boasting by the way He saves sinners.

First, boasting is excluded by faith. Romans 3:27 says, "Then what becomes of our boasting? It is excluded. By what kind of law? By a law of works? No, but by the law of faith." Why does faith exclude boasting? The reason is not merely because faith is a gift of God, which it is (Ephesians 2:8). But not all gifts exclude boasting in the same way. All the fruits of the Spirit are gifts of God—like love for people. But love for people is very different from faith in God's promises to help us love people. Love includes doing good things for people. This is virtuous action. But faith is different. Faith is unique among all the acts of the soul. It is the weakest and most helpless and most empty-handed. It is *all* dependence on Another. It is not the fruit of dependence as all the other virtues of the soul are. It is not the fruit of itself. In a sense, it is an acted non-act—an act that is entirely receiving. It is a doing, whose doing is the will to let another do all the doing.

I'll try to explain. I mean faith is an inclination of the soul to seek help from Christ with no expectation that any inclination of the soul is good enough to obtain help, not even the inclination of faith. It is unique among all the acts of the soul. Since it is empty-handed, it is not like a virtue. It looks to the virtue of another. It looks to the strength of another. It looks to the wisdom of another. It is entirely other-directed and other-dependent. Therefore, it can't boast in itself, for it can't even look at itself. It is the kind of thing that in a sense has no "self." As soon as the unique act of the soul exists, it is attached to Another from whom it gets all its reality.

Second, boasting is excluded by election. First Corinthians 1:27–29: "God *chose* [that is, *elected*] what is foolish in the world to shame the wise; God chose what is weak in the world to shame the strong; God chose what is low and despised in the world, even things that are not, to bring to nothing things that are, so that no human being might boast in the presence of God."

Notice the "so that." It signals the purpose of God's choosing. God's election is designed to remove boasting. The point is that God does not choose people with a view to any feature in us that would allow us to boast. In fact, Romans 9:11 makes clear that God's election is designed to make God's saving purpose rest finally on God alone, not any act of the human soul. "Though [Jacob and Esau] were not yet born and had done nothing either good or bad—in order that God's purpose of election might continue, not because of works but because of him who calls [God chose Jacob not Esau]." The contrast with works here is not faith, but "him who calls." The choice of God rests finally on God alone. He decides who will believe and undeservingly be saved.

Therefore, let us look away from ourselves and all human help. Let all boasting in man and man's accomplishments cease. "Let the one who boasts, boast in the Lord" (1 Corinthians 1:31).

60

ALL WE WILL GET IS MERCY

And It's All We Ever Need!

L et us make crystal clear at the beginning of each new day, all we will get from God as believers in Jesus is mercy. Whatever pleasures or pains may come our way in this day, they will all be mercy. This is why Christ came into the world—"in order that the Gentiles might glorify God for his mercy" (Romans 15:9). We were born again "according to his great mercy" (1 Peter 1:3), we pray daily "that we may receive mercy" (Hebrews 4:16), and we are now "waiting for the mercy of our Lord Jesus Christ that leads to eternal life" (Jude 1:21). If any Christian proves trustworthy, it is "by the Lord's mercy [he] is trustworthy" (1 Corinthians 7:25). In the end, when all is said and done, we will confess, "So then it depends not on human will or exertion, but on God, who has mercy" (Romans 9:16).

So as we face each day, let us humble ourselves and take the position of the blind man: "Jesus, Son of David, have mercy on me!" (Luke 18:38). Or the position of the leper: "Jesus, Master, have mercy on us" (Luke 17:13). And let us take heart that we will never obey God enough to put Him in debt to us. He will never owe us. "Who has given a gift to [God] that he might be repaid?" (Romans 11:35). And let us take heart that the smallest seed of true faith in Christ taps all the divine power of mercy—as the slightest touch of an electrical plug to the socket gets all the electricity.

Really? Did Jesus say that? He did. Consider.

In Luke 17:5, the apostles pleaded with the Lord, "Increase our faith!" And the Lord said, "If you had faith like a grain of mustard seed, you could say to this mulberry tree, 'Be uprooted and planted in the sea,' and it would obey you" (v. 6). In other words, the issue in your Christian life and ministry is not the strength or quantity of your faith, because that is not what uproots trees. God does. Therefore, the smallest faith that truly connects you with Christ will engage enough of His power for all you need. Moving trees is a small thing for Christ. The issue is not perfection for Christ, but connection to Christ. So take heart, the smallest seed of faith connects with all of Christ's mercy.

But what about your successes? When you succeed in obeying God, do you no longer need to be a supplicant of mercy? Jesus gives the answer in the next verses (vv. 7–10).

> Will any one of you who has a servant plowing or keeping sheep say to him when he has come in from the field, "Come at once and recline at table"? Will he not rather say to him, "Prepare supper for me, and dress properly, and serve me while I eat and drink, and afterward you will eat and drink"? Does he thank the servant because he did what was commanded? So you also, when you have done all that you were commanded, say, "We are unworthy servants; we have only done what was our duty."

What does he mean that after doing all his commands we should still say, "We are unworthy servants"? He means, you never cease to be dependent on mercy. Doing all we are called to do does not make us deserving in relation to God. "Unworthy" after all obedience means humans cannot earn anything good from God. If we get it, it's mercy.

Therefore, I conclude, the fullest obedience and the smallest faith obtain the same thing from God: mercy. A mere mustard seed of faith taps into the mercy of tree-moving power. And flawless obedience leaves us utterly dependent on mercy. God may withhold some blessings of mercy for our good, if we stray from the path of growing faith. But even this withholding is another form of mercy.

The point is: Whatever the timing or form of God's mercy, we never rise above the status of beneficiaries of mercy. We are always utterly dependent on the undeserved. God never owes us anything in ourselves. The smallest faith and the fullest obedience receive one thing: almighty mercy.

Therefore, let us humble ourselves and rejoice and "glorify God for his mercy"!

61

A Call for Coronary Christians

Thoughts on the Endurance of William Wilberforce

I am glad for adrenaline; I suspect it gets me through lots of Sundays. But it doesn't do much for Mondays. I am even more thankful for my heart. It just keeps on being a humble, quiet servant—during good days and bad days, happy and sad, high and low, appreciated and unappreciated. It never lets me down. It never says, "I don't like your attitude, Piper, I'm taking a day off." It just keeps humbly lubb-dubbing along.

Coronary Christians are like the heart in the causes they serve. Adrenal Christians are like adrenaline—a spurt of energy, and then fatigue. What the church and the world need today is marathoners, not just sprinters. People who find the pace to finish the (lifelong) race.

Oh, for coronary Christians! Christians committed to great causes, not great comforts. I plead with you to dream a dream that is bigger than you and your families and your churches. Un-deify the American family, and say boldly that our children are not our cause; they are given to us to train for a cause. They are given to us for a short season so that we can train them for the great causes of truth and mercy and justice in a prejudiced, pain-filled, and perishing world.

My blood is boiling on this issue of rugged, never-say-die, coronary Christian commitment to great causes, because I've been brimming these days with the life of William Wilberforce. Now *there* was a coronary Christian in the cause of racial justice. He was deeply Christian, vibrantly evangelical, and passionately political in the House of Commons over the long haul in the fight against the African slave trade. On October 28, 1787, he wrote in his diary at the age of 28, "God Almighty has set before me two great objects, the suppression of the Slave Trade and the Reformation of [Morals]." In battle after battle in Parliament he was defeated, because "the Trade" was so much woven into the financial interests of the nation. But he never gave up and never sat down. He was coronary, not adrenal.

On February 24, 1807, at 4:00 A.M., twenty years later, the decisive vote was cast (Ayes, 283, Noes, 16), and the slave trade became illegal. The House rose almost to a man and turned toward Wilberforce in a burst of parliamentary cheers, while the little man with the curved spine sat, head bowed, tears streaming down his face (John Pollock, *Wilberforce*, 211).

The coronary Christian, William Wilberforce, never gave up. There were keys to his relentlessness. The greatness and the certainty and the rightness of the cause sustained him. Abolishing the slave trade was "the grand object of my Parliamentary existence."

"Before this great cause," he wrote in 1796, "all others dwindle in my eyes, and I must say that the certainty that I am right here, adds greatly to the complacency with which I exert myself in asserting it. If it please God to honor me so far, may I be the instrument of stopping such a course of wickedness and cruelty as never before disgraced a Christian country" (Pollock, 143).

He saw that adrenal spurts would never prevail: "I daily become more sensible that my work must be affected by constant and regular exertions rather than by sudden and violent ones" (Pollock, 116). He had learned the secret of being strengthened, not stopped, by opposition. One of his adversaries said, "He is blessed with a very sufficient quantity of that Enthusiastic spirit, which is so far from yielding that it grows more vigorous from blows" (Pollock, 105). Most of all, the secret of his coronary commitment to the great Cause was his radical allegiance to Jesus Christ.

He prayed—and may this prayer rouse many coronary lovers of Christ to fight racism, abortion, hunger, ignorance, poverty, homelessness, alcoholism, drug abuse, crime, corruption, violence, AIDS, apathy, unbelief...with unwavering perseverance—"[May God] enable me to have a single eye and a simple heart, desiring to please God, to do good to my fellow creatures and to testify my gratitude to my adorable Redeemer" (Pollock, 210).

62

GOD IS NOT BORING

A Meditation on the Imagination

One of the great duties of the Christian mind is imagination. It is not the only thing the mind does. The mind observes. The mind analyzes and organizes. The mind memorizes. But imagination is different. It does not observe or analyze what we see; it imagines what we can't see, but what might really be there. Therefore, it is very useful in science, because it helps turn up unseen explanations for things we don't understand and leads to all kinds of discoveries. Or it imagines a new way of saying things that no one has said before, as in the case of creative writing and music and art.

I say that imagination is a Christian duty for two reasons. One is that you can't apply Jesus' golden rule without it. He said, "Whatever you wish that others would do to you, do also to them" (Matthew 7:12). We must imagine ourselves in their place and imagine what we would like done to us. Compassionate, sympathetic, helpful love hangs much on the imagination of the lover.

There are a thousand ways to say stupid and unhelpful things in a tense or tragic or joyful situation. How do we speak words that are fitly chosen? "A word fitly spoken is like apples of gold in a setting of silver" (Proverbs 25:11). One answer is that the Spirit of God gives us a "sympathetic imagination." *Sympathy* means we "feel with" someone. When we open our mouth, we spontaneously, with little reflection, imagine the right thing to say—or not to say—for the sake of others. Without imagination we would all be social klutzes.

The other reason I say that imagination is a Christian duty is that when a person speaks or writes or sings or paints about breathtaking truth in a boring way, it is probably a sin. The supremacy of God in the life of the mind is not honored when God and his amazing world are observed truly, analyzed duly, and communicated boringly. Imagination is the key to killing boredom. We must imagine ways to say truth for what it really is. And it is not boring.

God's world—all of it—rings with wonders. The imagination calls up new words, new images, new analogies, new metaphors, new illustrations, new connections to say old, glorious truth. Imagination is the faculty of the mind that God has given us to make the communication of his beauty beautiful.

Don't mistake what I am saying. Poets and painters and preachers don't make God's beauty more beautiful. They make it more visible. They cut through the dull fog of our finite, fallible, sin-distorted perception and help us see God's beauty for what it really is. Imagination is like a telescope to the stars: It doesn't make them big. They are big without the telescope. It makes them look like what they are.

Imagination may be the hardest work of the human mind. And perhaps the most Godlike. It is the closest we get to creation out of nothing. When we speak of beautiful truth, we must think of a pattern of words, perhaps a poem. We must conceive something that has never existed before and does not now exist in any human mind. We must think of an analogy or metaphor or illustration which has no existence. The imagination must exert itself to see it in our mind, when it is not yet there. We must create word combinations and music that have never existed before. All of this we do, because we are like God and because he is infinitely worthy of ever-new words and songs and pictures.

A college—or a church or a family—committed to the supremacy of

God in the life of the mind will cultivate fertile imaginations. And, oh, how the world needs God-besotted minds that can say and sing and play and paint the great things of God in ways that have never been said or sung or played or painted before.

Imagination is like a muscle. It grows stronger when you flex it. And .you must flex it. It does not usually put itself into action. It awaits the will. Imagination is also contagious. When you are around someone (alive or dead) who uses it a lot, you tend to catch it. So I suggest that you hang out with some people (mainly dead poets) who are full of imagination, and that you exert yourself to think up a new way to say an old truth. God is worthy. "Oh sing to the LORD a new song" (Psalm 98:1)— or picture, or poem, or figure of speech, or painting.

63

THANKSGIVING FOR THE LIVES
OF FLAWED SAINTS

The Value of Reading Inspiring Biographies

God ordains that we gaze on his glory, dimly mirrored in the ministry of his flawed servants. he intends for us to consider their lives and peer through the imperfections of their faith and behold the beauty of their God. "Remember your leaders, those who spoke to you the word of God. Consider the outcome of their way of life, and imitate their faith" (Hebrews 13:7).

The God who fashions the hearts of all men (Psalm 33:15) means for their lives to display his truth and his worth. From Phoebe (Romans 16:1) to St. Francis, the divine plan holds firm. Paul spoke it over the life of the pagan Pharaoh: "For this very purpose I have raised you up, that I might show my power in you, and that my name might be proclaimed in all the earth" (Romans 9:17). From David the king, to David Brainerd the missionary, extraordinary and incomplete specimens of godliness and wisdom have kindled the worship of sovereign grace in the hearts of reminiscing saints. "Let this be recorded for a generation to come, so that a people yet to be created may praise the LORD" (Psalm 102:18).

The history of the world is a field strewn with broken stones, which are sacred altars designed to waken worship in the hearts of those who will take the time to read and remember. "I will remember the deeds of the LORD; surely I will remember Your wonders of old. I will meditate on all Your work and muse on Your deeds. Your way, O God, is holy; what god is great like our God?" (Psalm 77:11–13, NASB).

The aim of God's providence in the history of the world is worship flowing from the people of God. Ten thousand stories of grace and truth are meant to be remembered for the refinement of faith and the sustaining of hope and the guidance of love. "Whatever was written in former days was written for our instruction, that by steadfastness and by the encouragement of the scriptures we might have hope" (Romans 15:4, RSV). Those who nurture their hope by the history of grace will live their lives to the glory of God.

The lives of our flawed Christian heroes are inspiring for two reasons: because they were flawed (like us) and because they were great (unlike us). Their flaws give us hope that maybe God could use us too. Their greatness inspires us to venture beyond the ordinary.

How does it come about that an ordinary person breaks out of the ruts of humdrum life to do something remarkable? It usually happens because of the inspiration of a man or woman they admire.

Do you have any heroes? Do you read about the lives of men and women who broke out of the mold and escaped the trap of the ordinary? Why not make a resolution now that you will read the biography of a Christian whom God made great. If you plan it, it is likely to happen. If you don't, it probably won't.

A few years ago, in preparation for our annual pastors' conference where I deliver a biographical address, I read *John G. Paton: Missionary to the New Hebrides*. It was worth all the hours even if only for one great paragraph. When Paton resolved to go to the unreached tribes of the South Sea Islands in 1856, a Christian gentleman objected, "You'll be eaten by cannibals!" To this Paton responded:

Your own prospect is soon to be laid in the grave, there to be eaten by worms; I confess to you, that if I can but live and die serving and honoring the Lord Jesus, it will make no difference to me whether I am eaten by Cannibals or by worms; and in the Great Day my resurrection body will arise as fair as yours in the likeness of our risen Redeemer. (p. 56)

This kind of abandon to the cause of Christ puts fire in my bones. If you don't know where to start, ask your pastor what biographies of Christians he would recommend. Or contact us at Desiring God for a list of the ones that have helped us.

64

WHY SATAN IS LEFT ON EARTH

Incentives to Battle for Joy in Jesus

Part of the problem of evil is the problem of why Satan is given so much freedom to harm the world, when God has the right and power to throw him in the pit. God will one day do away with Satan altogether (Revelation 20:3, 10). That will be no injustice to Satan. Nor would it be unjust for God to do it today. So why doesn't he, in view of how much misery Satan causes?

Satan roams around like a devouring lion seeking to destroy faith (1 Peter 5:8); he makes people sick and diseased (Acts 10:38); he tempts to sin (Luke 22:3–4); he blinds the minds of unbelievers (2 Corinthians 4:4); he takes people captive to do his will (2 Timothy 2:26); he kills (Revelation 2:10). One day God will stop him from doing this. Why doesn't he stop him now?

Could it be that there is a chance the devil and his angels will repent? Is God giving them time? No. The Bible teaches they are irredeemable. Jesus said that "the eternal fire...has been prepared for the devil and his angels" (Matthew 25:41, NASB). Jude confirms this when he says that the fallen angels are being "kept in eternal bonds under darkness for the judgment of the great day" (Jude 1:6, NASB).

Why then does God tolerate Satan? The key is that God aims to defeat Satan in a way that glorifies not only his power but also the superior beauty and worth and desirability of his Son over Satan. God could simply exert raw power and snuff Satan out. That would glorify God's power. But it would not display so clearly the superior worth of Jesus over Satan. That will be displayed as Christ defeats Satan by his death and then by winning allegiance from the saints because of his superior truth and beauty above the ugliness and lies of Satan.

Central to this plan is that God defeats Satan in stages through the work of Christ. First, we were forgiven all our trespasses by Christ's death on the cross. Paul said that in doing this God "disarmed the rulers and authorities and put them to open shame, by triumphing over them in him" (Colossians 2:15).

This was the first stage of Satan's defeat. The lethal weapon of soul-destroying sin and guilt is taken out of Satan's hand. He is disarmed of the single weapon that can condemn us—unforgiven sin. We see this in 1 Corinthians 15:55–57, "O death, where is your victory? O death, where is your sting? The sting of death is sin, and the power of sin is the law. But thanks be to God, who gives us the victory through our Lord Jesus Christ." What makes the sting of death powerful, that is, eternally lethal, is sin. The law sees to it that sin gets a just condemnation: eternal judgment. That is Satan's weapon: unforgiven sin, reinforced by the sanctions of the law. But if our sins could be forgiven, Satan could not condemn us. And, indeed, they are forgiven through faith in God's grace bought by the blood of Jesus.

Without sin and law to condemn us, Satan is a defeated foe. He is disarmed. Christ has triumphed over him, not yet by casting him into hell and nullifying his influence on earth, but by letting him live and watch while millions of saints find forgiveness for their sins and turn their back on Satan because of the greater glory of Christ.

That is the second stage of defeat: not only what happened on the cross for sinners but what happens in the hearts of those who are saved— the conversion of people by the power of the gospel of the cross. Jesus says to Paul that his mission to the Gentiles is "to open their eyes, so that they may turn from...the power of Satan to God" (Acts 26:18). This is what happens when God removes the blindness caused by the devil and gives us the light of the gospel of the glory of Christ (2 Corinthians 4:4–6). This enables people to see the ugliness of Satan and the beauty of Christ, so that their choosing Christ glorifies not only God's power but Christ's superior beauty and worth over Satan.

This way of defeating Satan is more costly than just snuffing him out. Christ suffered for this triumph, and the world suffers. But God's values are not so easily reckoned. If Christ obliterated all demons now (which he could do), his sheer power would be seen as glorious, but his superior beauty and worth would not shine so brightly as when God's people renounce the promises of Satan, trust in Christ's blood and righteousness, and take pleasure in the greater glory of Jesus over Satan.

This means that our treasuring Christ above all the promises of sin and Satan is part of the triumph that God designs for this age. Therefore, take up arms and defeat the devil by being bold and glad in the superior glory of the Son of God! I do not say it is easy. It is very costly. The path of love that leads from the cross of Christ to the glory of Christ is a road of sacrifice. Christ's superior beauty over Satan and sin is seen best when we are willing to suffer because we have tasted it and want to share it. One of the greatest blows against the power of darkness comes from the blood of martyrs. "They have conquered him [Satan!] by the blood of the Lamb and by the word of their testimony, for they loved not their lives even unto death" (Revelation 12:11).

65

THE PATH OF WISDOM MAY NOT BE THE MOST FRUITFUL PATH FOR GOD'S GLORY

Obedience in Making Plans and Decisions

We are held accountable for being wise, not influential.

The powers of our mind are simply not adequate for deciding which path of life will be most effective for God's kingdom purposes to save sinners, and transform lives, and exalt his name. The reason is that all the signs that we can see may point to a very fruitful ministry in one direction. It may seem to fit our gifts and meet the greatest need and be a God-given opportunity at this particular moment. It may get confirmation from wise counselors and seem to be part of a pattern of divinely orchestrated circumstances. And *yet*, in spite of all that wisdom, another path than the one that seemed so fruitful may lead to a single seemingly insignificant event that you could have never foreseen or planned but which God uses to bring about an effect for the glory of his name beyond anything the wise path would have produced.

For example, what if all the evidences pointed the southern preacher, Mordecai Fowler Ham, away from an evangelistic crusade in Charlotte, North Carolina, in September 1934? What if Scripture and prayer and counsel and circumstances all pointed to a larger, more fruitful ministry in Atlanta? If Mordecai Ham, who has been virtually forgotten by the world, had gone to Atlanta instead of Charlotte, the sixteen-year old William Franklin Graham would not have been converted under his preaching. But, as it happened, in the providence of God, Billy Graham became a Christian because Mordecai Ham came to Charlotte. That conversion was perhaps the most fruitful moment of Ham's entire ministry. No human can plan such things. And no human wisdom can see them coming.

So then what becomes of all our planning and all our strategic thinking? Clearly our planning does not render the last word on the fruitfulness of our lives. We simply do not know whether one path or the other will prove to be the path on which some remarkable turn of affairs may take place for the glory of God all out of proportion to what we planned or expected. A seemingly useless path may prove more effective than the best plan we could have made. You simply cannot know what God may do on any given path of faithfulness.

What conclusion can we draw from this observation? We should *not* draw the conclusion that thinking and planning about what is "wise" is a waste of time or is the wrong way to make decisions. If we abandon wisdom, thinking there is no way we can know the most effective path for our life, then we contradict the whole teaching of Scripture that it is good to be wise and to pursue wisdom.

But human wisdom is not omniscience. Wisdom does not equal knowing for sure that the path chosen will be the most fruitful path. Wisdom means doing the best you can with all the resources at your disposal to discern what the path of fruitfulness is for the glory of God.

This means that we are going to be held responsible by God to make our choices wisely, because that shows that in this moment our heart is obedient to God's Word and desirous of his glory. *That* is what we are held accountable for. But we are *not* responsible that the choices we make, with the best motives and knowledge available and with good counsel, will prove to be the most influential or effective choices in producing converts or changing lives. That is God's work, not ours.

We will be called to account at the last day for whether we have sought wisdom in reliance on God's Spirit and for the glory of God's Son. We will not be held accountable for whether our planning resulted in wonderful, serendipitous events like the conversion of a Billy Graham.

So what effect, then, should this observation have on our efforts to act wisely? It should at least give us an intense passion to honor God in *this* moment of decision-making. It should make us more zealous in this moment for God's glory to be shown in how we make decisions, not how they turn out. And then we should have a deep peace that the final effectiveness of our lives does not hang on our wisdom, but on God's sovereignty.

God will make it his rule to use our best efforts at wise, God-honoring choices to produce the most influential life. But not always. He can break that rule and make even a foolish decision fruitful. He has his ways to keep us humble and fearful of pride. He has his ways to keep us hopeful and protected from discouragement in view of our fallibility. We should be emboldened to move and act in faith, even if we think that our present choice may not have all the data possible, or all the counsel possible, or all the thought and prayer possible.

Our sovereign God is able to take the 80-percent-wise choice and make it more influential for Christ than the 90-percent-wise choice. This should not make us cavalier about the pursuit of wisdom, since we will be held accountable to pursue it, but it should make us bold that our wisdom is not what determines our influence or our fruitfulness in the end. God is. And he can take the worst detour and, for his wise and sometimes inscrutable purposes, make that route the most fruitful, even though we, in our folly, may be disciplined for taking it.

66

STORMS ARE THE TRIUMPH OF HIS ART

Thoughts on the Life of John Newton

John Newton wrote "Amazing Grace" after God saved him from a life—as he says—of being "a wretch" on the high seas for thirteen years. Then he became a pastor who faithfully loved two flocks for forty-three years in Olney and then in London, England.

Newton was a great and tender warrior against despair in other people's lives. He had been so hopeless and so beyond recovery in his sin that his own salvation constantly amazed him. If anyone should have despaired it was he. But God saved him. On March 21, 1748 a storm at sea wakened him from his folly. From that night at age twenty-three to the year he died at age eighty-two, he marked the day of his awakening on board the *Greyhound* with fasting and prayer and thankful rededication of his life to Jesus. As an old man he wrote, "The 21st in March is a day much to be remembered by me, and I have never suffered it to pass wholly unnoticed since the year 1748. On that day the Lord sent from on high, and delivered me out of the deep waters" (*Works*, I, 26–7).

He wrote his own epitaph to capture the wonder of his conversion and his undeserved ministry:

JOHN NEWTON, Clerk, Once an Infidel and Libertine, A Servant of Slaves in Africa, Was, by the rich mercy of our Lord and

Savior JESUS CHRIST, Preserved, restored, pardoned, And
appointed to preach the Faith He had long labored to destroy,
Near 16 years at Olney in Bucks; And...years in this church.
(*Works*, I, 90)

Newton's amazing rescue from utter wretchedness and hardness of
heart and blaspheming made him a rescuer of hopeless people all the rest
of his life. His first biographer and friend, Richard Cecil, closes his mem-
oir of Newton by pleading with young people:

> Mark the error of despair. We should see that the case of a pray-
> ing man cannot be desperate—that if a man be out of the pit of
> hell, he is on the ground of mercy. We should recollect that God
> sees a way of escape when we see none—that nothing is too hard
> for him—that he warrants our dependence, and invites us to call
> on him in the day of trouble, and gives a promise of deliverance.
> (*Works*, I, 126)

Newton had a favorite poet who died almost a hundred years before
Newton was born. His name was George Herbert. He was born in 1593
into a wealthy Welsh family, lost his father when he was three, became a
"public orator" in 1620 and a member of Parliament in 1625. But in
1630 he gave it all away to become a simple parish pastor in Bemerton.
For the rest of his life, he loved and served a flock as Newton did. Newton loved Herbert's poetry. Small wonder, when you read this verse from
his poem "The Bag." They were both enthralled with amazing grace that
banishes hopelessness from the sinner's heart. Herbert's poem captures
Newton's message and life:

> Away, Despair! My gracious Lord doth hear:
> Though winds and waves assault my keel,
> He doth preserve it: he doth steer,

Ev'n when the boat seems most to reel:
Storms are the triumph of his art:
Well may he close his eyes, but not his heart. (*Works*, I, 128)

It was certainly true in Newton's case: God's storm was a triumphant art of grace. For a season, God's face may turn away from his chosen ones, but not his heart. So let us learn from John Newton and George Herbert to say, "Away, Despair!" Let us embrace the precious truth of Jesus' words, "It is not those who are well who need a physician, but those who are sick. I have not come to call the righteous but sinners to repentance" (Luke 5:31–32, NASB). There is no condemnation to those who are in Christ Jesus. Listen as Paul adds, "It is a trustworthy statement, deserving full acceptance, that Christ Jesus came into the world to save sinners, among whom I am foremost" (1 Timothy 1:15, NASB). And finally, to double our hope, give heed to Hebrews 6:18: "By two unchangeable things in which it is impossible for God to lie, we who have taken refuge would have strong encouragement to take hold of the hope set before us" (NASB).

67

THE VALUE OF LEARNING HISTORY

A Lesson from Jude

The little New Testament letter of Jude teaches us something about the value of learning history. This is not the main point of the letter. But it is real and striking.

In this next-to-last book of the Bible, Jude writes to encourage the saints to "contend earnestly for the faith which was once for all handed down to the saints" (v. 3, NASB). The letter is a call to vigilance in view of "certain persons [who] have crept in unnoticed...ungodly persons who turn the grace of our God into licentiousness and deny our only Master and Lord, Jesus Christ" (v. 4). Jude describes these folks in vivid terms. They "revile the things which they do not understand" (v. 10). They "are grumblers, finding fault, following after their own lusts; they speak arrogantly, flattering people for the sake of gaining an advantage" (v. 16). They "cause divisions, [and are] worldly-minded, devoid of the Spirit" (v. 19).

This is a devastating assessment of people who are not outside the church but have "crept in unnoticed." Jude wants them to be spotted for who they really are so that the church is not deceived and ruined by their false teaching and immoral behavior.

One of his strategies is to compare them to other persons and events in history. For example, he says that "Sodom and Gomorrah...since they in the same way as these indulged in gross immorality and went after strange flesh, are exhibited as an example in undergoing the punishment of eternal fire" (v. 7). So Jude compares these people to Sodom and Gomorrah. His point in doing this is to say that Sodom and Gomorrah are "an example" of what will happen when people live like these intruders are living. So, in Jude's mind, knowing the history of Sodom and Gomorrah is very useful in helping detect such error and deflect it from the saints.

Similarly in verse 11, Jude piles up three other references to historical events as comparisons with what is happening in his day among Christians. He says, "Woe to them! For they have gone the way of Cain, and for pay they have rushed headlong into the error of Balaam, and perished in the rebellion of Korah." This is remarkable. Why refer to four different historical incidents like this that happened thousands of years earlier—Genesis 19 (Sodom), Genesis 3 (Cain), Numbers 22–24 (Balaam), Numbers 16 (Korah)? What's the point?

Here are three points:

1. Jude assumes that the readers know these stories! Is that not amazing? This was the first century! No books in anyone's homes. No Bibles available. No story tapes. Just oral instruction for almost all the common people. And he assumed that they would know "the way of Cain" and "the error of Balaam" and "the rebellion of Korah"? Do you know these stories? This is astonishing! He expects them to know these things. Surely, then, the standards of Bible knowledge in the church today are too low.

2. Jude assumes that knowing this history will illumine the present situation. The Christians will handle the error better today if they know similar situations from yesterday. In other words, history is valuable for Christian living. To know that Cain was jealous and hated his brother and resented his true spiritual communion with God will alert you to watch for such things even among brothers. To know that Balaam finally caved in and made the Word of God

a means of worldly gain makes you better able to spot that sort of thing. To know that Korah despised legitimate authority and resented Moses' leadership will protect you from factious folk who dislike anyone being seen as their leader.

3. Is it not clear, then, that God ordains for events to happen and be recorded as history so that we will know them and become wiser and more insightful in this present time for the sake of Christ and his church?

Therefore never debunk history. Never scorn the past. Never stop learning from the providence of God and what he has put forward as our lesson book. Knowing history will increase the urgency and preciousness of our present life, because it will make this life look very short against the unrelenting flow of centuries. That is a good lesson to learn. Life is a vapor. Anything to help us see this will make us wiser: "Teach us to number our days that we may get a heart of wisdom" (Psalm 90:12). Gain some knowledge of the past every day. And let us give ourselves and our children one of the best protections against the folly of the future, namely, a knowledge of the past.

68

ALREADY: DECISIVELY AND IRREVOCABLY FREE; NOT YET: FINALLY AND PERFECTLY FREE

The Reality of Union with Christ

Romans 6 and 7 teaches that when we trust in Christ as our Savior and Lord and Treasure of our lives, we are united to Christ (Romans 6:5; 7:4). In this union with Christ we die (Romans 6:8; Colossians 2:20; 3:3) and rise again (Romans 6:4; Colossians 2:12; Ephesians 2:6). Therefore, a decisive and irrevocable new creation comes into being (2 Corinthians 5:17), and a decisive and irrevocable liberation happens (Romans 6:14, 18). We pass from death to (eternal!) life. Our decisive judgment is behind us—at Golgotha (John 5:24). We have moved from the dominion of darkness into the kingdom of God's Son (Colossians 1:13).

But we also learn from these chapters that our liberation from sin is not yet final and perfect. Decisive and irrevocable, yes! But final and perfect, no! Sin still dwells within us (Romans 7:17, 20). Evil is present in us (Romans 7:21). The "flesh" is a daily troubler of our souls (Romans 7:25). We are not yet perfect, nor have we already obtained our crown and prize (Philippians 3:12). We are liars if we say we have no sin (1 John 1:8, 10).

How then does the apostle Paul teach us to live? Will he say, "You are decisively and irrevocably new, so you can coast through life with no fight to become new?" Or will he say, "You are not decisively and irrevocably new and must therefore fight to get to that place in Christ?" No, neither of these. He will say, By faith, embrace all that God is for you in Christ and all that you are for his glory in Christ. Believe that. And now, with that confidence, fight to take possession of the territory that Christ has conquered for you. Fight to become in practice what you are in Christ. Here are eight illustrations of this truth:

1. *Statement of newness:* Romans 6:14, "Sin shall not be master over you, for you are not under law but under grace" (NASB).
   Command to become new: Romans 6:12, "Do not let sin reign in your mortal body" (NASB).

2. *Statement of newness:* Romans 6:18, "Having been freed from sin, you became slaves of righteousness" (NASB).
   Command to become new: Romans 6:19, "Present your members as slaves to righteousness" (NASB).

3. *Statement of newness:* Romans 6:6, "Our old self was crucified with Him" (NASB).
   Command to become new: Romans 6:11, "Consider yourselves to be dead to sin" (NASB).

4. *Statement of newness:* Colossians 3:9, "You laid aside the old self with its evil practices" (NASB).
   Command to become new: Ephesians 4:22, "Lay aside the old self, which is being corrupted in accordance with the lusts of deceit" (NASB).

5. *Statement of newness:* Colossians 3:10, "[You] have put on the new self who is being renewed to a true knowledge according to the image of the One who created him" (NASB).
   Command to become new: Ephesians 4:24, "Put on the new self, which in the likeness of God has been created in righteousness and holiness of the truth" (NASB).

6. *Statement of newness:* Galatians 3:27, "All of you who were baptized into Christ have clothed yourselves with Christ" (NASB).
Command to become new: Romans 13:14, "But put on the Lord Jesus Christ" (NASB).

7. *Statement of newness:* Galatians 5:24, "Those who belong to Christ Jesus have crucified the flesh with its passions and desires" (NASB).
Command to become new: Romans 13:14, "Make no provision for the flesh in regard to its lusts" (NASB).

8. *Statement of newness:* 1 Corinthians 5:7, "Just as you are in fact unleavened" (NASB).
Command to become new: 1 Corinthians 5:7, "Clean out the old leaven so that you may be a new lump [of dough]" (NASB).

Knowing this and learning how to walk with confidence (because of our newness) and with urgency (because of the demand to become new) is the secret of the Christian life. This is the way the apostle Paul lived. He expressed it like this: "Not that I have already obtained this or am already perfect, but I press on to make it my own, because Christ Jesus has made me his own" (Philippians 3:12). Already Christ's own. But pressing on to make it his own.

God's will for us is not paralyzing frustration because of imperfection. His will is liberating courage because of the certainty of our future in him. The Not Yet makes us humble and vigilant. And sometimes the road seems long. But the Already makes us confident and bold and reminds us that the road is short. Jesus walked it. And in him, we are already home. While we live, this is our calling: brokenhearted boldness. Contrite confidence. The image of Christ on earth: the Lion and the Lamb.

69

IF YOU WANT TO LOVE, YOU MUST DIE TO THE LAW

Living out the "Glorious Gospel"

If you want to be a loving person, the way to pursue it is to die to the Law and to pursue a vital, all-satisfying union with Christ. Romans 7:4 says, "You also have died to the law through the body of Christ, so that you may belong to another, to him who has been raised from the dead, in order that we may bear fruit for God." Notice the exchange: die to the law and belong to the one who was raised from the dead, that is, Jesus. This leads, Paul says, to bearing fruit for God. And the preeminent fruit of the Christian life is love. Therefore the key to love is to die to the law and embrace Jesus Christ by faith as the Savior and Treasure of your life.

But this does not mean that the Law aimed at something other than love. Romans 13:10 says, "Love is the fulfillment of the law" (NASB). So it seems that death to the Law means something like: Stop using the Law unlawfully. That's the way Paul talks in 1 Timothy 1. There are folks who want to be "teachers of the Law" but "they do not understand...what they are saying" (v. 7, NASB). What are they doing wrong?

Paul explains in 1 Timothy 1:5 that "the goal of our instruction is love from a pure heart and a good conscience and a sincere faith" (NASB). So Paul's gospel ministry aims at the fruit of love. People who love from "sincere faith" are in sync with the gospel.

Where does this love come from? He says it comes "from a pure heart and a good conscience and a sincere faith." In other words, the way to pursue love is by focusing on the transformation of the *heart* and the *conscience* and the awakening and strengthening of *faith*. Love is not pursued first or decisively by focusing on a list of behavioral commandments and striving to conform to them. That is what we must die to.

Then in 1 Timothy 1:6–7, Paul describes some men who don't understand this and yet are trying to use the Law for moral transformation. They are making a mess of it. He says, "Some men, straying from these things [that is, from heart, the conscience, and faith], have turned aside to fruitless discussion, wanting to be teachers of the Law, even though they do not understand...what they are saying" (NASB). So their error is a misuse of the Law. They are trying to teach the Law, but they are turning aside from matters of the heart and conscience and faith. And so they are not arriving at love.

Is then the Law at fault? No. Paul absolves the Law, by saying in 1 Timothy 1:8, "We know that the Law is good, if one uses it lawfully." The "lawful" use of the Law is to use it as a pointer to the gospel of the risen Christ, which awakens love. Paul confirms this in verse 9 by saying, "Law is not made for a righteous person, but for those who are lawless, rebellious, for the ungodly and sinners" (NASB). What does he mean? He means that the Law does not need to do its job for those who are united to Christ by faith and are bearing the fruit of love. It needs to do its job by confronting sinners with the fact that their lives are contrary to the gospel and that they must pursue "the gospel of the glory of the blessed God" and belong to the one who was raised from the dead.

Paul says, with a sweeping statement in verses 10–11, that the Law is for pointing out, and convicting people of, "whatever is contrary to sound teaching, according to the glorious gospel of the blessed God" (NASB). This is very significant. Notice the connection between the Law and the gospel here. Who is the Law for? It is for "the lawless and rebellious, the ungodly and sinners," that is, for those whose lives are not "according to the glorious gospel" (NASB). That is, for those who do not love. For love is the aim of Paul's gospel (v. 5). The point is that the Law does not produce lives that accord with the gospel. The *gospel* produces lives that accord with the gospel. Used lawfully, the law sends us to the gospel. That's the point of Romans 7:4—you must die to the Law [as a way of producing the fruit of love] and be united to Christ by faith "in order that we might bear fruit [of love] for God" (NASB).

In other words, according to 1 Timothy 1:5–11, the Law is meant to accuse and convict people of breaking the gospel! "The law is... for...whatever else is contrary to...the glorious gospel" (v. 10–11, NASB). The law of commandments is not the first and decisive means of fruit-bearing for the Christian. Rather the Law brings us to Christ so that, as Romans 7:4 says, "you might be joined to...Him who was raised from the dead, in order that we might bear fruit [of love] for God." Oh, let us embrace the risen Christ!

Life is too brief to waste it romancing the Law of commandments. That marriage will not bear the offspring of love. Make haste to Christ. Let the Law be, not the wife, but the humble matchmaker between you and Jesus. Don't fall in love with, and don't hate, the humble go-between. Die to the Law. Belong to the living Christ.

70

THE LORD ALONE WILL
BE EXALTED

Making War on Pride

During our staff days of prayer and planning, one of our focuses in prayer was to wage war on pride. For help, we looked at God's attitude toward pride, the nature of pride and the remedy for pride. We are aware that our hearts are deceitful and that we must be relentlessly vigilant in the fight against pride.

God's Attitude Toward Pride

God is opposed to human pride and will eventually bring it all down.

> For the LORD of hosts will have a day of reckoning against everyone who is proud and lofty, and against everyone who is lifted up, that he may be abased. And it will be against all the cedars of Lebanon that are lofty and lifted up, against all the oaks of Bashan, against all the lofty mountains, against all the hills that are lifted up, against every high tower, against every fortified wall, against all the ships of Tarshish, and against all the beautiful craft. And the pride of man will be humbled, and the loftiness of men will be abased, and the LORD alone will be exalted in that day. (Isaiah 2:12–17, NASB)

The Nature of Pride
One part of pride is taking credit yourself for what God does.

> I will punish the fruit of the arrogant heart of the king of Assyria and the pomp of his haughtiness. For he has said, "By the power of my hand and by my wisdom I did this, for I have understanding." Is the axe to boast itself over the one who chops with it? Is the saw to exalt itself over the one who wields it? That would be like a club wielding those who lift it, or like a rod lifting him who is not wood. (Isaiah 10:12–15, NASB)

The Remedy for Pride
Take to heart that all you have is a gift of free grace.

> For who regards you as superior? And what do you have that you did not receive? But if you did receive it, why do you boast as if you had not received it? (1 Corinthians 4:7, NASB)

Trust God to exalt you in due time.

> Humble yourselves, therefore, under the mighty hand of God so that at the proper time he may exalt you. (1 Peter 5:6, NASB)

Remember that the true and full revelation of God comes only to the humble.

> At that time Jesus answered and said, "I praise You, O Father, Lord of heaven and earth, that Thou didst hide these things from the wise and intelligent and didst revealed them to babes." (Matthew 11:25, NASB)

Realize that entering the kingdom depends on humility.

Truly I say to you, unless you are converted and become like children, you shall not enter the kingdom of heaven. Whoever then humbles himself as this child, he is the greatest in the kingdom of heaven. (Matthew 18:3–4, NASB)

Rest in the truth that all things are already yours in Christ.

So then let no one boast in men. For all things belong to you, whether Paul or Apollos or Cephas or the world or life or death or things present or things to come; all things belong to you, and you belong to Christ; and Christ belongs to God. (1 Corinthians 3:21–23, NASB)

Pray with us that this will be a year of humble self-forgetfulness as we see and savor the greatness of God.

71

HOW TO QUERY GOD

Thoughts on Romans 9:19–20

You will say to me then, "Why does he still find fault? For who
can resist his will?" But who are you, O man, to answer back to
God? Will what is molded say to its molder, "Why have you
made me like this?"

Clearly Paul was displeased with this response to his teaching about
God. Does this mean that it's always wrong to ask questions in response
to biblical teaching? I don't think so.

Paul had said some controversial things. Peter admitted that Paul's
letters were sometimes hard to understand: "There are some things in
them that are hard to understand, which the ignorant and unstable twist
to their own destruction, as they do the other Scriptures" (2 Peter 3:16).
Paul had said that God "has mercy on whomever he wills, and hardens
whomever he wills" (Romans 9:18). The point was, God himself decides
finally whether we are hard-hearted or not. "Though they were not yet
born and had done nothing either good or bad" God had mercy on Jacob
and gave Esau over to hardness (Romans 9:11–13).

Someone hears this and objects in verse 19, "Why does he still find
fault? For who can resist his will?" To this Paul responds, "You, a mere
human being, have no right to answer back to God."

The word "answer back" (*antapokrinomenos*) occurs one other time
in the New Testament, namely, in Luke 14:5–6. Jesus is showing the

lawyers that it is lawful to heal on the Sabbath. He said to them, "'Which of you, having a son or an ox that has fallen into a well on a Sabbath day, will not immediately pull him out?' And they could not answer back (*antapokrithēnai*) to these things."

In what sense could they not "answer back"? They could not show him wrong. They could not legitimately criticize him. They could not truly contradict what he said. So the word "answer back" probably carries the meaning: "answer back with a view to criticizing or disagreeing or correcting."

That, I think, is what displeased Paul in Romans 9:20. This leaves open the possibility that a different kind of question would be acceptable, namely, a humble, teachable question that wants to understand more, if possible, but not rebuke or condemn or criticize what has been said.

For example, in Luke 1:31 the angel Gabriel comes to the virgin Mary and says, "Behold, you will conceive in your womb and bear a son, and you shall call his name Jesus." Mary is astounded and baffled. Virgins don't have sons. She could have scoffed and argued. But instead she said, "How will this be, since I am a virgin?" (Luke 1:34). She did not say it can't happen; she asked, "How?"

Contrast this with Gabriel's visit to Zechariah, the father of John the Baptist. The angel comes and tells him, "Your wife Elizabeth will bear you a son, and you shall call his name John" (Luke 1:13). But Zechariah knew that "Elizabeth was barren, and both were advanced in years" (Luke 1:7). Different from Mary, his skepticism gave rise to a different question. He said, "How shall I know this?" Not: "How will you do this?" But: "How can I know you'll do it?"

Gabriel did not like this answer. He said, "I am Gabriel. I stand in the presence of God, and I was sent to speak to you and to bring you this good news. And behold, you will be silent and unable to speak until the day that these things take place, because you did not believe my words, which will be fulfilled in their time" (Luke 1:19–20).

So I conclude that humble, teachable questions about how and why God does what he does are acceptable to God. God gave a very helpful answer to Mary, "The Holy Spirit will come upon you, and the power of the Most High will overshadow you" (Luke 1:35). This did not remove the mystery, but it helped.

I can't remove the mystery from Romans 9. But there is more to understand than we have seen, and I do not want to discourage you from pressing further up and further in to the heart and mind of God. Just do it with meekness and with willingness to affirm what he says, even if it is perplexing.

Don't let your prayers be an occasion for back-talking. Don't criticize or get angry at God. Soon enough we will be finished with this brief life of perplexity. "Now we see in a mirror dimly, but then face to face. Now I know in part; then I shall know fully, even as I have been fully known" (1 Corinthians 13:12). Be honest with God about your bewilderment. But put your hand on your mouth, if murmuring arises. Better to sit silently and wait for the explanation, than to say that one could not exist. "For God alone, O my soul, wait in silence, for my hope is from him" (Psalm 62:5).

72

WHY I DO NOT SAY, "GOD DID NOT CAUSE THE CALAMITY, BUT HE CAN USE IT FOR GOOD."

Thoughts on His Sovereignty

Many Christians spoke this way about the murderous destruction of the World Trade Towers on September 11, 2001: "God did not cause it, but he can use it for good." Of course God can and does use our calamities for our good. I am not denying that. But that is very different from saying, "God did not cause the calamity." There are two reasons I do not say, "God uses, but does not cause calamity." One is that it goes beyond, and is contrary to, what the Bible teaches. The other is that it undermines the very hope it wants to offer.

First, this statement goes beyond and against the Bible. For some, all they want to say in denying that God "caused" the calamity is that God is not a sinner and that God does not remove human accountability and that God is compassionate. That is all true—and precious beyond words. But for others, and for most people who hear this slogan, something far more is implied. Namely, God, by his very nature, cannot or would not act to bring about such a calamity. This view of God is what contradicts the Bible and undercuts hope.

How God governs all events in the universe without sinning, and without removing responsibility from man, and with compassionate outcomes is mysterious indeed! But that is what the Bible teaches. God "works all things according to the counsel of his will" (Ephesians 1:11).

This "all things" includes the fall of sparrows (Matthew 10:29), the rolling of dice (Proverbs 16:33), the slaughter of his people (Psalm 44:11), the decisions of kings (Proverbs 21:1), the failing of sight (Exodus 4:11), the sickness of children (2 Samuel 12:15), the loss and gain of money (1 Samuel 2:7), the suffering of saints (1 Peter 4:19), the completion of travel plans (James 4:15), the persecution of Christians (Hebrews 12:4–7), the repentance of souls (2 Timothy 2:25), the gift of faith (Philippians 1:29), the pursuit of holiness (Philippians 3:12–13), the growth of believers (Hebrews 6:3), the giving and taking of life (1 Samuel 2:6), and the crucifixion of His Son (Acts 4:27–28).

From the smallest thing to the greatest thing, good and evil, happy and sad, pagan and Christian, pain and pleasure—God governs them all for his wise and just and good purposes (Isaiah 46:10). As the twenty-seventh question to the *Heidelberg Catechism* says,

> The almighty and everywhere present power of God; whereby, as it were by his hand, he upholds and governs heaven, earth, and all creatures; so that herbs and grass, rain and drought, fruitful and barren years, meat and drink, health and sickness, riches and poverty, yea, and all things come, not by chance, but be his fatherly hand.

Lest we miss the point, the Bible speaks most clearly to this in the most painful situations. Amos asks, in time of disaster, "Does disaster come to a city unless the LORD has done it?" (Amos 3:6). After losing all ten of his children in the collapse of his son's house, Job says, "The LORD gave, and the LORD has taken away; blessed be the name of the LORD" (Job 1:21). After being covered with boils he says, "Shall we receive good from God, and shall we not receive adversity?" (Job 2:10).

Oh, yes, Satan is real and active and involved in this world of woe! In fact Job 2:7 says, "Satan went out from the presence of the LORD and smote Job with sore boils from the sole of his foot to the crown of his head" (NASB). Satan struck him. But Job did not get comfort from looking at secondary causes. He got comfort from looking at the ultimate cause. "Shall we not accept adversity from God?" And the author of the book agrees with Job when he says that Job's brothers and sisters "showed him sympathy and comforted him for all the evil that *the LORD* had brought upon him" (Job 42:11).

Then James underlines God's purposeful goodness in Job's misery: "You have heard of the steadfastness of Job, and you have seen the purpose of the Lord, how the Lord is compassionate and merciful" (James 5:11). Job himself concludes in prayer: "I know that you can do all things, and that no purpose of yours can be thwarted" (Job 42:2). Yes, Satan is real, and he is terrible—but he is on a leash.

The other reason I don't say, "God did not cause the calamity, but He can use it for good," is that it undercuts the very hope it wants to create. I ask those who say this: "If you deny that God could have 'used' a million prior events to save thousands of people from the World Trade Center collapse, what hope then do you have that God could now 'use' this terrible event to save you in the hour of trial?" Those who say God "can use the this calamity for good" nevertheless deny that he could "use" the events prior to 9/11 to prevent the evil itself. But the Bible teaches he could have restrained this evil (Genesis 20:6). "The LORD brings the counsel of the nations to nothing; he frustrates the plans of the peoples" (Psalm 33:10). Yet it was not in his plan to do it. Let us beware. We spare God the burden of his sovereignty and lose our only hope.

God is not like a firefighter who gets calls to show up at calamities when the damage is already happening. He is more like a surgeon who plans the cutting he must do and plans it for good purposes. Without the confidence that God rules over the beginning of our troubles, it is hard to believe that he could rule over their end. If we deny God his power and wisdom to govern the arrival of our pain, why should we think we can trust him with its departure?

All of us are sinners. We deserve to perish. Every breath we take is an undeserved gift in this vapor-length life. We have one great hope: that Jesus Christ died to obtain pardon and righteousness for us (Ephesians 1:7; 2 Corinthians 5:21) and that God will employ his all-conquering, sovereign grace to preserve us for our inheritance (Jeremiah 32:40). We surrender this hope if we sacrifice this sovereignty.

73

HOPE-GIVING PROMISES FOR TRIUMPH OVER SIN

Thoughts on the Nature of Sanctification

One of the reasons sin will not rule as lord over us while we are "under grace" (Romans 6:14) is that while we are under grace, God is at work in us to will and to do His good pleasure. I base this on Romans 6:17, which says, "But thanks be to God that though you were slaves of sin, you became obedient from the heart to that form of teaching to which you were committed" (NASB). Since Paul *thanks God* that the Romans became obedient from the heart, I conclude that God is the one who worked to bring about this obedience in their hearts. And if God works to bring about obedience in our heart, then sin won't be the lord over us—God will.

This does not mean we become perfect in this life (Philippians 3:12; 2 Corinthians 3:18; Romans 7:24), but it does mean that sin is dethroned in the castle of our lives and the defeat of sin is certain as we "fight the good fight of the faith" (1 Timothy 6:12) until we die or until Jesus comes (2 Timothy 4:7). I have heard the illustration that sanctification— our progressive war against sin and pursuit of holiness—is like a man spinning a yo-yo up and down as he goes up the stairs. Our lives have their ups and downs in the pursuit of godliness, but there is progress in rising overall toward the holiness we desire.

But I think the illustration needs one small correction. Halfway up the stairs we may have a temporary defeat in our warfare against unbelief and sin that sends the yo-yo of faith lower than it was on the first step. In other words, there is no guarantee in our battle with unbelief and sin that the defeats of our later years will not bring discouragements and desperation worse than those of the early years. The battle must be fought to the very end, whether progression is steady or not.

We must let the sovereignty of God make us hopeful that change is possible, not passive as if no change were necessary. So take the following texts as encouragements from God that you can and you will make progress in driving sin from your life.

Second Thessalonians 1:11–12, "*To this end we always pray for you, that our God may...fulfill every resolve for good and every work of faith by his power, so that the name of our Lord Jesus may be glorified in you.*" Remember, Christ gets the glory when it is manifest that God enables us to fulfill our good resolves through him.

Hebrews 13:20–21: "*Now may the God of peace...equip you with everything good that you may do his will, working in us that which is pleasing in his sight, through Jesus Christ, to whom be the glory forever and ever. Amen.*" Again, notice, since God enables us to do what is pleasing in his sight "through Jesus," it is Jesus who gets the glory, not us.

1 Peter 4:11, "*Whoever serves*" is to do so "*as one who serves by the strength which God supplies—in order that in everything God may be glorified through Jesus Christ. To him belong glory and dominion forever and ever. Amen.*" The giver gets the glory. Because God is the one who enables us to "serve" him, he gets the credit for the service.

Galatians 5:22–23, "*The fruit of the Spirit is love, joy, peace, patience, kindness, goodness, faithfulness, gentleness, self-control; against such things there is no law.*" Christian attitudes and behaviors are the fruit of the Spirit, not ultimately the fruit of our own efforts. Our efforts are essential but not finally decisive. See below on Philippians 2:12–13.

All these texts I have mentioned are examples of how God fulfills the

Old Testament promise of the New Covenant—the promise that God will work in his people to bring about obedience. Here are some examples of those Old Testament promises.

Jeremiah 31:31–33, "Behold, the days are coming, declares the LORD, when I will make a new covenant with the house of Israel.... I will put my law within them, and I will write it on their hearts." Once, the Law was external on stone and met rebellion in our rebellious hearts. In the New Covenant, however, God does not leave the Law outside, making demands; he also takes it inside, creating obedience.

Deuteronomy 30:6, "The LORD your God will circumcise your heart...so that you will love the LORD your God with all your heart and with all your soul."

Ezekiel 11:19–20, "A new spirit I will put within them. I will remove the heart of stone from their flesh and give them a heart of flesh, that they may walk in my statutes and keep my rules and obey them."

Ezekiel 36:26–27, "I will give you a new heart, and a new spirit I will put within you. And I will remove the heart of stone from your flesh and give you a heart of flesh. And I will put my Spirit within you, and cause you to walk in my statutes." Note the strong language of "cause you to walk in my statutes." That is what I think Paul was thanking God for in Romans 6:17.

Jeremiah 32:40, "I will make with them an everlasting covenant, that I will not turn away from doing good to them. I will put the fear of me in their hearts, that they may not turn from me." Our enduring to the end in the fear of God is owing to God's powerful grace to keep us.

How then should we pray and use our willpower? One example from Paul for how to pray if God has promised to work his holy will into our lives: "May the Lord make you increase and abound in love for one another and for all" (1 Thessalonians 3:12; see Philippians 1:9–11). We ask God to do in us the very thing that he commands: "O Lord, make us abound in love to each other! This is your work! Do it!"

But praying does not replace working. God's sovereignty does not mean there is no such thing as human willpower. We are commanded to exert our wills in the cause of righteousness. "Work out your own salvation with fear and trembling, for it is God who works in you, both to will and to work for his good pleasure" (Philippians 2:12–13). It is the promise (God will work in you!) that sustains and gives hope to the willpower (work out your salvation). Take heart. God will not leave you to yourself.

74

JONATHAN EDWARDS ON THE PILGRIM MIND-SET

Treasuring Christ Above All Else

The year 2003 was Jonathan Edwards' 300th birthday. It came as a timely reminder to me that this giant of the church, and one of my heroes, has much to teach the church today about treasuring Christ and about the pilgrim mind-set that marks the lives of those who treasure Christ above this world. In September 1733, he preached a sermon called "The Christian Pilgrim, Or, The True Christian's Life a Journey Toward Heaven." It was based on Hebrews 11:13–14:

> These all died in faith, not having received the things promised, but having seen them and greeted them from afar, and having acknowledged that they were strangers and exiles on the earth. For people who speak thus make it clear that they are seeking a homeland.

Let's listen in on Edwards' exposition, and let him shape our vision of what it means to live this vapor-length life as pilgrims on the way to heaven, treasuring Christ above all things.

Pilgrims are not diverted from their aim.

> A traveler...is not enticed by fine appearances to put off the thought of proceeding. No, but his journey's end is in his mind.

If he meets with comfortable accommodations at an inn, he entertains no thoughts of settling there. He considers that these things are not his own, that he is but a stranger, and when he has refreshed himself, or tarried for a night, he is for going forward. (Works, Banner of Truth, 243)

Pilgrims are to hold the things of this world loosely.

So should we desire heaven more than the comforts and enjoyments of this life.... Our hearts ought to be loose to these things, as that of a man on a journey, that we may as cheerfully part with them whenever God calls. (243)

Pilgrims become like what they hope to attain.

We should be endeavoring to come nearer to heaven, in being more heavenly, becoming more and more like the inhabitants of heaven in respect of holiness and conformity to God, the knowledge of God and Christ, in clear views of the glory of God, the beauty of Christ, and the excellency of divine things, as we come nearer to the beatific vision. We should labor to be continually growing in divine love—that this may be an increasing flame in our hearts, till they ascend wholly in this flame. (244)

Pilgrims will not be satisfied with anything less than God.

God is the highest good of the reasonable creature, and the enjoyment of him is the only happiness with which our souls can be satisfied. To go to heaven fully to enjoy God, is infinitely better than the most pleasant accommodations here. Fathers and mothers, husbands, wives, children, or the company of earthly friends, are but shadows. But the enjoyment of God is the substance. These are but scattered beams, but God is the sun. These are but streams, but God is the fountain. These are but drops, but God is the ocean.... Why should we labor for, or set our hearts on anything else, but that which is our proper end, and true happiness? (244)

Pilgrims are not grieved by their arrival at the journey's end.

To spend our lives so as to be only a journeying towards heaven, is the way to be free from bondage and to have the prospect and forethought of death comfortable. Does the traveler think of his journey's end with fear and terror? Is it terrible to him to think that he has almost got to his journey's end? Were the children of Israel sorry after forty years' travel in the wilderness, when they had almost got to Canaan? (246)

Pilgrims ponder what they pursue.

Labor to be much acquainted with heaven. If you are not acquainted with it, you will not be likely to spend your life as a journey thither. You will not be sensible of its worth, nor will you long for it. Unless you are much conversant in your mind with a better good, it will be exceeding difficult to you to have your hearts loose from these things, to use them only in subordination to something else, and be ready to part with them for the sake of that better good. Labor therefore to obtain a realizing sense of a heavenly world, to get a firm belief of its reality, and to be very much conversant with it in your thoughts. (246)

Pilgrims travel together.

Let Christians help one another in going this journey.... Company is very desirable in a journey, but in none so much as this.

Let them go united and not fall out by the way, which would be to hinder one another, but use all means they can to help each other up the hill. This would ensure a more successful traveling and a more joyful meeting at their Father's house in glory. (246)

These are precious words from a man who finished his journey well. He was a pilgrim. And we may learn from him how to see this life as a vapor and see heaven as an everlasting joy. To live is Christ and to die is gain. Therefore let us learn to treasure Christ now above all things, and count everything as rubbish by comparison, so that our hearts will "be loose to these things, as that of a man on a journey, that we may as cheerfully part with them whenever God calls."

75

Sown in Dishonor, Raised in Glory

The Two Sides of Death

R omantic death is rare. More common are involuntary groanings and screams of pain. The ignominy of dying is pathetic. It is more often hellish than heroic. The apostle Paul uses two words to capture death's degrading assault. The first is "dishonor." He says that the death of our physical body is like a seed being sown in the ground. How is it sown? "It is sown in dishonor" (1 Corinthians 15:43).

During my college days, my father's mother died, leaving my grandfather very alone in Pennsylvania. His youngest son, my father, brought him to South Carolina to live with us. I was glad, and my mother was gracious, as always. Over time, his condition worsened and my mother was unable to care for him in the absence of my dad, who traveled as an evangelist.

So the painful decision was made to move him to a nursing home. There I watched him decline from the strong toolmaker-turned-pastor to skin-and-bones. The last time I saw him alive was with my father while I was home from seminary. We drove to the nursing home together, expressing the expectation that this would be the last time I would see him alive. It was.

There he lay in a diaper, curled up in a fetal position. His eyes were glazed over and crusty. His breathing was labored. My father spoke with me about his dad for a few minutes and then suggested we pray very loudly by putting our mouths next to his seemingly deaf ears. Ignoring the others in the home, we almost shouted our prayer. When my father stopped, his father heaved with all his fading might and said, "AMEN!" That was the last sound I ever heard him make. If I had ever seen a body sown in "dishonor," this was it. And there are millions like him.

Then there is another word that Paul uses to describe the humiliating condition of death. In Philippians 3:21 he says that Christ "shall change our vile body, that it may be fashioned like unto his glorious body" (KJV). The word "vile" translates the Greek, *tapeinōseōs*. Before the New Testament transformed this word into a virtue, because of Christ's glorious "lowliness," the word had only negative connotations of "humiliation, debasement, defeat."

I recall reading a biography of Julius Schniewind, a German New Testament scholar who was born in 1883. He became deathly ill in the summer of 1948, but few knew how serious it was. Hans-Joakim Kraus was with him when he taught his last "lay Bible hour," and heard him groan as he was leaving, "*Soma tapeinōseōs! Soma tapeinōseōs!*"—the phrase from Philippians 3:21: "Body of humiliation! Body of humiliation!"

Christianity is deeply aware of the humiliation, degradation, and dishonor of the body in death. The death of Jesus stamped forever our expectation. "His appearance was so marred, beyond human semblance, and his form beyond that of the children of mankind" (Isaiah 52:14). Is the disciple above his Lord? Should we expect anything better? His back was torn from scourging, his face swollen from punching, his head bloodied from the thorns and chin ripped because of the beard-pulling, his hands and feet swollen and mangled with the spikes, his side pierced with a large spear. And he was shamefully naked. He died with a "loud cry" (Mark 15:37).

How precious, therefore, to all followers of Jesus, that he rose from the dead with a "body of glory," never to die again! And how precious is the promise of Romans 6:5 that "If we have become united with him in a death like his, we shall certainly be united with him in a resurrection like his." And the promise of 1 Corinthians 15:43, "It is sown in dishonor; *it is raised in glory.*" And the promise of Philippians 3:21, "[He] will transform our lowly body to be like his glorious body." And the promise of Matthew 13:43, "Then the righteous will shine like the sun in the kingdom of their Father."

76

THE FIERCE FRUIT OF SELF-CONTROL

The Key to Victory Is in God's Power

> *As the Hebrews were promised the land, but had to take it by force, one town at a time, so we are promised the gift of self-control, yet we also must take it by force.* *

The very concept of "self-control" implies a battle between a divided self. It implies that our "self" produces desires we should not gratify but instead "control." We should "deny" ourselves, and "take up [our] cross daily," Jesus says, and follow him (Luke 9:23). Daily our "self" produces desires that should be "denied" or "controlled."

The path that leads to heaven is narrow and strewn with suicidal temptations to abandon the way. Therefore, Jesus says, "Strive to enter through the narrow door" (Luke 13:24). The Greek word for "strive" is *agōnizesthe* in which you correctly hear the English word "agonize."

We get a taste of what is involved from Matthew 5:29, "If your right eye causes you to sin, tear it out and throw it away." This is the fierceness of self-control. This is what is behind the words of Jesus in Matthew

---

* Edward Welch, "Self-Control: The Battle Against 'One More,'" *The Journal of Biblical Counseling*, vol. 19, No. 2 (Winter, 2001): 30.

11:12, "The kingdom of heaven has suffered violence, and the violent take it by force." Are you laying hold on the kingdom fiercely?

Paul says that Christians exercise self-control like the Greek athletes, only our goal is eternal, not temporal. "Everyone who competes in the games (*agōnizomenos*) exercises self-control in all things. They then do it to receive a perishable wreath, but we an imperishable" (1 Corinthians 9:25, NASB). So he says, "I pommel my body and subdue it" (1 Corinthians 9:27, NASB). Self-control is saying no to sinful desires, even when it hurts.

But the Christian way of self-control is *not* "Just say no!" The problem is with the word "just." You don't *just* say no. You say no in a certain way: You say no by faith in the superior power and pleasure of Christ. The "No!" is just as ruthless. And maybe just as painful. But the difference between worldly self-control and godly self-control is crucial. Who will get the glory for victory? That's the issue. Will *we* get the glory? Or will *Christ* get the glory? If we exercise self-control by faith in Christ's superior power and pleasure, Christ will get the glory.

Fundamental to the Christian view of self-control is that it is a gift. It is the fruit of the Holy Spirit: "The fruit of the Spirit is love, joy, peace...self-control" (Galatians 5:22). How do we "strive" against our fatal desires? Paul answers: "I labor, striving (*agōnizomenos*) according to His power, which mightily works within me" (Colossians 1:29, NASB). The key is "according to his power." He "agonizes" by the power of Christ, not his own. Similarly he tells us, "If by the Spirit you put to death the deeds of the body, you will live" (Romans 8:13). "Not by might, nor by power, but by my Spirit, says the LORD of hosts" (Zechariah 4:6). We must be fierce! Yes, but not by *our* might. "The horse is made ready for the day of battle, but the victory belongs to the LORD" (Proverbs 21:31).

And how does the Spirit produce this fruit of self-control in us? By instructing us in the superior preciousness of grace, and enabling us to see and savor (that is, "trust") all that God is for us in Jesus. "The grace of God has appeared...training us to renounce...worldly passions...in the present age" (Titus 2:11–12). When we really see and believe what God is for us by grace through Jesus Christ, the power of wrong desires is broken. Therefore the fight for self-control is a fight of faith. "Fight the good fight of the faith. Take hold of the eternal life to which you were called" (1 Timothy 6:12).

77

THOUGHTS ON
GOD'S THOUGHTS

Nothing Matters More Than
Knowing What He Has Said

In a letter to George Bainton on October 15, 1888, Mark Twain said, "The difference between the almost right word and the right word is really a large matter—it's the difference between the lightning bug and the lightning."

So it is with the difference between the thought of a man and the thought of God. God's thoughts are our goal. We must be about finding, understanding, trusting, cherishing, obeying, and spreading the thoughts of God. Nothing matters more than what God has thought and spoken about everything, especially about himself.

Our thoughts are ephemeral, but God's are eternal.

Psalm 94:11, "The Lord knows the thoughts of man, that they are but a breath."

Isaiah 40:7–8, "The grass withers, the flower fades when the breath of the Lord blows on it; surely the people are grass. The grass withers, the flower fades, but the word of our God will stand forever."

God's thoughts are countless.

Psalm 40:5, "You have multiplied, O Lord my God, your wondrous deeds and your thoughts toward us; none can compare with you! I will proclaim and tell of them, yet they are more than can be told."

Psalm 139:17, "How precious to me are your thoughts, O God! How vast is the sum of them!"

God's thoughts are immeasurably higher than our thoughts.

Isaiah 55:7–9, "Let the wicked forsake his way, and the unrighteous man his thoughts.... For my thoughts are not your thoughts, neither are your ways my ways, declares the Lord. For as the heavens are higher than the earth, so are my ways higher than your ways, and my thoughts than your thoughts."

God's thoughts are unsearchable and unfathomable.

Romans 11:33–36, "Oh, the depth of the riches and wisdom and knowledge of God! How unsearchable are his judgments and how inscrutable his ways! For who has known the mind of the Lord, or who has been his counselor? Or who has given a gift to him that he might be repaid? For from him and through him and to him are all things. To Him be glory forever. Amen."

God's thoughts can only be found out by God.

1 Corinthians 2:11, "For who knows a person's thoughts except the spirit of that person, which is in him? So also no one comprehends the thoughts of God except the Spirit of God."

God's thoughts are revealed to whom he pleases.

Matthew 11:25–27, "At that time Jesus declared, 'I thank you, Father, Lord of heaven and earth, that you have hidden these things from the wise and understanding and revealed them to little children; yes, Father, for such was your gracious will. All things have been handed over to me by my Father; and no one knows the Son except the Father, and no one knows the Father except the Son and anyone to whom the Son chooses to reveal him.'"

God's thoughts are revealed through inspired spokesmen in the Bible.

1 Corinthians 2:12–13, "Now we have received not the spirit of the world, but the Spirit who is from God, that we might understand the things freely given us by God. And we impart this in words not taught by human wisdom but taught by the Spirit, interpreting spiritual truths to those who are spiritual."

But the thoughts of God are ridiculed by the natural man.

1 Corinthians 2:14, "The natural person does not accept the things of the Spirit of God, for they are folly to him, and he is not able to understand them because they are spiritually discerned."

We need a renewed mind to grasp the thoughts of God.

Romans 12:2, "Do not be conformed to this world, but be transformed by the renewal of your mind, that by testing you may discern what is the will of God, what is good and acceptable and perfect."

We are transformed to receive the thoughts of God by beholding God's glory.

2 Corinthians 3:18, "And we all, with unveiled face, beholding the glory of the Lord, are being transformed into the same image from one degree of glory to another. For this comes from the Lord who is the Spirit."

We behold the glory of God by a miracle of God's creative act through the gospel.

2 Corinthians 4:4–6, "In their case the god of this world has blinded the minds of the unbelievers, to keep them from seeing the light of the gospel of the glory of Christ, who is the image of God. For what we proclaim is not ourselves, but Christ Jesus as Lord, with ourselves as your servants for Jesus' sake. For God, who said, 'Let light shine out of darkness,' has shone in our hearts to give the light of the knowledge of the glory of God in the face of Jesus Christ."

Thus renewed, we pursue the thoughts of God like silver and gold.

Proverbs 2:1–6, "My son, if you receive my words and treasure up my commandments within you, making your ear attentive to wisdom and inclining your heart to understanding; yes, if you call out for insight and raise your voice for understanding, if you seek it like silver and search for it as for hidden treasures, then you will understand the fear of the LORD and find the knowledge of God. For the LORD gives wisdom; from his mouth come knowledge and understanding."

The Lord gives understanding of his thoughts through serious thinking about them.

2 Timothy 2:7, "Think over what I say, for the Lord will give you understanding in everything."

Knowledge of God's thoughts puffs up, but love builds up.

1 Corinthians 8:1–3, "Now concerning food offered to idols: we know that 'all of us possess knowledge.' This 'knowledge' puffs up, but love builds up. If anyone imagines that he knows something, he does not yet know as he ought to know. But if anyone loves God, he is known by God."

All knowledge of God's thoughts is for the sake of love.

1 Timothy 1:5, "The aim of our charge is love that issues from a pure heart and a good conscience and a sincere faith."

But all love is for the sake of the glory of and praise of God.

Philippians 1:9–11, "It is my prayer that your love may abound more and more, with knowledge and all discernment, so that you may approve what is excellent, and so be pure and blameless for the day of Christ, filled with the fruit of righteousness that comes through Jesus Christ, to the glory and praise of God."

Now this is remarkable—all of God's thoughts aiming to help us love each other; and all of our love aiming at "the praise and glory of God." This double truth is one of God's great thoughts. God has acted and spoken so that we might love each other and in loving each other show God to be glorious.

But how can this be? How does this great thought of God work? Isn't love an end in itself? How can you really love someone and have an ulterior motive—that God be glorified? The answer is one of God's thoughts toward us that is precious beyond words. It goes like this: Love is doing what will enthrall the beloved with the greatest and longest joy. What will enthrall the beloved this way is the glory of God. Love *means* doing all we can, at whatever cost to ourselves, to help people be enthralled with the glory of God. When they are, they are satisfied and God is glorified. Therefore loving people and glorifying God are one.

This is only one of the many discoveries we will make as we spend our days thinking the thoughts of God after him. Seeing a thought of God for what it really is and seeing a thought of a mere man is the difference between seeing lightning and a lightning bug.

78

Is God's Demand for Worship Vain?

An Open Letter to Michael Prowse

Dear Mr. Prowse,
It would be my great joy to persuade you that God's demand for worship is beautiful love, not ugly pride. On March 30, 2003, you wrote in the *London Financial Times:*

> Worship is an aspect of religion that I always found difficult to understand. Suppose we postulate an omnipotent being who, for reasons inscrutable to us, decided to create something other than Himself. Why should he...expect us to worship him? We didn't ask to be created. Our lives are often troubled. We know that human tyrants, puffed up with pride, crave adulation and homage. But a morally perfect God would surely have no character defects. So why are all those people on their knees every Sunday?

I don't understand why you assume that the only incentive for God to demand praise is that he is needy and defective. This is true for mere humans. But with God there is another possibility.

What if, as the atheist Ayn Rand once said, admiration is the rarest and best of pleasures? And what if, as I wish Ayn Rand could have seen, God really is the most admirable being in the universe? Would this not imply that God's summons for our praise is the summons for our highest joy? And if the success of that summons cost him the life of his Son, would that not be love (instead of arrogance)?

The Bible says God should be greatly praised because he *is* great. "Great is the LORD, and greatly to be praised" (Psalm 96:4). He is more admirable than anything he has made. That is what it means to be God.

Moreover, the Bible says that praise—overflowing, heartfelt admiration—is a pleasure. "Praise the LORD! For it is good to sing praises to our God; for it is pleasant" (Psalm 147:1). And this pleasure is the best there is and lasts forever. "In [God's] presence there is fullness of joy; at your right hand are pleasures forevermore" (Psalm 16:11).

The upshot of this is that God's demand for supreme praise is his demand for our supreme happiness. Deep in our hearts we know that we were not made to be made much of. We were made to make much of something great. The best joys are when we forget ourselves, enthralled with greatness. The greatest greatness is God's. Every good that ever thrilled the heart of man is amplified ten thousand times in God, its Maker. God is in a class by himself. He is the only being for whom self-exaltation is essential to love. If he "humbly" sent us away from his beauty, suggesting we find our joy in another, we would be ruined.

Great thinkers have said this long before I did. For example, Jonathan Edwards said:

> It is easy to conceive how God should seek the good of the creature...even his happiness, from a supreme regard to himself; as his happiness arises from...the creature's exercising a supreme regard to God...in loving it, and rejoicing in it.... God's respect to the creature's good, and his respect to himself, is not a divided respect; but both are united in one, as the happiness of the creature aimed at is happiness in union with himself. (Jonathan Edwards, *The End for Which God Created the World*, in John Piper, *God's Passion for His Glory* [Wheaton, Ill.: Crossway Books, 1998], 248f.)

C. S. Lewis broke through to the beauty of God's self-exaltation (thinking at first, like you, that the Psalms sounded like an old woman craving compliments). He finally saw the obvious:

> My whole, more general, difficulty about the praise of God
> depended on my absurdly denying to us, as regards the supremely
> Valuable, what we delight to do, what indeed we can't help doing,
> about everything else we value. I think we delight to praise what
> we enjoy because the praise not merely expresses but completes
> the enjoyment; it is its appointed consummation. (C. S. Lewis,
> *Reflections on the Psalms* [New York: Harcourt, Brace and World,
> 1958], 93–5)

Both Edwards and Lewis saw that praising God is the consummation of joy in God. This joy flows from the infinite beauty and greatness of God. There is no one who surpasses him in any truly admirable trait. He is absolutely enjoyable. But we are sinners and do not see it, and do not want it. We want ourselves at the center. But Jesus Christ taught us to be human in another way and then died for our sin, absorbed God's wrath against us, and opened the way to see and savor God. "Christ suffered once for sins, the righteous for the unrighteous, that he might bring us to God" (1 Peter 3:18).

Therefore, the reason God seeks our praise is not because he won't be complete until he gets it. He is seeking our praise because we won't be complete until we give it. This is not arrogance. It is love.

I pray that you will see and savor the beauty of your Maker and your Redeemer.

John Piper

79

TAKING THE SWAGGER OUT OF CHRISTIAN CULTURAL INFLUENCE

The Role of Happy, Brokenhearted Exiles

The fact that Christians are exiles on the earth (1 Peter 2:11), does not mean that they don't care what becomes of culture. But it does mean that they exert their influence as very happy, brokenhearted outsiders. We are exiles. "Our citizenship is in heaven, and from it we await a Savior, the Lord Jesus Christ" (Philippians 3:20). "Here we have no lasting city, but we seek the city that is to come" (Hebrews 13:14). Life is a vapor, lived in a foreign land.

But we are very happy sojourners, because we have been commanded by our bloody Champion to rejoice in exile miseries. "Blessed are you when others...persecute you...on my account. Rejoice and be glad, for your reward is great in heaven" (Matthew 5:11–12). We are happy because the apostle Paul showed us that "the sufferings of this present time are not worth comparing with the glory that is to be revealed to us" (Romans 8:18). We are happy because there are merciful foretastes everywhere in this fallen world, and God is glad for us to enjoy them (1 Timothy 4:3; 6:17). And we are happy because we know that the exiles will one day inherit the earth (Matthew 5:5). Christ died for sinners so that "all things" might one day belong to his people (Romans 8:32).

But our joy is a *brokenhearted* joy. Christ is worthy of so much better

271

obedience than we Christians render. Our joy is a brokenhearted joy because so many people around the world have not heard the good news that "Christ Jesus came into the world to save sinners" (1 Timothy 1:15). And our joy is a brokenhearted joy because human culture—in every society—dishonors Christ, glories in its shame, and is bent on self-destruction.

This includes America. American culture does not belong to Christians, neither in reality nor in biblical theology. It never has. The present tailspin toward Sodom is not a fall from Christian ownership. "The whole world lies in the power of the evil one" (1 John 5:19). It has since the fall, and it will till Christ comes in open triumph. God's rightful ownership will be manifest in due time. The Lordship of Christ over all Creation is being manifest in stages, first the age of groaning, then the age of glory. "We ourselves, who have the firstfruits of the Spirit, groan inwardly as we wait eagerly for adoption as sons, the redemption of our bodies" (Romans 8:23). The exiles are groaning with the whole Creation. We are waiting.

But Christian exiles are not passive. We do not smirk at the misery or the merrymaking of immoral culture. We weep. Or we should. This is my main point: Being exiles does not mean being cynical. It does not mean being indifferent or uninvolved. The salt of the earth does not mock rotting meat. Where it can, it saves and seasons. And where it can't, it weeps. And the light of the world does not withdraw, saying "good riddance" to godless darkness. It labors to illuminate. But not dominate.

Being Christian exiles in American culture does not end our influence; it takes the swagger out of it. We don't get cranky that our country has been taken away. We don't whine about the triumphs of evil. We are not hardened with anger. We understand. This is not new. This was the way it was in the beginning—Antioch, Corinth, Athens, Rome. The Empire was not just degenerate; it was deadly. For three explosive centuries Christians paid for their Christ-exalting joy with blood. Many still do. More will.

It never occurred to those early exiles that they should rant about the ubiquity of secular humanism. The Imperial words were still ringing in their ears: "You will be hated by all for my name's sake. But the one who endures to the end will be saved" (Mark 13:13). This was a time for indomitable joy and unwavering ministries of mercy.

Yes, it was a time for influence—as it is now. But not with huffing and puffing as if to reclaim our lost laws. Rather with tears and persuasion and perseverance, knowing that the folly of racism, and the exploitation of the poor, and the de-God-ing of education, and the horror of abortion, and the collapse of heterosexual marriage are the tragic death-tremors of joy, not the victory of the left or the right.

The greatness of Christian exiles is not success but service. Whether we win or lose, we witness to the way of truth and beauty and joy. We don't own culture, and we don't rule it. We serve it with brokenhearted joy and longsuffering mercy, for the good of man and the glory of Jesus Christ.

80

THE SWEET COMMANDS OF GOD TO DEMONS, WIND, RAVENS, AND LOVE

Everything That Befalls the Elect Is for Their Good

If, by God's grace, you are assured that God is for you and not against you, then the more evidences you find of God's sovereignty, the happier you are. And the wider the scope of God's sovereignty, the more secure you feel in all the perils of love.

And he *is* for us. The gospel is the good news that, because of Christ's blood and righteousness, we are justified by faith alone, and God is for us forever. In Romans 8:31–33 Paul says, "If God is for us, who can be against us?... Who shall bring any charge against God's elect?"

So, if God is for us, then all his power is on our side. All his sovereignty is exerted for our good and never against us. All his decrees are for our ultimate benefit. How sovereign is God over the things that threaten our lives? When God commands, who and what must obey?

Let's start at the highest enemy level. Good angels and evil spirits must obey God when he commands them with omnipotent authority: "Bless the Lord, O you his angels, you mighty ones who do his word, obeying the voice of his word!" (Psalm 103:20). "He commands even the unclean spirits, and they obey him" (Mark 1:27). So no demon can do anything to God's elect except serve the ultimate purposes of God, who is for us. For example, consider 2 Corinthians 12:7–9,

> To keep me from becoming conceited because of the surpassing greatness of the revelations, a thorn was given me in the flesh, a messenger of Satan to harass me, to keep me from becoming conceited. Three times I pleaded with the Lord about this, that it should leave me. But he said to me, "My grace is sufficient for you, for my power is made perfect in weakness." Therefore I will boast all the more gladly of my weaknesses, so that the power of Christ may rest upon me.

Paul's thorn in the flesh is "a messenger of Satan." Satan's design is Paul's misery and the ruin of his faith. He wants Paul to curse God the way he wanted Job to curse God. Paul prayed that this "messenger of Satan" be removed. The risen Christ said no three times. Then he gave his reason: his own divine power would be magnified in Paul's weakness. In other words, Christ's design for this thorn and Satan's design are exactly the opposite. Satan wants to ruin Paul's faith and dishonor Christ. Christ wants it to refine Paul's faith and honor his power. The irony here is that Satan's torment backfires and becomes a means of sanctification— it must gall him when God does this. God knew he would do this when he permitted Satan to afflict Paul. Therefore, even Satan is part of God's design to bless Paul with greater usefulness and glorify the power of Christ.

Then let's consider the apparent enemy of the natural world that often hurts us with calamity and disaster and disease and obstruction. How sovereign is God over nature? What parts of nature can he command with effective power? Here are some biblical examples:

"I have commanded the ravens to feed you there" (1 Kings 17:4). "Have you commanded the morning since your days began, and caused the dawn to know its place?" (Job 38:12). "He commanded the skies above...and he rained down on them manna" (Psalm 78:23–24). "[He] commands the sun, and it does not rise; [he] seals up the stars" (Job 9:7). "The LORD appointed a great fish to swallow up Jonah" (Jonah 1:17). "The LORD God appointed a plant and made it come up over Jonah" (Jonah 4:6). "God appointed a worm that attacked the plant, so that it withered" (Jonah 4:7). "He commanded and raised the stormy wind, which lifted up the waves of the sea" (Psalm 107:25). "Who then is this, that he commands even winds and water, and they obey him?" (Luke 8:25). "He sends out his command to the earth; his word runs swiftly. He gives snow like wool; he scatters hoarfrost like ashes" (Psalm 147:15). "He hurls down his crystals of ice like crumbs; who can stand before his cold?" (Psalm 147:17). "I will also command the clouds that they rain no rain upon it" (Isaiah 5:6). "He covers his hands with the lightning and commands it to strike the mark" (Job 36:32).

If God commands all demons and all natural elements and they obey Him, and if God is always for us and not against us, then everything that befalls the elect is for our good. Everything. "All things work together for good for those who love him and are called according to his purpose" (Romans 8:28) because he rules all things and is only for us and not against us.

Is that not the point of Jesus' logic when he said, "Are not two sparrows sold for a penny? And not one of them will fall to the ground apart from your Father.... Fear not, therefore; you are of more value than many sparrows" (Matthew 10:29, 31)? The logic here is that fear would be warranted if God did not rule tiny events like sparrow deaths. But since he does rule over them and since you are more valuable than sparrows, fear is *not* warranted. It's the sovereignty of God (no bird dies without him) and the mercy of God (he cherishes you more) that takes away fear when it feels like the world is out of control.

But the sweetest commands of God are not commands to demons and ravens and wind. They are the commands to his own love and blessing and covenant. "By day the LORD commands his steadfast love, and at night his song is with me" (Psalm 42:8). "For there the LORD has commanded the blessing, life forevermore" (Psalm 133:3). "He sent redemption to his people; he has commanded his covenant forever. Holy and awesome is his name!" (Psalm 111:9). The sweetest commands God gives to his own love: Love, go out to my people with omnipotent power!

Awesome indeed!

81

CHRIST SUFFERED AND DIED TO DELIVER US FROM THE PRESENT EVIL AGE

Meditation on Galatians 1:4

> *[He] gave himself for our sins to deliver us from the present evil age, according to the will of our God and Father.*

Until we die, or until Christ returns to establish his kingdom, we live in "the present evil age." Therefore, when the Bible says that Christ gave himself "to deliver us from the present evil age," it does not mean that he will take us out of the world but that he will deliver us from the power of the evil in it. Jesus prayed for us like this: "I do not ask that you take them out of the world, but that you keep them from the evil one" (John 17:15).

The reason Jesus prays for deliverance from "the evil one" is that "this present evil age" is the age when Satan is given freedom to deceive and destroy. The Bible says, "The whole world lies in the power of the evil one" (1 John 5:19). This "evil one" is called "the god of this world," and his main tactic is blinding people to truth. "The god of this world has blinded the minds of the unbelievers, to keep them from seeing the light of the gospel of the glory of Christ" (2 Corinthians 4:4).

Until we waken to our darkened spiritual condition, we live in sync with "the present evil age" and the ruler of it. "You once walked, following the course of this world, following the prince of the power of the air, the spirit that is now at work in the sons of disobedience" (Ephesians 2:2). Without knowing it, we were lackeys of the devil. What felt like freedom was bondage. The Bible speaks straight to twenty-first-century fads, fun, and addictions when it says, "They promise them freedom, but they themselves are slaves of corruption. For whatever overcomes a person, to that he is enslaved" (2 Peter 2:19).

The resounding cry of freedom in the Bible is: "Do not be conformed to this world, but be transformed by the renewal of your mind" (Romans 12:2). In other words, be free! Don't be duped by the gurus of the age. They are here today and gone tomorrow. One enslaving fad follows another. Thirty years from now today's tattoos will not be marks of freedom, but indelible reminders of conformity.

The wisdom of this age is folly in view of eternity. "Let no one deceive himself. If anyone among you thinks that he is wise in this age, let him become a fool that he may become wise. For the wisdom of this world is folly with God.... The word of the cross is folly to those who are perishing" (1 Corinthians 3:18–19; 1:18). What then is the wisdom of God in this age? It is the great liberating death of Jesus Christ. The early followers of Jesus said, "We preach Christ crucified...the power of God and the *wisdom of God*" (1 Corinthians 1:23–24).

When Christ went to the cross, he set millions of captives free. He unmasked the devil's fraud and broke his power. That's what he meant on the eve of his crucifixion when he said, "Now will the ruler of this world be cast out" (John 12:31). Don't follow a defeated foe. Follow Christ. It is costly. You will be an exile in this age. But you will be free.

And it will all be very soon. "With the Lord one day is as a thousand years, and a thousand years as one day" (2 Peter 3:8). Life is a vapor. Even two thousand years of lives are a vapor with God. "As for man, his days are like grass; he flourishes like a flower of the field; for the wind passes over it, and it is gone, and its place knows it no more" (Psalm 103:15–16). "Only one life, 'twill soon be past; only what's done for

Christ will last," wrote missionary C. T. Studd. What a tragedy when we fail to see that Christ, by his death and resurrection, has freed us from this evil age—from everything that we would look back on and say: wasted.

Therefore, attach yourself to the gospel of Christ. This alone will turn your earthly vapor into everlasting life. "For 'all flesh is like grass and all its glory like the flower of grass. The grass withers, and the flower falls, but the word of the Lord remains forever.' And this word is the good news that was preached to you" (1 Peter 1:24–25).

82

GOD'S WORK IN OUR WEAKNESSES

Paul's Humility and Christ's Power

I want to encourage you to identify and exploit your weaknesses for the glory of Christ. I would like to give you an illustration from my own life, but first let me clarify what I mean.

These days, millions of people read books and take inventories designed to find their *strengths*. These are useful for positioning people in places of maximum effectiveness. But I am calling you to give attention and effort in finding your weaknesses and maximizing their God-given purpose. The Bible tells us what that purpose is in 2 Corinthians 12:7–10. Paul had been given a thorn in the flesh, which was one instance of a weakness. Why?

A thorn was given me in the flesh, a messenger of Satan to harass me, *to keep me from becoming conceited*. Three times I pleaded with the Lord about this, that it should leave me. But he said to me, "My grace is sufficient for you, for *my power is made perfect in weakness*." Therefore I will boast all the more gladly of my weaknesses, so that the power of Christ may rest upon me. For the sake of Christ, then, I am content with weaknesses, insults, hardships, persecutions, and calamities. For *when I am weak, then I am strong*.

Paul mentions four purposes for his weaknesses.

1. "To keep me from becoming conceited" (v. 7).
2. "[Christ's] power is made perfect in weakness" (v. 9).
3. "So that the power of Christ may rest upon me" (v. 9).
4. "When I am weak, then I am strong" (v. 10).

Even though this weakness of the thorn is called "a messenger of Satan," the purposes are clearly not Satan's. Satan does not want Christ's power to be made perfect! God does. So God is overruling Satan's design with his own. In other words, wherever the Christian's weaknesses come from, they have a *God-given* purpose. They are not fortuitous.

We can sum up the purpose of Paul's weakness like this: securing *Paul's humility* and showing *Christ's power*. That's why God made sure Paul had weaknesses, to keep him "from becoming conceited" and to give him a more obvious experience of the power of Christ resting on him.

What is your goal for the next year? I hope it is to be humble and to magnify the power of Christ. If it is, then one key strategy is to identify and exploit your weaknesses.

What does this mean? Negatively, it means that we stop complaining (to God and to people) about the things we are constitutionally not good at. And, positively, it means that we look for ways to turn our weaknesses into Christ-exalting experiences.

When I say "constitutionally not good at," I mean that we have done our best to overcome the weakness, but we can't. God has ordained that, through genetics or life-experience, we are limited, broken, weak. Paul asked that God would take his weakness away (v. 8), but God said no. Which means that sooner or later, we should stop praying against the weakness and accept it as God's design for our humility and the glory of Christ.

I'll use myself as a simple example. I read slowly—about as fast as I speak. Many people read five or ten times faster than I do. I tried for years to overcome this weakness, with special classes and books and techniques. After about two decades of bemoaning this weakness (from age seventeen to thirty-seven or so), I saw there would be no change. This is one reason I left college teaching and the academic life. I knew I could never be what scholars ought to be: widely read.

What did it mean for me to identify and exploit this weakness? It meant first that I accept this as God's design for my life. I will never read fast. It meant I stop complaining about it. It meant that I take my love for reading and do with it what I can for the glory of Christ. If I can only read slowly, I will do all I can to read deeply. I will exploit slowness. I will ask Jesus to show me more in reading little than many see in reading much. I will ask Jesus to magnify his power in making my slowness more fruitful than speed.

In realizing I cannot read many books, I will pour my limited scope into reading one book better than any other: the Bible. If I must read fewer of many books, then I will read more carefully the greatest book.

Now after all these years, I say with Paul, "I will boast all the more gladly of my weaknesses, so that the power of Christ may rest upon me" (v. 9). Christ has been faithful to fulfill his purpose. He has magnified himself in this weakness.

If I had angrily resented God all these years that he did not let me be a comprehensively well-read scholar, I would not have exploited this weakness. I would have wasted it.

So this year, don't focus too much on finding your strengths. Give attention to identifying and exploiting your weaknesses. God has not given them to you in vain. Identify them. Accept them. Exploit them. Magnify the power of Christ with them. Don't waste your weaknesses.

83

GOD IS THE GOSPEL

Why Do We Want Eternal Life?

Have you ever asked why God's forgiveness is of any value? Or what about eternal life? Have you ever asked why a person would want to have eternal life? Why should we want to live forever? These questions matter because it is possible to want forgiveness and eternal life for reasons that prove you don't have them.

Take forgiveness, for example. You might want God's forgiveness because you are so miserable with guilt feelings. You just want relief. If you can believe that he forgives you, then you will have some relief, but not necessarily salvation. If you only want forgiveness because of emotional relief, you won't have *God's* forgiveness. He does not give it to those who use it only to get his gifts and not himself.

Or you might want to be healed from a disease or get a good job or find a spouse. Then you hear that God can help you get these things but that first your sins would have to be forgiven. Someone tells you to believe that Christ died for your sins and that if you believe this, your sins will be forgiven. So you believe it in order to remove the obstacle to health and job and spouse. Is that gospel salvation? I don't think so.

In other words, it matters what you are hoping for through forgiveness. It matters why you want it. If you want forgiveness only for the sake of savoring the creation, then the Creator is not honored and you are not saved. Forgiveness is precious for one final reason: It enables you to enjoy fellowship with God. If you don't want forgiveness for that reason, you won't have it at all. God will not be used as currency for the purchase of idols.

Similarly, we ask: Why do we want eternal life? One might say: Because hell is the alternative and that's painful. Another might say: Because there will be no sadness there. Another might say: My loved ones have gone there, and I want to be with them. Others might dream of endless sex or food. Or more noble fortunes. In all these aims one thing is missing: God.

The saving motive for wanting eternal life is given in John 17:3: "This is eternal life, that they know you the only true God, and Jesus Christ whom you have sent." If we do not want eternal life because it means joy in God, then we won't have eternal life. We simply kid ourselves that we are Christians if we use the glorious gospel of Christ to get what we love more than Christ. The "good news" will not prove good to any for whom God is not the chief good.

Here is the way Jonathan Edwards put it in a sermon to his people in 1731. Read this slowly and let it waken you to the true goodness of forgiveness and life.

> The redeemed have all their objective good in God. God Himself
> is the great good which they are brought to the possession and
> enjoyment of by redemption. He is the highest good, and the
> sum of all that good which Christ purchased. God is the inheri-
> tance of the saints; he is the portion of their souls. God is their
> wealth and treasure, their food, their life, their dwelling place,
> their ornament and diadem, and their everlasting honor and
> glory. They have none in heaven but God; he is the great good
> which the redeemed are received to at death, and which they are
> to rise to at the end of the world. The Lord God, he is the light
> of the heavenly Jerusalem; and is the "river of the water of life"
> that runs, and the tree of life that grows, "in the midst of the par-
> adise of God." The glorious excellencies and beauty of God will

be what will forever entertain the minds of the saints, and the love of God will be their everlasting feast. The redeemed will indeed enjoy other things; they will enjoy the angels, and will enjoy one another: but that which they shall enjoy in the angels, or each other, or in anything else whatsoever, that will yield them delight and happiness, will be what will be seen of God in them.*

* Wilson H. Kimnach, Kenneth P. Minkema, and Douglas A. Sweeney, eds., *The Sermons of Jonathan Edwards: A Reader* (New Haven, CT: Yale University Press, 1999), 74–75.

84

PIERCED BY THE WORD OF GOD

A Meditation on Hebrews 4:12

> *For the word of God is living and active and sharper than*
> *any two-edged sword, and piercing as far as the division of*
> *soul and spirit, of both joints and marrow, and able to*
> *judge the thoughts and intentions of the heart.*

Oh, how we need to know ourselves. Are we saved? Are we alive in Christ? There is only one instrument that creates, detects, and confirms eternal life in the soul of man; namely, the Word of God. What Hebrews 4:12 says about this Word is, therefore, all important. Consider it with me phrase by phrase.

"The word of God"
The term "word of God" may mean a word spoken by God without a human mouthpiece. But in the New Testament it regularly means a word or a message that a human speaks on God's behalf. So, for example, Hebrews 13:7 says, "Remember your leaders, those who spoke to you the word of God. Consider the outcome of their way of life, and imitate their faith." So the "word of God" in Hebrews 4:12 probably refers to the truth of God revealed in Scripture that humans speak to each other with reliance on God's help to understand it and apply it.

"Living and active"

The Word of God is not a dead word or an ineffective word. It has life in it. And because it has life in it, it produces effects. There is something about the Truth, as God has revealed it, that connects it to God as a source of all life and power. God loves his Word. He is partial to his Word. He honors his Word with his presence and power. If we want our teaching or witness to have power and produce effects, let us stay close to the revealed Word of God.

"Sharper than any two-edged sword, and piercing as far as the division of soul and spirit, of both joints and marrow"

What does this living and effective Word do? It pierces. For what purpose? To divide. To divide what? Soul and spirit. What does that mean?

The writer gives an analogy: It's like dividing joints and marrow. Joints are the thick, hard outer part of the bone. Marrow is the soft, tender, living inner part of the bone. That is an analogy of "soul and spirit." The Word of God is like a sword that is sharp enough to cut right through the outer, hard, tough part of a bone to the inner, soft living part of the bone. Some swords, less sharp, may strike a bone and glance off and not penetrate. Some swords may penetrate partway through the tough, thick joint of a bone. But a very sharp, powerful double-edged sword (sharp on each side of the point) will penetrate the joint all the way to the marrow. "Soul and spirit" are like "bone joint and bone marrow." "Soul" is that invisible dimension of our life that we are by nature. "Spirit" is what we are by supernatural rebirth. Jesus said, "That which is born of the flesh is flesh, and that which is born of the Spirit is spirit" (John 3:6). Without the awakening, creative, regenerating work of the Spirit of God in us we are merely "natural" rather than "spiritual" (1 Corinthians 2:14–15). So the "spirit" is that invisible dimension of our life that we are by the regenerating work of the Spirit.

What then is the point in saying that the "word of God" pierces to the "division of soul and spirit"? The point is that it's the Word of God that reveals to us our true selves. Are we spiritual or are we natural? Are we born of God and spiritually alive, or are we deceiving ourselves and spiritually dead? Are the "thoughts and intentions of our hearts" spiritual thoughts and intentions or only natural thoughts and intentions? Only the "word of God" can "judge the thoughts and intentions of the heart" as Hebrews 4:12 says (NASB).

Practically speaking, when we read or hear "the word of God" we sense ourselves pierced. The effect of this piercing is to reveal whether there is spirit or not. Is there marrow and life in our bones? Or are we only a "skeleton" with no living marrow? Is there "spirit," or only "soul"? The Word of God pierces deep enough to show us the truth of our thoughts and our motives and our selves.

Give yourselves to this Word of God, the Bible. Use it to know yourself and confirm your own spiritual life. If there is life, there will be love and joy and a heart to obey the Word. Give yourself to this Word so that your words become the Word of God for others and reveal to them their own spiritual condition. Then in the wound of the Word, pour the balm of the Word.

85

BE NOT MERE SHADOWS AND ECHOES

Break Free from the Spirit of the Age

We are not God. So by comparison to ultimate, absolute Reality, we are not much. Our existence is secondary and dependent on the absolute reality of God. He is the only given in the universe. We are derivative. He always was and had no beginning. So he was not given form by another. We were. He simply is. But we become. "I AM WHO I AM" is his name (Exodus 3:14).

Nevertheless, because he made us with the highest creaturely purpose in mind—to enjoy and display the Creator's glory—we may have a very substantial life that lasts forever. This is why we were made ("All things were created through him and *for him*," Colossians 1:16). This is why our sexuality was redeemed ("Flee from sexual immorality.... You are not your own, for you were bought with a price. So *glorify God in your body*," [1 Corinthians 6:18, 20]). This is why we eat and drink ("So, whether you eat or drink, or whatever you do, *do all to the glory of God*," [1 Corinthians 10:31]). This is why we pray ("Whatever you ask the Father in my name, this I will do, *that the Father may be glorified in the Son*," [John 14:13]). This is why we do all good deeds ("Let your light shine before others, so that they may see your good works and *give glory to your Father* who is in heaven," [Matthew 5:16]).

That is why we exist—to display the glory of God. Human life is all

290

about God. That is the meaning of being human. It is our created nature to make much of God. It is our glory to worship the glory of God. When we fulfill this reason for being, we have substance. There is weight and significance in our existence. Knowing, enjoying, and thus displaying the glory of God is a sharing in the glory of God. Not that we become God. But something of his greatness and beauty is on us as we realize this purpose for our being—to image-forth his excellence. This is our substance.

Not to fulfill this purpose for human existence is to be a mere *shadow* of the substance we were created to have. Not to display God's worth by enjoying him above all things is to be a mere *echo* of the music we were created to make.

This is a great tragedy. Humans are not made to be mere shadows and echoes. We were made to have Godlike substance and make Godlike music and have Godlike impact. That is what it means to be created in the image of God (Genesis 1:27). But when humans forsake their Maker and love other things more, they become like the things they love—small, insignificant, weightless, inconsequential, and God-diminishing.

Listen to the way the psalmist puts it: "The idols of the nations are silver and gold, the work of human hands. They have mouths, but they do not speak; they have eyes, but they do not see; they have ears, but they do not hear, nor is there any breath in their mouths. *Those who make them become like them, so do all who trust in them*" (Psalm 135:15–18; see also 115:4–8).

Think and tremble. You become like the man-made things that you trust: mute, blind, deaf. This is a shadow existence. It is an echo of what you were meant to be. It is an empty mime on the stage of history, with much movement and no meaning.

Dear reader, be not shadows and echoes. Break free from the epidemic of the manward spirit of our age. Set your face like flint to see and know and enjoy and live in the light of the Lord. "O house of Jacob, come, let us walk in the light of the LORD" (Isaiah 2:5). In his light you will see *him* and all things as they truly are. You will wake up from the slumbers of shadowland existence. You will crave and find substance. You will make Godlike music with your life. Death will but dispatch you to paradise. And what you leave behind will not be a mere shadow or echo but a tribute on earth, written in heaven, to the triumphant grace of God.

86

How To Drink Orange Juice to the Glory of God

Apart from Grace We Are Morally Ruined

W hen I am asked, "Is the doctrine of Total Depravity biblical?" my answer is, "Yes." One thing I mean by this is that all of our actions (apart from saving grace) are morally ruined. In other words, everything an unbeliever does is sinful and thus unacceptable to God.

One of my reasons for believing this comes from 1 Corinthians 10:31. "So, whether you eat or drink, or whatever you do, do all to the glory of God." Is it sin to disobey this biblical commandment? Yes.

So I draw this somber conclusion: It is sin to eat or drink or do anything *not* for the glory of God. In other words, sin is not just a list of harmful things (killing, stealing, etc.). Sin is leaving God out of account in the ordinary affairs of your life. Sin is anything you do that you don't do for the glory of God.

But what do unbelievers do for the glory of God? Nothing. Therefore everything they do is sinful. That is what I mean by saying that, apart from saving grace, all we do is morally ruined.

This, of course, raises the practical question: Well, how *do* you "eat and drink" to the glory of God? Say, orange juice for breakfast?

One answer is found in 1 Timothy 4:3–5:

[Some] forbid marriage and require abstinence from foods that God created to be received with thanks-giving by those who believe and know the truth. For everything created by God is good, and nothing is to be rejected if it is received with thanks-giving, for it is made holy by the word of God and prayer.

Orange juice was "created to be received with *thanksgiving* by those who *believe*...the truth." Therefore, *un*believers cannot use orange juice for the purpose God intended—namely, as an occasion for heartfelt *thanksgiving* to God from a true heart of *faith*.

But believers can, and this is how they glorify God. Their drinking orange juice is "made holy by the word of God and prayer" (1 Timothy 4:5). The *Word of God* teaches us that juice, and even our strength to drink it, is a free gift of God (1 Corinthians 4:7; 1 Peter 4:11). The *prayer* is our humble response of thanks from the heart. *Believing* this truth in the Word and offering *thanks* in prayer is one way we drink orange juice to the glory of God.

The other way is to drink lovingly. For example, don't insist on the biggest helping. This is taught in the context of 1 Corinthians 10:33, "I try to please everyone in everything I do, *not seeking my own advantage, but that of many, that they may be saved.*" "Be imitators of me, as I am of Christ" (1 Corinthians 11:1). Everything we do—even drinking orange juice—can be done with the intention and hope that it will be to the advantage of many that they may be saved.

Let us praise God that we have escaped by his grace from the total ruin of all our deeds. And let us do everything, whether we eat or drink, to the glory of our great God!

87

BIG, SWEEPING—BUT NOT INSIPID—PRAYERS

What Should We Really Want from God?

One of the amazing things about the prayers of the Bible is how big and sweeping they often are. Yet they don't have the vague ring of "God bless the missionaries" that sounds so weak. We sometimes try to remedy this by saying, "We should pray specific prayers for specific people and specific needs and not vague general prayers." There is truth to that. We should pray that way.

But there is another reason why our big general prayers seem insipid, while the big Bible prayers don't. Ours often don't have much of God in them and don't articulate what the great spiritual things are that we want God to do for "the missionaries" or "the nations" or "the world" or "the lost." The words "God bless" would not sound so weak and vague if we said what the blessing would look like. There is a world of difference between "Lord, help our missionaries" and "Lord, help our missionaries to drink deep at the river of Your delights." Or, "Lord, help our missionaries rejoice in tribulations and remember that tribulation works endurance and endurance hope."

Big general prayers become powerful when they are filled up with concrete, radical biblical goals for the people we are praying for. "Hallowed be thy name...thy will be done on earth as in heaven," is a huge, sweeping prayer. But it asks for two concrete things: that in all the world

God's name would be regarded as precious, and that hearts would be changed to do God's will with the same zeal and purity that the angels have in heaven.

It is mentioning these spiritual goals with passion that turns insipid generalizations into dynamite generalizations. So don't shrink back from praying huge, sweeping prayers. For example, in Ephesians 6:18 Paul says that we should be "praying at all times in the Spirit, with all prayer and supplication...for all the saints." Think of it! What an incredible breadth and generality. ALL the saints! Do you do that? Pray for *all* the saints? I admit I do not do it often enough. My heart is too small. But I am trying to get my heart around it. The Bible commands it.

This will not sound silly, like "God bless all the saints." It will sound robust and cataclysmic, like, "God, look upon your entire church everywhere and have mercy to waken her and give her new life and hope and doctrinal purity and holiness so that all the saints stand strong for your glory in the day of temptation and distress."

Let's pray some huge prayers for billions of lost people and thousands of peoples in the "10/40 Window." Paul said, "Finally, brothers, pray for us, that the word of the Lord may speed ahead and be honored, as happened among you" (2 Thessalonians 3:1). Oh, that God would do that speeding work in our day! I encourage all of my readers to go out and buy Patrick Johnstone's *Operation World*—a truth-laden prayer guide for all the countries of the world. Then pray some huge, sweeping prayers for the peoples and the missionaries of this vast region called the 10/40 Window.

The 10/40 Window extends from West Africa to East Asia, and from ten degrees north to forty degrees south of the equator. This specific region contains three of the world's dominant religious blocs. The majority of those darkened in unbelief by Islam, Hinduism, and Buddhism live within the 10/40 Window. It is home to the majority of the world's unevangelized people.

While it constitutes only one-third of earth's total land area, the

10/40 Window is home to nearly two-thirds of the world's people, with a total population nearing four billion. Of the world's 50 least evangelized countries, 37 are within the 10/40 Window. Yet those 37 countries comprise 95 percent of the total population of the 50 least evangelized countries!

Of the poorest of the poor, more than eight out of ten live in the 10/40 Window. On average, they exist on less than $500 per person per year. Although 2.4 billion of these people live within the 10/40 Window, only 8 percent of all missionaries work among them. Surely this is worth some big, sweeping, biblical prayers!

88

WHAT IS HUMILITY?

How God Defines It

In 1908 the British writer G. K. Chesterton described the embryo of today's full-grown, adolescent culture called postmodernism. It's already a worn-out phrase. Someday readers will have to look it up in a history book. One mark of its "vulgar relativism" (as Michael Novak calls it)* is the hijacking of the word *arrogance* to refer to conviction and *humility* to refer to doubt. Chesterton saw it coming:

> What we suffer from today is humility in the wrong place. Modesty has moved from the organ of ambition. Modesty has settled upon the organ of conviction; where it was never meant to be. A man was meant to be doubtful about himself, but undoubting about the truth; this has been exactly reversed. Nowadays the part of a man that a man does assert is exactly the part he ought not to assert—himself. The part he doubts is exactly the part he ought not to doubt—the Divine Reason.... The new skeptic is so humble that he doubts if he can even learn.... There is a real humility typical of our time; but it so happens that it's practically a more poisonous humility than the wildest prostrations of the ascetic.... The old humility made a man doubtful about his

---

* Michael Novak, "Awakening from Nihilism," *First Things*, no. 45 (August/September, 1994), 20–21 (available atwww.firstthings.com/ftissues/ft9408/articles/novak.html).

efforts, which might make him work harder. But the new humility makes a man doubtful about his aims, which make him stop working altogether.... We are on the road to producing a race of man too mentally modest to believe in the multiplication table.*

We have seen it, for example, in the resentment over Christians expressing the conviction that Jewish people (like everyone else) need to believe on Jesus to be saved. The most common response to this conviction is that Christians are arrogant. Modern-day humility is firmly rooted in the relativism that recoils from knowing truth and naming error. But that is not what humility used to mean.

Well, if humility is not compliance with the popular demands of relativism, what is it? This is important, since the Bible says, "God opposes the proud but gives grace to the humble" (1 Peter 5:5), and "Everyone who exalts himself will be humbled, and he who humbles himself will be exalted" (Luke 14:11). So humility is tremendously important. God has told us at least five things about humility.

1. Humility begins with a sense of subordination to God in Christ. "A disciple is not above his teacher, nor a servant above his master" (Matthew 10:24). "Humble yourselves, therefore, under the mighty hand of God" (1 Peter 5:6).

2. Humility does not feel it has a right to better treatment than Jesus got. "If they have called the master of the house Beelzebul, how much more will they malign those of his household" (Matthew 10:25). Therefore humility does not return evil for evil. It is not a life based on its perceived rights. "Christ also suffered for you, leaving you an example, so that you might follow in his steps.... When he suffered, he did not threaten, but continued entrusting to him who judges justly" (1 Peter 2:21–23).

---

* G. K. Chesteron, *Orthodoxy* (Garden City, NY: Doubleday, 1957), 31–32.

3. Humility asserts truth not to bolster the ego with control or with triumphs in debate, but as service to Christ and love to the adversary. Love "rejoices with the truth" (1 Corinthians 13:6). "What I [Jesus] tell you in the dark, say in the light.... Do not fear" (Matthew 10:27–28). "What we proclaim is not ourselves, but Jesus Christ as Lord, with ourselves as your servants for Jesus' sake" (2 Corinthians 4:5).

4. Humility knows it is dependent on grace for all knowing and believing. "What do you have that you did not receive? If then you received it, why do you boast as if you did not receive it?" (1 Corinthians 4:7). "In humility receive the word implanted, which is able to save your souls" (James 1:21, NASB).

5. Humility knows it is fallible and so considers criticism and learns from it, but also knows that God has made provision for human conviction and that he calls us to persuade others.

"Now we see in a mirror dimly, but then face to face. Now I know in part; then I shall know fully, even as I have been fully known" (1 Corinthians 13:12). "A wise man listens to advice" (Proverbs 12:15). "Therefore, knowing the fear of the Lord, we persuade others" (2 Corinthians 5:11).

89

WILDERNESS, WORSHIP, TREASON, AND GOD

A Meditation on Psalm 63

A Psalm of David, when he was in the wilderness of Judah.

O God, you are my God; earnestly I seek you; my soul thirsts for you; my flesh faints for you, as in a dry and weary land where there is no water. So I have looked upon you in the sanctuary, beholding your power and glory. Because your steadfast love is better than life, my lips will praise you. So I will bless you as long as I live; in your name I will lift up my hands. My soul will be satisfied as with fat and rich food, and my mouth will praise you with joyful lips, when I remember you upon my bed, and meditate on you in the watches of the night; for you have been my help, and in the shadow of your wings I will sing for joy. My soul clings to you; your right hand upholds me. But those who seek to destroy my life shall go down into the depths of the earth; they shall be given over to the power of the sword; they shall be a portion for jackals. But the king shall rejoice in God; all who swear by him shall exult, for the mouths of liars will be stopped.

The writer is David when he was king (vv. 1, 11). The situation is that someone was seeking to destroy his life (v. 9). This corresponds to the time when Absalom, his own son, drove him out of Jerusalem (2 Samuel 15:23). Put yourself in David's place. His son is not just alienated, but hostile enough to want to see his father killed. Here is mortal danger mixed with heartbreaking estrangement from his son.

Learn from David what to do in this brokenhearted, terrifying moment. He prays. The whole psalm is addressed to God. He asks for one thing—not protection, not victory, but God himself, satisfying his soul, like water satisfies thirst in a dry and weary land. "O God, you are my God; earnestly I seek you; my flesh faints for you, as in a dry and weary land where there is no water" (v.1). There are seasons of pain and loss and grief and darkness when nothing is worth asking for but God. Everything else seems trivial, even life.

That's why David said in verse 3, "Because your steadfast love is better than life, my lips will praise you." David may well be killed during the night by some plotting traitor sold out to Absalom. How do you sleep? You remind yourself that the love of God in the presence of God is better than not being stabbed to death in the night. But this rest in God's steadfast love is not easily felt. We say the words. But do we feel the reality? David did not feel it as he wanted to feel it. That is why he cried out, "Earnestly I seek you; my soul thirsts for you." David desperately needed God to answer his cry to come and help him taste—not just know, but feel—that God's steadfast love is better than life.

Oh, to know God like this! Would this not be everything to us? Would this not be more than all riches and fame and success and health, indeed, all the world can offer? God himself coming near and making our souls drink from his love until all else fades from view, and fear is swallowed up in the unshakable security of everlasting enjoyment at the right hand of God. Oh, that we would come to this place in our walk with God! When the saving of David's own life and the rescue of his own son cease to be his gods, and God alone engulfs him in the solid joy of unshakable love, then he will sing for joy in the sorrows of this night, and even perhaps, if God wills, win back his son.

The Satisfied Soul

How did God come to David and awaken his spiritual taste, so that he could see God and "be satisfied as with fat and rich food" (v. 5)? The answer is that David remembered the days of worship in the house of God: "So I have looked upon you in the sanctuary, beholding your power and glory" (v. 2). David had been driven from Jerusalem, the place of corporate worship with God's people. And in his distress, he remembers what it was like and what he saw of God in worship.

Here is a great longing I have for the corporate worship in our churches—that when we meet and sing and pray and hear the Word of God, God himself will be so manifestly present in "power and glory" that in the years to come, when any of you is cut off from this immeasurable privilege, the very memory of seeing God in worship will bring him home to you again.

Would you pray with me that God will meet us like that? Would you pray for your pastors and other worship leaders that God would give them songs and prayers and silence and Scriptures and sermons that are so full of the truth of God and the Spirit of God that we will all taste and see that the steadfast love of God is better than life—and all that life can give?

And would you pray for yourselves and for all the people that Saturday nights and Sunday mornings would become seasons of preparation for meeting God—vestibules of the holy place of worship? Pray with David, "O God, you are my God; earnestly I seek you; my soul thirsts for you, my flesh faints for you, as in a dry and weary land where there is no water." If this were on our lips Saturday night and Sunday morning, would not God open the springs of heaven and show us mightily that his "steadfast love is better than life"?

90

How to Be a Refuge for Your Children

A Meditation on Proverbs 14:26

> *In the fear of the LORD one has strong confidence,*
> *and his children will have a refuge.*

If Daddy is afraid, where can a little child turn? Daddies are supposed to be safe. They are supposed to know what to do and how to solve problems and fix things and, most of all, how to protect the children from harm. But what happens if a child sees fear in Daddy's face? What if Daddy is as scared as the child and doesn't know what to do? Then the child is utterly distraught and feels panic. He feels that the one strong and good and reliable place of safety is no longer safe.

But if Daddy is confident, then the children have a refuge. If Daddy is not panicking, but calm and steady, all the walls can come tumbling down, and all the waves can break, and all the snakes hiss and the lions roar and the winds blow, and there will still be a safe place in Daddy's arms. Daddy is a refuge, as long as Daddy is confident. That's why Proverbs 14:26 says that "his children will have a refuge," if Daddy has a "strong confidence." Daddy's confidence is the refuge of his children.

Dads, the battle to be confident is not just about us; it is about the security of our children. It is about their sense of security and happiness. It's about whether they grow up fretful or firm in faith. Until children can know God in a deep, personal way, we are the image and the embodiment of God in their lives. If we are confident and reliable and safe for them, they will much more likely cleave to God as their refuge when the storms break over them later.

So how shall we have "strong confidence"? After all, we, too, are little children; clay pots, weak and broken and battling anxieties and doubts. Is the solution to put on the best show we can and hide our true selves? That will lead to ulcers at best and God-dishonoring, teenager-repelling duplicity at worst. That is not the answer.

Proverbs 14:26 gives another answer: "In the fear of the LORD one has strong confidence." This is very strange. It says that the solution to fear is fear. The solution to timidity is fear. The solution to uncertainty is fear. The solution to doubt is fear.

How can this be?

Part of the answer is that the "fear of the LORD" means fearing to dishonor the Lord. Which means fearing to distrust the Lord. Which means fearing to fear anything that the Lord has promised to help you overcome. In other words, the fear of the Lord is the great fear destroyer.

If the Lord says, "Fear not, for I am with you; be not dismayed, for I am your God; I will strengthen you, I will help you" (Isaiah 41:10), then it is a fearful thing to worry about the problem he says he will help you with. Fearing that problem when he says, "Fear not...I will help you," is a vote of no confidence against God's Word, and that is a great dishonor to God. And the fear of the Lord trembles to dishonor God like that.

The Lord says, "I will never leave you nor forsake you.' So we can confidently say, 'The Lord is my helper; I will not fear; what can man do to me?'" (Hebrews 13:5–6). If the Lord says that to you, then not to be confident in the Lord's promised presence and help is a kind of pride. It puts our reckoning of the trouble above God's. That is why we read the amazing words of the Lord in Isaiah 51:12, "I, I am he who comforts you; who are you that you are afraid of man who dies, of the son of man who is made like grass?" Who are you to fear man, when God has promised to help you? So it is pride to fear man. And pride is the exact opposite of the fear of God.

So, yes, the proverb is true and a great help to us. Fear God, dads. Fear God. Fear dishonoring him. Fear distrusting him. Fear putting your assessment of the problem above his. He says he can help. He is smarter. He is stronger. He is more generous. Trust him. Fear not to trust him.

Why? He works for those who wait for him (Isaiah 64:4). He will solve the problem. He will rescue the family. He will take care of the little ones. He will meet your needs. Fear distrusting that promise. Then your children will have a refuge. They will have a daddy who "has strong confidence"—not in himself, but in the promises of God, which he trembles not to trust.

91

GOING DEEP WITH GOD BY HAVING HIM CARRY OUR LOADS

No Challenge too Great, No Burden too Heavy

One of the reasons we don't know God deeply is that we don't venture much on his pledge to carry things for us. Knowing God with a sense of authentic personal reality is not merely a matter of study. It is a matter of walking with him through fire and not being burned. It is a matter of not being crushed under a load because he carries it for you at your side. What, then, does he carry?

1. God Has Carried Our Sins

Isaiah 53:11, "By his knowledge shall the righteous one, my servant, make many to be accounted righteous, and *he shall bear their iniquities.*" Hebrews 9:28, "Christ, having been offered once *to bear the sins of many.*" 1 Peter 2:24, "*He himself bore our sins* in his body on the tree."

Believing this and experiencing its liberating effect is crucial *for life now.* Guilt feelings do not have the last word! It is also crucial *for the hour of our dying.* The sting of death is sin, but thanks be to God, it was removed. It is crucial, too, *for everlasting joy.* Christ's sin-bearing work secures for us never-ending compensation for every so-called "loss" in this life of sacrificial love. This confidence is the foundation of knowing God.

2. God Pledges to Carry Our Anxieties

1 Peter 5:7, "[*Cast*] *all your anxiety on him*, because he cares for you." The only other place this word for "cast" occurs is in Luke 19:35, where the disciples threw their coats on the colt for Jesus to ride.

What worries does God aim to take from our backs and carry for us? Every kind. For example, anxieties about lacking necessities (Philippians 4:4–7), uselessness (Isaiah 55:11), weakness (2 Corinthians 12:9), decisions (Psalm 32:8), opponents (Romans 8:31), affliction (Psalm 34:19; Romans 5:3–5), aging (Isaiah 46:4), dying (Romans 14:7–9), and not persevering (Philippians 1:6; Hebrews 7:25).

When George Müller was asked how he could be so calm in the middle of a hectic day with so many uncertainties in the orphanage, he answered something like, "I rolled sixty things onto the Lord this morning." When Hudson Taylor was told about missionaries in his charge being in trouble, he was heard soon after whistling his favorite hymn, "Jesus, I Am Resting, Resting in the Joy of What Thou Art."

3. God Pledges to Carry Our Burdens

Psalm 55:22, "*Cast your burden on the LORD,* and he will sustain you; he will never permit the righteous to be moved." The word for "burden" here is *lot*. What is your lot in life today? What has providence brought you? In the end, this is of the Lord. And he will carry it for you. It is not meant to carry you away, but to test your trust in God to carry it for you.

For Amy Carmichael the "lot" was singleness. There were several chances to leave it and take "the other life." But she heard the inner voice, *No, no, no.* She handed this over to the Lord, and he carried it for her and made her fruitful and full of joy.

4. God Pledges to Carry the Cause of Justice for Us

1 Peter 2:23, "When he was reviled, [Jesus] did not revile in return; when he suffered, he did not threaten, but continued *handing over to him who*

judges justly" (author's translation).

In almost every relationship of life, you will be treated unjustly. "Jesus never called us to a fair fight" (George Otis, Jr.). How will you not be embittered? By letting God carry your cause and settle accounts either on the cross or in hell. Peter said that Jesus handled the wrongs done to him by "handing over" to God who would judge all things justly. God will manage our cause. "'Vengeance is mine, I will repay' says the Lord" (Romans 12:19). Leave it to him. Prepare to be treated unjustly, whether it is someone breaking in front of you in line or bearing false witness at the final trial of your life.

5. God Pledges to Carry You—All Your Life

Isaiah 46:3–4, "Hearken to me, O house of Jacob, all the remnant of the house of Israel, who have been borne by me from your birth, carried from the womb; even to your old age I am He, and to gray hairs I will carry you. I have made, and I will bear; I will carry and will save" (RSV). (See also Exodus 19:4; Psalm 18:35; 94:18.)

The Christian life is a life of being carried from beginning to end. We work. Yet it is not we, but God who works within us (1 Corinthians 15:10).

Conclusion

So come to him, all you who labor and are heavy laden, and find rest for your soul. Go deep with God and know him better by venturing more on his pledge to carry you and all your concerns.

92

PERSEVERE IN PRAYER!

A Meditation on Colossians 4

> *Continue steadfastly in prayer,*
> *being watchful in it with thanksgiving.*
> *At the same time, pray also for us,*
> *that God may open to us a door for the word,*
> *to declare the mystery of Christ...*
> *that I may make it clear, which is how I ought to speak.*
>
> —COLOSSIANS 4:2–4

This text gives five guidelines for prayer that we need to hear.

First, "Continue steadfastly in prayer." There is so much power to be had in persevering prayer. Don't forget the "importunate friend" of Luke 11:8 ("Because of his persistence he will get up and give him as much as he needs" NASB), and don't forget the parable Jesus told to the effect that we "ought always to pray and not lose heart" (Luke 18:1–8). Perseverance is the great test of genuineness in the Christian life. I praise God for Christians who have persevered in prayer sixty, seventy, or eighty years! Oh, let us be a praying people, and let this year—and all our years—be saturated with prayers to the Lord of all power and all good. It will be good to say in the end, "I have finished the race, I have kept the faith"—through prayer.

Second, be watchful in your prayers. This means, Be alert! Be mentally awake! Paul probably learned this from the story of what happened in Gethsemane. Jesus asked the disciples to pray, but found them sleeping. So he said to Peter, "Could you not watch one hour? Watch and pray that you may not enter into temptation" (Mark 14:37–38). We must be on the watch as we pray—on the watch against wandering minds, against vain repetitions, against trite and meaningless expressions, against limited, selfish desires. And we should also watch for what is good. We should especially be alert to God's guidance of our prayers in Scripture. It is God who works in us the will to pray, but we always experience this divine enabling as our own resolve and decision.

Third, be thankful in all your prayers. The stories of what God has done in so many lives through renewed prayer are amazing. They have often stirred me up to press on in prayer with thanksgiving. Keep sharing with others these good things.

Fourth, pray that a door would be opened for the Word in your life. In two senses: (1) that there be open, receptive hearts in your church from week to week, and (2) that your neighbors will be open to the gospel as you share it. "The Lord opened [Lydia's] heart to give heed to what was said by Paul" (Acts 16:14). That is what we should want to happen on Sundays and during the week.

Fifth, pray for the preachers of our land, that they may make the mystery of Christ clear. "Great…is the mystery of godliness" (1 Timothy 3:16). And oh, what a calling to proclaim it! I love the preaching office! But it is above me. I, and every preaching pastor, need prayer—that we understand the mystery of Christ, that we choose needed texts, that we preach in the power of the Holy Spirit, that we speak the truth in love. Without Christ we can do nothing.

93

WHY HELL IS A NONNEGOTIABLE

Dorothy Sayers on Loving the
Eternal Truths of God

Today belongs to the sound bite; tomorrow belongs to marketing; eternity belongs to the Truth. If you live only for this world, you will care little for truth. "Let us eat and drink, for tomorrow we die." And if that's all there is, we may as well call the ideas that protect our appetites "truths." But if you live for eternity, you will forego a few fads in order to be everlastingly relevant.

We need to prize truth above temporary successes. Where truth is minimized and people are not rooted and grounded in it, successes are superficial and the growing tree is hollow even while it blooms in the sunshine of prosperity. May God give us a humble, submissive love for the truth of God's Word in the depth and fullness of it.

Listen to Paul's warning about our day: "The time is coming when people will not endure sound teaching; but having itching ears they will accumulate for themselves teachers to suit their own passions (2 Timothy 4:3). "[They] are perishing, because *they refused to love the truth* and so be saved" (2 Thessalonians 2:10).

Take one truth that is not popular and is being abandoned by many who fly the banner of "evangelical" over their tent—the truth of hell. Oh, what a difference it makes when one believes in hell—with trembling and with tears. There is a seriousness over all of life, and an urgency in all our endeavors, and a flavor of blood-earnestness that seasons every-thing and makes sin feel more sinful, and righteousness feel more right-eous, and life feel more precious, and relationships feel more profound, and God appear more weighty.

Nevertheless, as in every generation, there are fresh abandonments of the truth. Clark Pinnock, a Canadian theologian who still calls him-self an evangelical, wrote:

> I was led to question the traditional belief in everlasting con-scious torment because of moral revulsion and broader theologi-cal considerations, not first of all on scriptural grounds. It just does not make any sense to say that a God of love will torture people forever for sins done in the context of a finite life…. It's time for evangelicals to come out and say that the biblical and morally appropriate doctrine of hell is annihilation, not everlast-ing torment."*

Dorothy Sayers, who died in 1957, speaks a necessary antidote to this kind of abandonment of truth.

> There seems to be a kind of conspiracy, especially among middle-aged writers of vaguely liberal tendency, to forget, or to conceal, where the doctrine of Hell comes from. One finds frequent refer-ences to the "cruel and abominable mediaeval doctrine of hell," or "the childish and grotesque mediaeval imagery of physical fire and worms."…
>
> But the case is quite otherwise; let us face the facts. The doc-trine of hell is not "mediaeval": it is Christ's. It is not a device of "mediaeval priestcraft" for frightening people into giving money

---

* Clark Pinnock and Delwin Brown, *Theological Crossfire: An Evangelical/Liberal Dialogue* (Grand Rapids, MI: Zondervan, 1990), 226–27.

to the church: it is Christ's deliberate judgment on sin. The imagery of the undying worm and the unquenchable fire derives, not from "mediaeval superstition," but originally from the Prophet Isaiah, and it was Christ who emphatically used it.... It confronts us in the oldest and least "edited" of the gospels: it is explicit in many of the most familiar parables and implicit in many more: it bulks far larger in the teaching than one realizes, until one reads the Evangelists through instead of picking out the most comfortable texts: one cannot get rid of it without tearing the New Testament to tatters. We cannot repudiate Hell without altogether repudiating Christ.*

I would only add: There are many other things which, if abandoned, will also mean the eventual repudiation of Christ. It is not out of antiquarian allegiance that we love the truths of Scripture—even the hard ones. It is out of love to Christ—and love to the people that only the Christ of truth can save.

---

* Dorothy Sayers, *A Matter of Eternity*, ed. Rosamond Kent Sprague (Grand Rapids, MI: Eerdmans, 1973), 86.

The Satisfied Soul

94

TO YOU WHO BELIEVE, HE IS PRECIOUS

A Meditation on 1 Peter 2:7

To you...who believe, [Christ] is precious" (1 Peter 2:7, RSV). The mark of a child of God is not perfection, but hunger for Christ. If we have tasted the kindness of the Lord, we will desire him (1 Peter 2:2–3). The reason for this is that a child has the nature of its father. We are partakers of the divine nature (2 Peter 1:4) if we are born of God and have his seed abiding in us (1 John 3:9). We are, as it were, chips off the Old Block. For 1 Peter 2:4 says Christ is precious to God, and 1 Peter 2:7 says therefore he is precious to believers. Therefore, belief which saves is not just agreeing that the Bible is true. Belief which saves signifies a new nature that cherishes what God cherishes.

In light of this, consider John 17:26. What a promise this is! Here Jesus is praying for his disciples and all who would believe on him through their word (John 17:20). He concludes his prayer with the highest petition of all: "I made known to them your name, and I will make it known, that the love with which you have loved me may be in them, and I in them."

Look carefully. Jesus' request to God is that God's love for the Son be in us. Have you ever thought that Jesus wants you to love him not merely with your love but with the love which God the Father has for him? How is this possible? It is possible because of the new birth.

Becoming a Christian means getting a new nature, which is given by God. Practically speaking this means that God comes into our lives by the Holy Spirit and begins to give us new affections, new emotions, namely, the emotions of God. It is the presence of God the Spirit in our lives that causes us to love Jesus with the love of God the Father. Indeed, the Holy Spirit may be viewed as the love of God in a Person. To be ruled by the Spirit is to be ruled by a divine love for Jesus. Jesus is simply praying that we may be filled with the Spirit, who is the divine Person who expresses the love that the Father has for the Son. Thus we will be filled with the very love with which the Father loves the Son.

And what a love that is! There is no greater love in all the universe than the love flowing between the Father and the Son in the holy Trinity. No love is more powerful, more intense, more continuous, more pure, more full of delight in the beloved than the love God the Father has for the Son. It is an energy of joy that makes atom bombs look like firecrackers. Oh, how the Father delights in the Son! Oh, how precious the Son is to the Father! "This is my beloved Son, with whom I am well pleased," God said at Jesus' baptism (Matthew 3:17). "This is my beloved Son, with whom I am well pleased; listen to him," God said at the transfiguration (Matthew 17:5).

In all the universe, none is more precious to God the Father than his Son, Jesus Christ. That is how precious he should be to us. And with what infinite energy does the Father love the Son! That is the greatness to which we are moving in our delight in the Son. Oh, Christian, join the Father in this greatest of all loves! If you are born of God, see Jesus with the eyes of God. "To you...who believe, he is precious."

95

WHAT DOES JESUS WANT?

A Meditation on Seeing and Savoring Christ's Glory

What does Jesus want? We can see the answer in his prayers. What does he ask God for? His longest prayer is John 17. Here is the climax of his desire:

> Father, I desire that they also, whom you have given me, may be with me where I am. (v. 24)

Among all the undeserving sinners in the world, there are those whom God has "given to Jesus." These are those whom God has drawn to the Son (John 6:44, 65). These are *Christians*—people who have "received" Jesus as the crucified and risen Savior, Lord, and Treasure of their lives (John 1:12; 3:17; 6:35; 10:11, 17–18; 20:28). Jesus says he wants them to be with him.

Sometimes we hear people say that God created man because he was lonely. So they say, "God created us so that we would be *with Him*." Does Jesus agree with this? Well, he *does* say that he really wants us to be with him! Yes, but why? Consider the rest of the verse. Why does Jesus want us to be with him?

> [Father, I desire that they may be with me] *to see my glory* that you have given me because you loved me before the foundation of the world.

That would be a strange way of expressing his loneliness. "I want them with me so they can see my glory." In fact, it doesn't express his loneliness. It expresses his concern for the satisfaction of *our* longing, not his loneliness. Jesus is not lonely. He and the Father and the Spirit are profoundly satisfied in the fellowship of the Trinity. We, not he, are starving for something. And what Jesus wants is for us to experience what we were really made for—seeing and savoring his glory.

Oh, that God would make this sink into our souls! Jesus made us (John 1:3) to see his glory. Just before he goes to the cross he pleads his deepest desires with the Father: "Father, I *desire*—I desire!—that they…may be with me where I am, *to see my glory*."

But that is only half of what Jesus wants in these final, climactic verses of his prayer. I just said we were really made for seeing *and savoring* his glory. Is that what he wants—that we not only see his glory but savor it, relish it, delight in it, treasure it, love it? Consider verse 26, the very last verse:

I made known to them your name, and I will continue to make it known, *that the love with which you have loved me may be in them*, and I in them.

That is the end of the prayer. What is Jesus' *final* goal for us? Not that we simply see his glory, but that we love him with the same love that the Father has for him: "that the love with which you [Father] have loved me may be in them." Jesus' longing and goal is that we see his glory and then that we be able to love what we see with the same love that the Father has for the Son. And he doesn't mean that we merely *imitate* the love of the Father for the Son. He means the Father's very love becomes our love for the Son—that we love the Son with the love of the Father for the Son. This is what the Spirit becomes and bestows in our lives: Love for the Son by the Father through the Spirit.

What Jesus wants most is that his elect be gathered in (John 10:16;

11:52) and then get what *they* want most—to *see* his glory and then *savor* it with the very savoring of the Father for the Son.

What I want most is to join you (and many others) in seeing Christ in all his fullness and that we together be able to love what we see with a love far beyond our own half-hearted human capacities.

This is what Jesus prays for us: "Father, show them my glory and give them the very delight in me that you have in me." Oh, may we *see* Christ with the eyes of God and *savor* Christ with the heart of God. That is the essence of heaven. That is the gift Christ came to purchase for sinners at the cost of his death in our place.

96

HOW DOES THE LAW HELP
ME KNOW MY SIN?

A Meditation on Romans 7 : 7 – 8

What then shall we say? That the law is sin? By no means!
Yet if it had not been for the law, I would not have known sin.
I would not have known what it is to covet if the law had not said,
"You shall not covet." But sin, seizing an opportunity through the
commandment, produced in me all kinds of covetousness.
Apart from the law, sin lies dead.

Let's begin by looking at the context of Romans 7:7–8.

1. Paul is defending the law after saying some pretty negative things
   about it (like: You need to die to the law, 7:4; sinful passions are
   aroused by the law, 7:6; the law came in so that transgressions
   would increase, 5:20).
2. His defense is that the law is not sin but exposes sin as sin and, in
   doing so, often makes sin flare up and then gets blamed for it.
3. There is a sinful condition beneath our sins that we need to know
   about. Paul says in verse 8, "Sin...produced in me all kinds of covetousness." In other words, the sin of coveting is produced by a condition called "sin." This is our "depravity," or "fallenness," or (for
   Christians) our "remaining corruption."

4. Paul uses the commandment against covetousness to illustrate how the law shows us our sinful condition.

5. "Covetousness" simply means desires that you shouldn't have. At root, what makes bad desires bad is that they come as a loss of satisfaction in all that God is for us in Jesus. Desires are bad that come from a loss of contentment in God.

6. Until God's law comes in and prohibits some of our desires ("You shall not covet"), our desires are not experienced as sin but as imperial demands that seem to have their own lawful standing. Until God's law confronts this mutinous "law" we don't experience our desires as sin ("apart from the law sin lies dead," 7:8). "I want it, so I should have it." This is inborn. "Desire equals deserve," until God's law says no. You see this clearly in little children for whom it is very painful to learn that their desires are not law.

7. This points to the root sinful condition: independence from God, rebellion against God. At root our sinful condition is the commitment to be our own god. I will be the final authority in my life. I will decide what is right and wrong for me, and what is good and bad for me, and what is true and false for me. My desires express my sovereignty, my autonomy, and—though we don't usually say it—my presumed deity.

This independence from God—this rebellion and presumed sovereignty and autonomy and deity—produces *all kinds* of covetousness. This word *all* (kinds) sets us to thinking about how deviously covetousness can express itself. We need to know this or we won't know our sin or ourselves.

In general, there are two kinds of bad desire (covetousness) that the law stirs up, and both are expressions of our love affair with independence and self-exaltation.

1. One is more obvious, namely, desires for the very things that are forbidden. Proverbs 9:17 says, "Stolen water is sweet, and bread eaten in secret is pleasant." St. Augustine confessed that as a youth,

"I was willing to steal, and steal I did, although I was not compelled by any lack, unless it were the lack of a sense of justice or a distaste for what was right and a greedy love of doing wrong.... *I had no wish to enjoy the things I coveted by stealing, but only to enjoy the theft itself and the sin.*"* So one form of desire that the commandment stirs up is the desire to do the very thing forbidden. This is owing to our ingrained love of being our own god and our distaste for submission.

2. The other kind of bad desire that the law stirs up is the desire to keep the law by our own strength with a view to exalting our own moral prowess. This looks very *different*. No stealing, no murder, no adultery, no lying. Instead, just self-righteousness. Not that keeping the law is evil or covetous. No, the problem is the desire to keep it by *my* power, not in childlike reliance on *God's* power. The problem is desiring the glory of my achievement, not God's. That is a subtle form of covetousness.

So know yourself! Know your sins. Know your sinful condition of rebellion and insubordination. If this leads you (again and again) to the cross and the gospel of justification by grace alone through faith alone, it will exalt Christ, be healing to your soul, and sweetening to all your relationships.

---

* Augustine, *Confessions,* II, 4, emphasis added.

97

A Passion for Purity Versus Passive Prayer

The Necessity of Vicious Mental Warfare

> *I say to you that everyone who looks at a woman with lustful*
> *intent has already committed adultery with her in his heart.*
> *If your right eye causes you to sin, tear it out and throw it*
> *away. For it is better that you lose one of your members than*
> *that your whole body be thrown into hell.*
>
> —MATTHEW 5:28–29

When you are enticed sexually, do you fight with your mind to say no to the image and then mightily labor to fill your mind with counter-images that kill off the seductive image? "If by the Spirit you put to death the deeds of the body, you will live" (Romans 8:13).

Too many people think they have struggled with temptation when they have prayed for deliverance and hoped the desire would go away. That is too passive. Yes, God works in us to will and to do his good pleasure! But the effect is that we "work out [our] own salvation with fear and trembling" (Philippians 2:12–13). Gouging out your eye may be a metaphor, but it means something very violent. The brain is a "muscle" to be flexed for purity, and in the Christian it is supercharged with the Spirit of Christ.

What this means is that we must not give a sexual image or impulse more than five seconds before we mount a violent counterattack with the mind. I mean that! Five seconds. In the first two seconds we shout, "NO! Get out of my head!" In the next two seconds we cry out: "O God, in the name of Jesus, help me. Save me now. I am yours."

Good beginning. But then the real battle begins. This is a mind war. The absolute necessity is to get the image and the impulse out of our mind. How? Get a Christ-exalting, soul-captivating counter-image into the mind. Fight. Push. Strike. Don't ease up. It must be an image that is so powerful that the other image cannot survive. There are lust-destroying images and thoughts.

For example, have you ever in the first five seconds of temptation demanded of your mind that it look steadfastly at the crucified form of Jesus Christ? Picture this. You have just seen a peek-a-boo blouse inviting further fantasy. You have five seconds. "No! Get out of my mind! God help me!" Now, immediately, demand of your mind—you can do this by the Spirit (Romans 8:13)—demand of your mind that it fix its gaze on Christ on the cross. Use all your fantasizing power to see his lacerated back. Thirty-nine lashes left little flesh intact. He heaves with his breath up and down against the rough vertical beam of the cross. Each breath puts splinters into the lacerations. The Lord gasps. From time to time he screams out with intolerable pain. He tries to pull away from the wood, and the massive spokes through his wrists rip into the nerve endings, and he screams again with agony and pushes up with his feet to give some relief to his wrists. But the bones and nerves in his pierced feet crush against each other with anguish, and he screams again. There is no relief. His throat is raw from screaming and thirst. He loses his breath and thinks he is suffocating, and suddenly his body involuntarily gasps for air, and all the injuries unite in pain. In torment, he forgets about the crown of two-inch thorns and throws his head back in desperation, only to hit one of the thorns perpendicular against the cross beam and drive it half an inch into his skull. His voice reaches a soprano pitch of pain and sobs break over his pain-wracked body as every cry brings more and more pain.

Now, I am not thinking about the blouse anymore. I am at Calvary. These two images are not compatible. If you will use the muscle of your brain to pursue—violently pursue with the muscle of your mind—images of Christ crucified with the same creative energy that you use to pursue sexual fantasies, you will kill them. But it must start in the first five seconds—and not give up.

So my question is: Do you fight, rather than only praying and waiting and trying to avoid? It is image against image. It is ruthless, vicious mental warfare, not just prayer and waiting. Join me in this bloody warfare to keep my mind and body pure for my Lord and my wife and my church. Jesus suffered beyond imagination to "purify for himself a people for his own possession" (Titus 2:14). Every scream and spasm was to kill my lust—"He himself bore our sins in his body on the tree, that we might die to sin and live to righteousness" (1 Peter 2:24).

98

THE BATTLE FOR BREAKFAST BLESSING

A Meditation on Ephesians 4:29–5:2

This is for families. The rest of you will, I hope, be helped also. I am assuming that Christian families try to eat breakfast together—or have some kind of family moment in the Word and prayer before going their different ways. Even if there are seasons in life when this is hard or impossible, not to work toward it seems contrary to Deuteronomy 6:7, "You shall teach [God's Word] diligently to your sons and shall talk of them...when you rise up" (NASB).

This takes effort. Everybody likes to get up at different times. So you have to decide how important you think these family moments in the Word are. It is possible—for little ones and teenagers and parents. You may have to work at it. But it can be done.

But once you are there, then what? For many of us, morning is our moodiest, least cheerful time of day. Teenagers, some say, are not fully human till midmorning. Dad may feel tremendous pressure looming ahead. Mom may be exhausted from a hundred pressures. Little ones may be cranky.

What then is the point of this family event? Dad, the point is for you to dispense grace to your family. If there's no dad, then, mom, it's your job. How do you dispense grace?

Here's a key part of the answer from Ephesians 4:29:

Let no unwholesome word proceed from *your mouth*, but only such a word as is good for edification according to the need of the moment, *so that it will give grace to those who hear.* (NASB)

The key dispenser of grace is the dad's mouth. Oh, Fathers! What a treasure is the grace that comes from your mouth at the breakfast table!

1. Speak no unwholesome word.

No spoiled word. No unhelpful word. What does this mean? Well, perhaps the best interpretation is simply the next phrase where it is put positively:

2. Speak only words that are good for edification.

Aim always to build the faith of your family by what you say. Don't confuse this with building their egos. We are not talking here about self-esteem. We are talking about building faith and hope in Jesus Christ. "Edification" means growing confidence in the promises of God purchased by the blood of Christ. Dads, come to breakfast with some word of hope for your family. Tell them something about God and Christ that will help them be strong that day.

3. Speak words that fit the need of the moment.

Some promises are more fitting than others. If they are old enough, ask your children what their needs and challenges will be for that day. Or ask them the night before. Give them something from God that will help them be strong in the strength in the Lord that day.

4. This is the way you dispense grace to your family.

But it assumes something. Namely, that anger is not the dominant feeling in your heart. Some anger is godly. Most is not. So Paul continues, "Let all bitterness and wrath and anger and clamor and slander be put away from you, along with all malice" (Ephesians 4:31, NASB). Malicious anger is deadly. One of its most deadly effects is to ruin a dad's ability to bless his family with his mouth. His heart is so angry that his mouth is continually sour. Oh, for sweetness in the mouth of a dad! Oh, for deeply delighting dads! "I will bless the LORD at all times; his praise shall continually be in my mouth" (Psalm 34:1). That is what blessing the family assumes.

How can you get there, dads? Answer:

> [Forgive, just] as God in Christ forgave you. Therefore be imitators of God, as beloved children. And walk in love, as Christ loved us and gave himself up for us. (Ephesians 4:32–5:2)

Dads, do you know the sweetness of being forgiven a million-dollar debt? Have you seen Jesus suffering horrifically to purchase your forgiveness? Do you know the wonder of hearing God call to you, "Beloved child"? Not just child. But *loved* child. So, dads, get up early enough to soak in these things for your own soul. Then you will bring the aroma of Christ to the table. In the long run, no matter how grumpy the family may seem, this blessing will come back on your head a thousandfold.

99

You Have One Precious Life

Is TV Too Big a Part of It?

If all other variables are equal, your capacity to know God deeply will probably diminish in direct proportion to how much television you watch. There are several reasons for this. One is that television reflects American culture at its most trivial. And a steady diet of triviality shrinks the soul. You get used to it. It starts to seem normal. Silly becomes funny. And funny becomes pleasing. And pleasing becomes soul-satisfaction. And in the end, the soul that is made for God has shrunk to fit snugly around triteness.

This may be unnoticed, because if all you've known is American culture, you can't tell there is anything wrong. If you have only read comic books, it won't be strange that there are no novels in your house. If you live where there are no seasons, you won't miss the colors of fall. If you watch fifty TV ads each night, you may forget there is such a thing as wisdom. TV is mostly trivial. It seldom inspires great thoughts or great feelings with glimpses of great Truth. God is the great, absolute, all-shaping Reality. If he gets any air time, he is treated as an opinion. There is no reverence. No trembling. God and all that he thinks about the world is missing. Cut loose from God, everything goes down.

Just think how new TV is. In the 2000 years since Christ, TV has shaped only the last 2.5 percent of that history. For 97.5 percent of the time since Jesus, there was no TV. And for 95 percent of this time there was no radio. It arrived on the scene in the early 1900s. So for 1900 years of Christian history, people spent their leisure time doing other things. We wonder, what could they possibly have done? They may have read more. Or discussed things more. For certain they were not bombarded with soul-shrinking, round-the-clock trivialities.

Do you ever ask, "What could I accomplish that is truly worthwhile if I did not watch TV?" You see, it isn't just what TV does to us with its rivers of emptiness; it is also what TV keeps us from doing. Why not try something? Make a list of what you might accomplish if you took the time you spend watching TV and devoted it to something else. For example:

- You might be inspired to some great venture by learning about the life of a noble saint like Amy Carmichael and how she found courage to go alone to serve the children of India. Where do such radical dreams come from? Not from watching TV. Open your soul to be blown away by some unspeakable life of dedication to a great cause.

- You might be inspired by a biography of a businessman or doctor or nurse to work hard for the skills to bless others with the excellence of your profession devoted to a higher end than anything you will see commended on TV, which never includes Jesus Christ.

- You might memorize the eighth chapter of Paul's letter to the Romans, and penetrate to the depths of his vision of God, and discover the precious power of memorized Scripture in your life and ministry to others. No one could estimate the power that would come to a church if we all turned the TV off for one month and devoted that same amount of time to memorizing Scripture.

- You might write a simple poem or a letter to a parent or a child or a friend or a colleague expressing deep gratitude for their life or a longing for their soul.

- You might make a cake or a casserole for new neighbors and take it to them with a smile and an invitation to visit some time and get to know each other.

So there are good reasons to try a TV fast. Or to simply wean yourself off of it entirely. We have not owned a TV for thirty-four years of marriage except for three years in Germany when we used it for language learning. There is no inherent virtue in this. I only mention it to prove that you can raise five culturally sensitive and biblically informed children without it. They never complained about it. In fact, they often wondered out loud how people found the time to watch as much as they did.

100

TERRORISM, JUSTICE, AND LOVING OUR ENEMIES

Thoughts on September 11, 2001

S omeone asked me after our Tuesday prayer service in response to the terrorist attacks on September 11, 2001, "Can we pray for justice and yet love our enemy at the same time?" The answer is yes.

But let's start with our own guilt. Christians know that if God dealt with us only according to justice, we would perish under his condemnation. We are guilty of treason against God in our sinful pride and rebellion. We deserve only judgment. Justice alone would condemn us to everlasting torment.

But God does not deal with us only in terms of justice. Without compromising his justice he "justifies the ungodly" (Romans 4:5). That sounds unjust. And it *would* be if it were not for what God did in the life and death of Jesus Christ. The mercy of God moved him to send the Son of God to bear the wrath of God so as to vindicate the justice of God when he justifies sinners who have faith in Jesus. So we have our very life because of mercy *and* justice (Romans 3:25–26). They met in the cross.

So we are not quick to demand justice unmingled with mercy. Jesus demands, "Love your enemies and pray for those who persecute you, so that you may be sons of your Father who is in heaven. For he makes his sun rise on the evil and on the good, and sends rain on the just and the unjust" (Matthew 5:44–45). And, of course Jesus modeled this for us as a perfect man. "*While we were enemies* we were reconciled to God by the death of his Son" (Romans 5:10). And even as he died for his enemies he prayed, "*Father, forgive them,* for they know not what they do" (Luke 23:34).

So the resounding command of the apostles is, "Bless those who persecute you; bless and do not curse.... Repay no one evil for evil.... Never avenge yourselves, but leave it to the wrath of God, for it is written, 'Vengeance is mine, I will repay, says the Lord.' To the contrary, 'if your enemy is hungry, feed him; if he is thirsty, give him something to drink'" (Romans 12:14–20). When we live this way, we magnify the glory of God's mercy and the all-satisfying Treasure that he is to our souls. We show that because of his supreme value to us, we do not need the feeling of personal vengeance in order to be content.

But it does not compromise this truth to say that God should also be glorified as the one who governs the world and delegates some of his authority to civil states. Therefore, some of God's divine rights as God are given to governments for the purposes of restraining evil and maintaining social order under just laws. This is what Paul means when he writes, "There is no authority except from God, and those that exist have been instituted by God.... [This authority is] God's servant for your good...he does not bear the sword in vain. For he is the servant of God, an avenger who carries out God's wrath on the wrongdoer" (Romans 13:1–4).

God wills that human justice hold sway among governments and between citizens and civil authority. He does not prescribe that governments always turn the other cheek. The government "does not bear the sword in vain." Police have the God-given right to use force to restrain evil and bring lawbreakers to justice. And legitimate states have the God-given right to restrain life-threatening aggression and bring criminals to justice. If these truths are known, this God-ordained exercise of divine prerogative would glorify the justice of God who mercifully ordains that the flood of sin and misery be restrained in the earth.

Therefore, we will magnify the *mercy* of God by praying for our enemies to be saved and reconciled to God. At the personal level we will be willing to suffer for their everlasting good and we will give them food and drink. We will put away malicious hatred and private vengeance. But at the public level we will also magnify the *justice* of God by praying and working for justice to be done on the earth, if necessary through wise and measured force from God-ordained authority.

101

How Is God's Love Experienced in the Heart?

Look, Pray, Renounce, Enjoy

Experiencing the love of God, not just thinking about it, is something we should desire with all our hearts. This is an experience of great joy because in it we taste the very reality of God and his love. It is the ground of deep and wonderful assurance—the assurance that our hope "does not disappoint" (Romans 5:5, NASB). This assurance helps us "rejoice in hope of the glory of God" (Romans 5:2). It carries us through terrible trials of faith.

Is this experience of the love of God the same for all believers? No, not in degree. If all believers had the same experience of the love of God, Paul would not pray for the Ephesians that they "have strength to comprehend with all the saints what is the breadth and length and height and depth, and to know the love of Christ that surpasses knowledge" (Ephesians 3:18–19). He prayed this, because some (or all!) were deficient in their experience of this love of God in Christ. And, presumably, we are not all deficient in exactly the same way.

How then do we pursue the fullness of the experience of the love of God poured out in our hearts by the Holy Spirit? One key is to realize that the experience is not like a hypnosis or electric shock or drug-induced hallucinations or shivers at a good tune. Rather it is mediated through knowledge. It is not the same as knowledge. But it comes through knowledge. Or to say it another way, this experience of the love of God is the work of the Spirit giving unspeakable joy in response to the mind's perception of the demonstration of that love in Jesus Christ. In this way, Christ gets the glory for the joy that we have. It is a joy in what we see in him.

Where can you see this in the Scriptures? Consider 1 Peter 1, "Though you have not seen him, you love him. Though you do not now see him, you believe in him and rejoice with joy that is inexpressible and filled with glory" (v. 8). Here is an experience of great and inexpressible joy. Joy beyond words. It is not based on a physical seeing of Christ. But it is based on believing in Christ. Christ is the focus and content of the mind in this inexpressible joy.

In fact, 1 Peter 1:6 says that the joy itself is "in" the truth that Peter is telling us about the work of Christ. It says, "In *this* you rejoice." And what is "this"? It is the truth that (1) in "his great mercy, [God] has caused us to be born again to a living hope through the resurrection of Jesus Christ from the dead" (v. 3); and (2) we will obtain "an inheritance that is imperishable, undefiled, and unfading" (v. 4); and (3) we "are being guarded through faith for a salvation ready to be revealed in the last time" (v. 5). In *this* we greatly "rejoice with joy that is inexpressible and filled with glory" (v. 8). We know something. In *this* we rejoice! The experience of unspeakable joy is a mediated experience. It comes through knowledge of Christ and his work. It has content.

Consider also Galatians 3:5, "Does he who supplies the Spirit to you and works miracles among you do so by the works of the law, or by hearing with faith?" We know from Romans 5:5 that the experience of the love of God is "through the Holy Spirit who has been given to us." But now Galatians 3:5 tells us that this supply of the Spirit is not without content. It is "by *hearing* with *faith*." Two things: hearing and faith. There is the hearing of the truth about Christ, and there is the faith in that truth. This is how the Spirit is supplied. He comes *through knowing*

The Satisfied Soul

and believing. His work is a mediated work. It has mental content. Beware of seeking the Spirit by emptying your head.

Similarly Romans 15:13 says that the God of hope fills us with joy and peace "*in believing*." And believing has content. The love of God is experienced in knowing and believing Christ because, as Romans 8:39 says, the love of God is "in Christ Jesus our Lord." Nothing will be able to separate us from the love of God, which *is in Christ Jesus* our Lord.

So do four things: look, pray, renounce, enjoy.

1. Look to Jesus. Consider Christ. Meditate on his glory and his work, not just casually, but intentionally. Think about the promises he made and guaranteed by his death and resurrection.

2. Pray that God would open your eyes to the wonder of his love in these things.

3. Renounce all known attitudes and behaviors that contradict this demonstration of love to you.

4. Then enjoy the experience of the love of God poured out in your heart by the Holy Spirit.

102

REASONS BELIEVERS IN CHRIST NEED NOT BE AFRAID

God Will Take Care of You

Over a hundred times in the Bible we are told not to be afraid. "Fear not, for I am with you; be not dismayed, for I am your God" (Isaiah 41:10). When we are young we are easily made afraid, though our knowledge of what can harm us is small. As we get older, our knowledge of risk and peril increases. Must our fears increase? One might answer no, because we also become wiser and more able to avoid danger and avert peril and overcome assault.

But there are better reasons not to let our fears increase. It is not so much because we become smarter or more able to avoid danger but that we become more confident that, by faith in Jesus, God will take care of us in the way he sees best. It does not guarantee safety or comfort in this life. But it does guarantee everlasting joy, as we trust in him. Trusting God, through Jesus Christ, is the key to fearlessness. And promises from God are the key that leads from the dungeon of fear. So consider these and be courageous.

1. We will not die apart from God's gracious decree for his children.

If the Lord wills, we will live and do this or that. (James 4:15)

Are not two sparrows sold for a penny? And not one of them will fall to the ground apart from your Father. But even the hairs of your head are all numbered. Fear not, therefore; you are of more value than many sparrows. (Matthew 10:29–31)

See now that I, even I, am he, and there is no god beside me; I kill and I make alive; I wound and I heal; and there is none that can deliver out of my hand. (Deuteronomy 32:39) (See also Job 1:21; 1 Samuel 2:6; 2 Kings 5:7.)

2. Curses and divination do not hold sway against God's people.

For there is no enchantment against Jacob, no divination against Israel. (Numbers 23:23)

3. The plans of terrorists and hostile nations do not succeed apart from our gracious God.

The LORD brings the counsel of the nations to nothing; he frustrates the plans of the peoples. (Psalm 33:10)

Take counsel together [you peoples], but it will come to nothing; speak a word, but it will not stand, for God is with us. (Isaiah 8:10) (See also 2 Samuel 7:14; Nehemiah 4:15.)

4. Man cannot harm us beyond God's gracious will for us.

The LORD is on my side; I will not fear. What can man do to me? (Psalm 118:6)

In God I trust; I shall not be afraid. What can man do to me? (Psalm 56:11)

5. God promises to protect his own from all that is not finally good for them.

Because he holds fast to me in love, I will deliver him; I will protect him, because he knows my name. (Psalm 91:14)

6. God promises to give us all we need to obey, enjoy, and honor him forever.

Therefore do not be anxious, saying, "What shall we eat?" or "What shall we drink?" or "What shall we wear?"...Your heavenly Father knows that you need them all. But seek first the kingdom of God and his righteousness, and all these things will be added to you. (Matthew 6:31–33)

And my God will supply every need of yours according to his riches in glory in Christ Jesus. (Philippians 4:19)

7. God is never taken off guard.

Behold, he who keeps Israel will neither slumber nor sleep. (Psalm 121:4)

8. God will be with us, help us, and uphold us in trouble.

Fear not, for I am with you; be not dismayed, for I am your God; I will strengthen you, I will help you, I will uphold you with my righteous right hand. (Isaiah 41:10)

For I, the LORD your God, hold your right hand; it is I who say to you, "Fear not, I am the one who helps you." (Isaiah 41:13)

9. Terrors will come, some of us will die, but not a hair of our heads will perish.

> Then [Jesus] said to them, ". . . there will be terrors and great signs from heaven.... and some of you they will put to death.... But not a hair of your head will perish." (Luke 21:10–11, 18)

10. Nothing befalls God's own but in its appointed hour.

> So they were seeking to arrest him, but no one laid a hand on him, because his hour had not yet come. (John 7:30) (See also John 8:20; 10:18.)

11. When God Almighty is your helper, none can harm you beyond what He decrees.

> So we can confidently say, "The Lord is my helper; I will not fear; what can man do to me?" (Hebrews 13:6)

> If God is for us, who can be against us? (Romans 8:31)

12. God's faithfulness is based on the firm value of his name, not the fickle measure of their obedience.

> And Samuel said to the people, "Do not be afraid; you have done all this evil.... For the Lord will not forsake his people, for his great name's sake." (1 Samuel 12:20–22)

13. The Lord, our protector, is great and awesome.

> Do not be afraid of them. Remember the Lord, who is great and awesome. (Nehemiah 4:14)

103

EMBRACING THE PAIN OF SHAME

A Meditation on Acts 5:41

There is a kind of shame that you should not be ashamed of. You might say, "Well, then it is not really shame." But the Bible calls it shame, and it really feels like shame—until the miracle happens in our heart that turns our felt values upside down.

The reason this is important to me is that I am still learning—sometimes I think, just beginning to learn—how to embrace this shame. I mean really embrace, not just tolerate, the unpleasant feeling of being shamed. Until I learn this more fully, I will never be the kind of witness among unbelievers that God calls me to be.

Where do I get this strange notion of embracing shame? I get it from the story of Peter and the apostles in Acts 5. They were arrested and put in jail for healing and for preaching Christ (v. 18). That night the angel of the Lord released them and told them to go preach in the temple "all the words of this Life" (v. 20). But again the Council and the High Priest took them into custody and accused them of "filling Jerusalem with [their] teaching" (v. 28). "We strictly charged you not to teach in this name."

Peter spoke up with boldness and said, "We must obey God rather than men" (v. 29). The Council was ready to kill them when Gamaliel, a teacher of the law, stood up and said, "If this plan or this undertaking is of men, it will fail; but if it is of God, you will not be able to overthrow them. You might even be found opposing God" (vv. 38–39). At this they changed their plans and "beat them and charged them not to speak in the name of Jesus, and let them go" (v. 40).

Now comes one of the most stunning verses in the New Testament: "So they went on their way from the presence of the Council, rejoicing that they had been considered worthy to suffer shame for His name" (v. 41, NASB). Read that slowly and let it sink in. Notice two things.

First, they were shamed. They suffered shame. To be made a spectacle by the respected leaders of your people and to be treated like wicked criminals and to be stripped to the waist (at least) and to be hurt so badly that you probably scream out and cry with deep sobs of pain—that is a shame-filled moment. The Bible calls it shame. It feels like shame. And it is horrible.

Second, they rejoiced over this shame. Use your imagination. This is not light. It is not romantic. It is not a noble, heroic moment with soaring music and lots of admirers watching. This is terrifying. The pain is excruciating. Death may follow. There is no recourse. It is humiliating. But the apostles did not sue. They did not seethe at the loss of their rights. They did not swear at their enemies. Instead they sang. They rejoiced "that they had been considered worthy to suffer shame for His name" (NASB).

That is what I mean by "embracing the pain of shame." Are you there yet? If not, take heart. Not many of us are. Do you want to be? So do I. What shall we do? Three things:

1. Let's pray for each other. Be specific. Pray, *Father, work a deep transforming work in us so that we actually feel joy when we are shamed for the name of Christ.*
2. Meditate often on the infinite worth of Christ, the sweetness of his promises, and the great suffering that he endured for your salvation.
3. Take a step into uncharted territory to witness to Christ. If the painful feelings of shame come, transpose that dirge into a song of triumph.

Then the world will begin to see what is really most valuable in the universe, Jesus Christ. Until then, we look so much like them in what we enjoy, they see little reason to pay any attention.

104

How Jesus Helped His Disciples Increase Their Faith

A Meditation on Luke 17:5–10

The apostles said to the Lord, "Increase our faith!" And the Lord said, "If you had faith like a grain of mustard seed, you could say to this mulberry tree, 'Be uprooted and planted in the sea,' and it would obey you. Will any one of you who has a servant plowing or keeping sheep say to him when he has come in from the field, 'Come at once and sit down at table'? Will he not rather say to him, 'Prepare supper for me, and dress properly, and serve me while I eat and drink, and afterward you will eat and drink'? Does he thank the servant because he did what was commanded? So you also, when you have done all that you were commanded, say, 'We are unworthy servants; we have only done what was our duty.'"

In Luke 17:5 the apostles ask Jesus to increase their faith. How does Jesus help them? In two ways, both of which are by telling them truth. So even in the way he responds he shows us that faith comes by hearing. Knowing certain things should increase our faith.

First, he strengthens our faith by telling us in verse 6 that the crucial issue in accomplishing great things to advance the kingdom of God is not the *quantity* of our faith but the power of God. He says, "If you had faith like a grain of mustard seed, you could say to this mulberry tree, 'Be uprooted and be planted in the sea,' and it would obey you." By referring to the tiny mustard seed after being asked about increased faith, He deflects attention away from the quantity of faith to the object of faith. *God* moves mulberry trees. And it does not depend decisively on the quantity of our faith, but on His power and wisdom and love. In knowing this, we are helped not to worry about our faith and are inspired to trust God's free initiative and power.

Second, he helps our faith grow by telling us in verses 7–10 that when we have done all we are commanded to do, we are still radically dependent on grace. Jesus gives an illustration. You might want to read it again in verses 7–10. The gist of it is that the owner of a slave does not become a debtor to the slave no matter how much work the slave does. The meaning is that God is never our debtor. Verse 10 sums it up: "So you also, when you have done all that you were commanded, say, 'We are unworthy servants; we have only done what was our duty.'" We are always his debtor. And we will never be able to pay this debt, nor are we ever meant to. We will always be dependent on grace. We will never work our way up out of debt to a place where God is in *our* debt. "Who has given a gift to [God] that he might be repaid?" (Romans 11:35).

When it says in verse 9 that the owner does not "thank" the slave, the idiom for "thank" is provocative. I think the idea is that "thanks" is a response to grace. The reason the owner does not thank the slave is that the servant is not giving the owner more than what the owner deserves. He is not treating the owner with *grace*. Grace is being treated better than you deserve. That's how it is with us in relation to God. We can *never* treat God with grace. We can never give him more than he deserves. Which means that he never owes us thanks. God never says "Thank you" to us. Instead he is always giving us more than what we deserve, and *we* are always owing *him* thanks.

So the lesson for us is that when we have done all we should do— when we have solved all our church problems, and fixed the attitudes of all Christian people, and mobilized many missions, and loved the poor, and saved marriages, and reared godly children, and kept every promise we've made, and fulfilled all business responsibilities, and boldly proclaimed Christ—God owes us no thanks. Instead, we will at that moment relate to him as debtors to grace just as we do now.

This is a great encouragement to faith. Why? Because it means that God is just as free to bless us *before* we get our act together as he is *after*. Since we are "unworthy" slaves before we have done what we should, and "unworthy" slaves afterwards as well, it is only grace that would prompt God to help us. Therefore he is free to help us before and after. This is a great incentive to trust him for help when we feel like our act is not together. And this trust is exactly what obtains the power to get our act together.

So two things increase our faith.

1. God himself, and not the quantity of our faith, is the decisive factor in flinging mulberry trees out of the way.
2. Free grace is decisive in how God treats us before and after we have done all we ought to do.

We never move beyond the need for grace. Therefore, let us trust God for great things in our little faith, and let us not be paralyzed by what is left to be done in our personal lives, and in our church, and in our vocations, and in the global cause of missions.

105

THE STRANGE WAYS OF OUR WONDERFUL BUILDER

How Deep the Wisdom, Riches, and Knowledge of God

Was Christ building his church on September 11, 2001 when the World Trade Center towers came down? Or when your own world collapsed? The reason this question rises is the absolute, universal authority behind Jesus' promise in Matthew 16:18, "I will build my church." Who said this? The one who spoke and fevers departed (Luke 4:39), trees withered (Mark 11:21), demons obeyed (Mark 1:27), Satan was plundered (Mark 3:27), wind ceased (Mark 4:41), the dead were raised (Luke 7:14; John 11:43), thousands ate from five loaves and two fish (Matthew 14:19–21), and water became wine (John 4:46) or a walkway for his feet (Matthew 14:25).

This power over heaven and earth and hell is explicitly related to Christ's missionary commitment to build his church. "I will build my church, and the gates of hell shall not prevail against it" (Matthew 16:18). "All authority in heaven and on earth has been given to me. Go therefore and make disciples of all nations" (Matthew 28:18–19). In other words, Jesus is firmly committed to using his power over heaven and earth and hell to make disciples. No event in the universe which Christ produces or permits is outside his purpose to build his church.

But it doesn't look that way. His ways are not our ways. He seldom moves in a straight line from A to B. The way up is almost always down. The river turns back on itself flowing away from the sea even as it moves toward the sea. I tried to catch this once in a poem about Hosea's pain-filled life:

> Think not, my son, that God's great river
>   Of love flows simply to the sea,
> He aims not straight, but to deliver
>   The wayward soul like you and me.
> Follow the current where it goes,
>   With love and grace it ever flows.

The surprising, convoluted path of God in redemptive history brings Paul to these words, "Oh, the depth of the riches and wisdom and knowledge of God! How unsearchable are his judgments and how inscrutable his ways!" (Romans 11:33).

For example, was Christ triumphantly building his church when he was killed by his enemies and buried for three days? Jesus answers: "Destroy this temple, and in three days I will raise it up" (John 2:19). "I lay down my life for the sheep. And I have other sheep that are not of this fold.... No one takes it from me...I have authority to lay it down, and I have authority to take it up again" (John 10:15–16, 18). In other words, what looked like failure and tragedy was total authority—plus the purchase of "other sheep." By the worst sin that has ever been committed—the murder of the Son of God—Jesus was triumphantly building his church.

Was Christ building his church when the apostle Paul was imprisoned in Rome? Paul answers: "What has happened to me has really served to advance the gospel, so that it has become known throughout the whole imperial guard and to all the rest that my imprisonment is for Christ. And most of the brothers, having become confident in the Lord by my imprisonment, are much more bold to speak the word without fear" (Philippians 1:12–14). I am "bound with chains as a criminal. But the word of God is not bound!" (2 Timothy 2:9). In other words, what looked like defeat was Christ's strange design for victory.

Was Christ building his church in China when the Communists triumphed in 1949, ending 150 years of Protestant missionary presence?

> The growth of the Church in China since 1977 has no parallels in history.... Mao Zedong unwittingly became the greatest evangelist in history.... [He] sought to destroy all religious 'superstition' but in the process cleared spiritual roadblocks for the advancement of Christianity. Deng [Xiaoping] reversed the horrors inflicted by Mao and in freeing up the economy, gave more freedom to the Christians.... [Today] the Church of the Lord Jesus is larger than the Communist Party of China.*

So then, was this all-ruling Christ building his church on September 11? I answer with questions that are not merely hypothetical. What if Christ saw the planes heading for the destruction of thousands and the upheaval of nations? What if, at the same time, he saw 200 million Hindu untouchables in India, the Dalits? What if he saw that his centuries-long work of dislodging them from Hindu bondage was about to come to consummation in our day and they were contemplating embracing Islam or possibly Christianity or Buddhism? And what if he foresaw that this Islam-related terror against civilians in New York would have a mass effect of tilting millions of Dalits away from Islam toward Christ? What if he withheld his power from stopping the terrorists because (along with ten thousand other hope-filled effects) he had a view to the everlasting life of millions of untouchables in India? And if not this, perhaps my grandchildren will tell a better story of sovereign grace, which only time reveals.

---

* Patrick Johnstone and Jason Mandryk, *Operation World: When We Pray God Works*, 21st Century Edition (Waynesboro, GA: Paternoster, 2001), 161. The second sentence is from the 1993 edition of *Operation World*, 164.

106

A • N • T • H • E • M:
STRATEGIES FOR FIGHTING LUST
An Acronym for Purity

I have in mind men and women. For men it's obvious. The need for warfare against the bombardment of visual temptation to fixate on sexual images is urgent. For women it is less obvious, but just as great if we broaden the scope of temptation to food or figure or relational fantasies. When I say "lust" I mean mainly the realm of thought, imagination, and desire that envisions what God forbids and often leads to sexual misconduct.

I don't mean sex is bad. God created it. He blessed it. He made it pleasurable. And he defined the place for it, to protect the beauty and power of it, namely, marriage between a man and a woman. But it has become disordered with the fall of man into sin. Therefore, we must exercise restraint and make war on what would destroy us. Here is one set of strategies in the war against wrong desires. I put it in the form of an acronym,

A • N • T • H • E • M.

A—AVOID as much as is possible and reasonable the sights and situations that arouse unfitting desire. I say "possible and reasonable" because some exposure to temptation is inevitable. And I say "unfitting desire" because not all desires for sex, food, and family are bad. We know when they are unfitting and unhelpful and on their way to becoming enslaving. We know our weaknesses and what triggers them. "Avoiding" is a biblical strategy. "Flee youthful passions and pursue righteousness" (2 Timothy 2:22). "Make no provision for the flesh, to gratify its desires" (Romans 13:14).

N—Say NO to every lustful thought within five seconds.* And say it with the authority of Jesus Christ. "In the name of Jesus, NO!" You don't have much more than five seconds. Give it more unopposed time than that, and it will lodge itself with such force as to be almost immovable. Say it out loud if you dare. Be tough and warlike. As John Owen said, "Be killing sin or it will be killing you."† Strike fast and strike hard. "Resist the devil, and he will flee from you" (James 4:7).

T—TURN the mind forcefully toward Christ as a superior satisfaction. Saying no will not suffice. You must move from defense to offense. Fight fire with fire. Attack the promises of sin with the promises of Christ. The Bible calls lusts "*deceitful* desires" (Ephesians 4:22). They lie. They promise more than they can deliver. The Bible calls them "passions of your former *ignorance*" (1 Peter 1:14). Only fools yield. "All at once he follows her, as an ox goes to the slaughter" (Proverbs 7:22). Deceit is defeated by truth. Ignorance is defeated by knowledge. It must be glorious truth and beautiful knowledge. This is why I wrote *Seeing and Savoring Jesus Christ* (Crossway, 2001). I need short portraits of Christ to keep myself awake spiritually to the superior greatness of Jesus. We must stock our minds with the promises and pleasures of Jesus. Then we must turn to them immediately after saying, "NO!"

H—HOLD the promise and the pleasure of Christ firmly in your mind until it pushes the other images out. "Fix your eyes on Jesus" (Hebrews 3:1). Here is where many fail. They give in too soon. They say, "I tried to push the fantasy out, and it didn't work." I ask, "How long did

---

* For more on this, see devotion 97.
† John Owen, *The Mortification of Sin,* in *The Works of John Owen,* ed. William H. Gould, vol. 6 (London: Johnstone & Hunter, 1852; reprint, Edinburgh and Carlisle, Penn.: Banner of Truth, 1959), 9.

A • N • T • H • E • M: Strategies for Fighting Lust

you try?" How hard did you exert your mind? Remember, the mind is a muscle. You can flex it with vehemence. Take the kingdom violently (Matthew 11:12). Be brutal. Hold the promise of Christ before your eyes. Hold it. Hold it! Don't let it go! Keep holding it! How long? As long as it takes. Fight! For Christ's sake, fight till you win! If an electric garage door were about to crush your child you would hold it up with all your might and holler for help, and hold it and hold it and hold it and hold it. More is at stake, Jesus said, in the habit of lust (Matthew 5:29).

E—ENJOY a superior satisfaction. Cultivate the capacities for pleasure in Christ. One reason lust reigns in so many is that Christ has so little appeal. We default to deceit because we have little delight in Christ. Don't say, "That spiritual talk is just not me." What steps have you taken to waken affection for Jesus? Have you fought for joy? Don't be fatalistic. You were created to treasure Christ with all your heart—more than you treasure sex or chocolate or sugar. If you have little taste for Jesus, competing pleasures will triumph. Plead with God for the satisfaction you don't have: "Satisfy us in the morning with your steadfast love, that we may rejoice and be glad all our days" (Psalm 90:14). Then look, look, look at the most magnificent Person in the universe until you see him the way he is.

M—MOVE into a useful activity away from idleness and other vulnerable behaviors. Lust grows fast in the garden of leisure. Find a good work to do, and do it with all your might. "Do not be slothful in zeal, be fervent in spirit, serve the Lord" (Romans 12:11). "Be steadfast, immovable, always abounding in the work of the Lord" (1 Corinthians 15:58). Abound in work. Get up and do something. Sweep a room. Hammer a nail. Write a letter. Fix a faucet. And do it for Jesus' sake. You were made to manage and create. Christ died to make you "zealous for good deeds" (Titus 2:14). Displace deceitful lusts with a passion for good deeds.

107

MEALTIME PRAYERS WITH THE PIPERS

Some Suggestions on Giving Thanks

I wrote the following mealtime prayers for my own family to use. There is a short one and a longer one for each of the three meals in the day. The three longer ones have been used by our family for over twenty years, and all the children know the prayers by heart now so that they are able to say them together without reading.

For example, in August of 2001, when Benjamin, my second oldest son, was married in Brazil, I was asked to say a table grace at a large family gathering in Fortaleza. Instead of praying by myself, I said, "I think what I would like to do is ask all my children (Karsten, Benjamin, Abraham, Barnabas, Talitha) to pray with Noël and me the evening prayer that we have used during all their growing-up years." Then we all prayed the prayer from memory. The people were so moved that the whole family could say the prayer together in unison on the spur of the moment that they asked me to pray it again slowly and have it translated into Portuguese one phrase at a time. It proved to be a wonderful witness for Christ to all the people there.

So I offer them here, not with the expectation that everyone will use them, but with the hope they will stir up serious reflection on what we really want God to do at mealtimes and what we are truly thankful for.

Morning Meal
(short)

Lord Jesus, thank You for this day,
And for the night of rest,
And for this food, and for the way
That we are always blessed.

Morning Meal
(longer)

Our Father, every day You give
The food by which our bodies live.
For this we thank You from our heart
And pray that as we this day start,
You might allow our eyes to see
Your endless generosity.
And grant that when we thus are filled,
We may do only what You've willed.

Midday Meal
(short)

Lord Jesus, thank You for these gifts
And what each one displays;
For Your own steady love which lifts
Our hearts in midday praise.

MIDDAY MEAL
(LONGER)

We're grateful, Father, for this hour
To rest and draw upon Your power
Which You have shown in sun and rain
And measured out to every grain.
Let all this food which You have made
And graciously before us laid
Restore our strength for these next hours
That You may have our fullest power.

EVENING MEAL
(SHORT)

Lord Jesus, come now to our meal,
And bless to us this food;
Where faith is weak, dear Lord, reveal
That all You give is good.

EVENING MEAL
(LONGER)

How faithful, Father, is Your care;
Again as always food is there.
Again You have set us before
A meal we pray will mean much more
Than single persons filled with food;
Let there be, Lord, a loving mood.
And as You make our bodies new,
Come now and feed our oneness too.

108

IT IS NEVER RIGHT TO BE ANGRY WITH GOD

Because He Is Righteous and Perfect in His Ways

R ecently I said those words to a group of several hundred people: "It is never, ever, ever, right to be angry with God." There was an incredulous look on many faces. This was not landing well. Clearly many did not agree.

Some were obviously tracking with me, but others looked baffled. I have given a lot of thought to those baffled looks since then. What assumptions were out there that made this statement so difficult to accept? To me nothing could be more obvious. Why is it then so confusing to some others?

There are two possible assumptions that may be common in many heads today, which would make people balk at what I said.

First, many assume that feelings are not right or wrong, that they are neutral. So to say that anger (whether at God or anybody else) is "not right" is like saying sneezing is not right. You don't apply the labels right and wrong to sneezing. It just happens to you. That is the way many people think about feelings: they just happen to you. Therefore, they are not moral or immoral; they are neutral. So for me to say that it is never right to be angry with God is to put the feeling of anger in a category where it doesn't belong, the category of morality.

This kind of thinking about feelings is one of the reasons there is so much shallow Christianity. We think the only things that have moral significance in the world are acts of reflection and volition. And we think feelings like desire and delight and frustration and anger are not acts of volition but waves that break on the shore of our souls with no moral significance. Small wonder that many people do not earnestly seek to be transformed at the level of feelings but only of "choices." That makes for a superficial saint (at best).

This assumption is contrary to what the Bible teaches. In the Bible, many feelings are treated as morally good and many as morally bad. What makes them good or bad is how they relate to God. If they show that God is true and valuable, they are good, and if they suggest that God is false or foolish or evil, they are bad. For example, delight in the Lord is not neutral, it is commanded (Psalm 37:4). Therefore, it is good. But to "take pleasure in wickedness" is wrong (2 Thessalonians 2:12), because it signifies that sin is more desirable than God, which is not true.

It's the same with anger. Anger at sin is good (Mark 3:5), but anger at goodness is sin. That is why it is never right to be angry with God. he is always and only good, no matter how strange and painful his ways with us. Anger toward God signifies that he is bad or weak or cruel or foolish. None of those is true, and all of them dishonor him. Therefore, it is never right to be angry at God. When Jonah and Job were angry with God, Jonah was rebuked by God (Jonah 4:9), and Job repented in dust and ashes (Job 42:6).

The second assumption that may cause people to stumble over the statement that it is never right to be angry with God is the assumption that God really does things that ought to make us angry at him. But, as painful as his providence can be, we should trust that he is good, not get angry with him. That would be like getting angry at the surgeon who cuts us. It might be right if the surgeon slips and makes a mistake. But God never slips.

I have learned over the years that when a person uses the words, "Is it right to be angry at God?" he may be asking a very different question.

He may be asking, "Is it right to *express* anger at God?" These are not the same question, and the answer is not always the same.

The question usually arises in times of great suffering and loss. Disease threatens to undo all your dreams. Death takes a precious child from your family. Utterly unexpected desertion and divorce shake the foundations of your world. At these times people can become very angry at God.

Is this right? To answer this question we might, perhaps, ask the angry person, Is it *always* right to get angry at God? In other words, can a person get angry at God for every reason, and still be right? Was it right, for example, for Jonah to be angry at God's mercy on Nineveh? "God relented of the disaster that he had said he would do to them, and he did not do it. But it displeased Jonah exceedingly, and he was *angry*" (Jonah 3:10–4:1). I assume the answer would be no. We should not get angry at God for just any reason.

But then we would ask: Which deeds of God should make us angry with him, and which should not? Now this is harder to answer. The truth begins to close in on the angry heart.

What about the things that displease us? Are these the acts of God that justify our anger at him? Is it the acts of God that hurt us? "I kill and I make alive; I wound and I heal; and there is none that can deliver out of my hand" (Deuteronomy 32:39). Are these the acts that justify us in directing our anger at God? Or is it his choice to permit the devil to harass and torture us? "The LORD said to Satan, 'Behold, [Job] is in your hand; only spare his life.' So Satan went out from the presence of the LORD and struck Job with loathsome sores from the sole of his foot to the crown of his head" (Job 2:6–7). Does the decision of God to permit Satan to hurt us and our children justify our anger *at him*?

Or come at it from the other side. What is anger? The common definition is: "An intense emotional state induced by displeasure" (Merriam-Webster). But there is an ambiguity in this definition. You can be "displeased" by a *thing* or by a *person*. Anger at a thing does not contain indignation at a choice or an act. We simply don't like the effect of the

The Satisfied Soul

thing: the broken clutch, or the grain of sand that just blew in our eye, or rain on our picnic. But when we get angry at a person, we are displeased with a choice they made and an act they performed. Anger at a person always implies strong disapproval. If you are angry at me, you think I have done something I should not have done.

This is why being angry at God is never right. It is wrong—always wrong—to disapprove of God for what he does and permits. "Shall not the Judge of all the earth do what is just?" (Genesis 18:25). It is arrogant for finite, sinful creatures to disapprove of God for what he does and permits. We may weep over the pain. We may be angry at sin and Satan. But God is always righteous in what he does and what he permits. "Yes, O Lord God, the Almighty, true and righteous are Your judgments" (Revelation 16:7).

But many who say that it is right to *be* angry with God really mean it is right to *express* anger at God. When they hear me say it is wrong to *be* angry with God, they think I mean "stuff your feelings and be a hypocrite." That's not what I mean. I mean it is always wrong to disapprove of God in any of his judgments.

But if we do experience the sinful emotion of anger at God, what then? Shall we add the sin of hypocrisy to the sin of anger? No. If we feel it, we should confess it to God. He knows it anyway. He sees our hearts. If anger at God is in our heart, we may as well tell him so and then tell him we are sorry, and ask him to help us put it away by faith in his goodness and wisdom.

When Jesus died on the cross for our sins, he removed forever the wrath of God from all who trust him. God's disposition to us now is entirely mercy, even when severe and disciplinary (Romans 8:1). Therefore, doubly shall those in Christ turn away from the terrible specter of anger at God. We may cry, in agony, "My God, My God, where are you?" But we will follow soon with, "Into your hands I commit my spirit."

So I say it again: It is never right to be angry with God. But if you sin in this way, don't compound it by hypocrisy. Tell him the truth and repent.

109

THE CHURCH WAS SPOKEN AGAINST EVERYWHERE

Opposition Need Not Stall the

Advance of the Gospel

C an the gospel spread, and thousands be converted, and churches grow, and love abound where Christianity is continually spoken against? Yes. It not only can; it has. I say this not to discourage winsomeness but to encourage hope. Do not assume that seasons of hostility or controversy will be lean seasons with little power or growth. They may be seasons of explosive growth and great spiritual blessing.

How do we know this? Consider the way Luke reports the state of the church in the book of Acts. When Paul finally gets to Rome near the end of his life, he invites the "local leaders of the Jews" to come hear his gospel. What these leaders say about the "sect" of Christians is very significant. They say, "With regard to this sect we know that it is spoken against everywhere" (Acts 28:22).

This is not surprising to disciples who knew that Jesus said, "You will be hated by all nations for my name's sake" (Matthew 24:9). And, "Woe to you, when all men speak well of you" (Luke 6:26). And, "If they have called the master of the house Beelzebul, how much more will they malign those of his household!" (Matthew 10:25).

The early church was an embattled church. Yes, there were seasons of calm (Acts 9:31), but that was the exception. Most of the time there were slanders and misunderstandings and accusations and persecutions, not to mention internal disputes about ethics and doctrine. Virtually all of Paul's letters reflect controversy in the church as well as affliction from outside. The point is not that this is desirable but that it need not hinder great power and growth. In fact, it may be the occasion and reason for great power and growth.

This seems to be Luke's view, because, even though he portrayed Christianity as "spoken against everywhere," he also portrayed relentless growth throughout the book of Acts. "The Lord added to their number day by day those who were being saved" (2:47). "The disciples were increasing in number" (6:1). "The word of God continued to increase, and the number of the disciples multiplied greatly" (6:7). "The hand of the Lord was with them, and a great number who believed turned to the Lord" (11:21). "The word of God increased and multiplied" (12:24). "The churches…increased in number daily" (16:5). "All the residents of Asia heard the word of the Lord" (19:10). "The word of the Lord continued to increase and prevail mightily" (19:20).

Therefore, we must not think that controversy and conflict keep the church from experiencing the power of the Holy Spirit and dramatic growth. We are taught in Romans 12:18, "If possible, so far as it depends on you, live peaceably with all." But we are not taught to sacrifice truth for peace. So Paul said, "Even if we or an angel from heaven should preach to you a gospel contrary to the one we preached to you, let him be accursed" (Galatians 1:8).

And if there is enough conflict and hostility that those who speak the gospel are even imprisoned, that very moment of bad press may be the occasion of gospel triumph. Why? Because, Paul said, "I am suffering, bound with chains as a criminal [for the gospel]. But the word of God is not bound!" (2 Timothy 2:9). In fact, it may be that when God and truth are loved enough that we are willing to take stands that incur slander and hostility, the Spirit may move more powerfully than in times of peace and popularity.

Sometimes Christians have favor with society, and sometimes we "are spoken against everywhere." In either case, God can, and often does, pour out his power for effective witness. Both peace and slander can be the occasion of blessing. Therefore, let us not embrace the assumption that times of social ridicule must be times of weakness and fruitlessness for Christianity. They may be a sign of faithfulness and occasions of great harvest. The church was "spoken against everywhere," and "the word of the Lord continued to increase and prevail mightily."

110

BY WHAT DEATH WILL YOU GLORIFY GOD?

A Meditation on John 21:18–19

When John wrote his gospel, Peter had probably already been killed by the Roman emperor Nero. So when he recorded the words of Jesus about Peter's coming death, he was able to look back and interpret the symbolism Jesus had used. Here's what Jesus said to Peter, with John's interpretation:

> "Truly, truly, I say to you, when you were young, you used to dress yourself and walk wherever you wanted, but when you are old, you will stretch out your hands, and another will dress you and carry you where you do not want to go." (This he said to show by what kind of death he was to glorify God.) And after saying this he said to him, "Follow me." (John 21:18–19)

It is a sobering thing to be told by your Master and friend that you will die in his service. It was oblique, but Peter probably got the message. And who knows what look was on Jesus' face when he said it. But such is the price of following Jesus Christ. This isn't that different from what he predicts for each of us. "If anyone comes to me and does not hate…his own life, he cannot be my disciple" (Luke 14:26). "Whoever loves his life loses it, and whoever hates his life in this world will keep it for life eternal" (John 12:25). "If anyone would come after me, let him deny himself and take up his cross and follow me" (Matthew 16:24). "Some of you will be put to death. You will be hated by all for my name's sake" (Luke 21:16–17).

Tradition says that Peter was crucified upside down in Rome during one of Nero's persecutions in the midsixties. The early church historian Eusebius wrote, "Peter seems to have preached in Pontus and Galatia and Bithynia and Cappadocia and Asia, to the Jews of the Dispersion, and at last, having come to Rome, he was crucified head downward, for so he himself had asked to suffer."*

Jesus predicted the martyrdom of Peter. Jesus knew what sort of death it would be, and he knew the time frame. This much knowledge could discourage Peter. Or it could serve to remind him that, come what may, the Lord Jesus is never taken off guard. Not only that, Jesus spoke these words to Peter after rising triumphant from the dead. This meant that "Christ being raised from the dead will never die again; death no longer has dominion over him" (Romans 6:9). Therefore, Jesus will be alive and ruling when Peter comes to die. He will be there to help him. "I am with you always, even to the end of the age" (Matthew 28:20). And not only to help him die, but raise him: "If the Spirit of him who raised Jesus from the dead dwells in you, he who raised Christ Jesus from the dead will also give life to your mortal bodies" (Romans 8:11).

Jesus knew that there would be part of Peter's will that would not want this death. "Another...will carry you where you do not want to go" (John 21:18). Even Jesus cried, "If it be possible, let this cup pass from me" (Matthew 26:39). So it is with all who follow in his steps. Pain is pain, not pleasure. Only a higher love brings you to embrace it when you could avoid it by denying Christ.

John said Peter's death was to glorify God, "This he said to show by what kind of death he was to *glorify God*" (John 21:19). The way John

---

* Eusebius, *Ecclesiastical History,* III, I.

said this seems to show that he considers all our deaths as appointed for the glory of God. The difference is, With what kind of death will we glorify God?

Are you ready for this? Will you show God great in the way you die? Will you say, "To live is Christ, and to die is gain" (Philippians 1:21)? Will you call this ugly, defeated, torturing enemy sweet names? Will the loss of all your earthly family, friends, and possessions fade at the prospect of seeing and being with Christ?

After Jesus had predicted the horrible death of Peter, he said to him, "Follow me."

"Let us go to him outside the camp" (Hebrews 13:13).

111

JOHN G. PATON'S FATHER

A Key to His Courage

John G. Paton was a missionary to the New Hebrides, today called Vanuatu, in the South Seas. He was born in Scotland in 1824. I write about him because of the courage he showed throughout his eighty-two years of life. I want to be courageous in the cause of Christ. I want you to be. And I especially want my children to be. So I ponder courage in others. Where does it come from? When I dig for the reasons that John Paton was so courageous, one reason I find is the deep love he had for his father.

The tribute Paton pays to his godly father is, by itself, worth the price of his autobiography, which is still in print.* Maybe it's because I have four sons (and Talitha), but I wept as I read this section. It filled me with such longing to be a father like this.

There was a "closet" where his father would go for prayer as a rule after each meal. The eleven children knew it, and they reverenced the spot and learned something profound about God. The impact on John Paton was immense.

---

* James C. Paton, *John G. Patton: Missionary to the New Hebrides, An Autobiography Edited by His Brother* (Edinburgh: The Banner of Truth Trust, 1965, orig. 1889, 1891). I have tried to retell Paton's story in a message available at DesiringGod.org, titled, "'You Will Be Eaten by Cannibals!' Courage in the Cause of World Missions: Lessons in the Life of John G. Paton."

Though everything else in religion were by some unthinkable catastrophe to be swept out of memory, were blotted from my understanding, my soul would wander back to those early scenes, and shut itself up once again in that Sanctuary Closet, and, hearing still the echoes of those cries to God, would hurl back all doubt with the victorious appeal, "He walked with God, why may not I?"

...How much my father's prayers at this time impressed me I can never explain, nor could any stranger understand. When, on his knees and all of us kneeling around him in Family Worship, he poured out his whole soul with tears for the conversion of the Heathen world to the service of Jesus, and for every personal and domestic need, we all felt as if in the presence of the living Savior, and learned to know and love him as our Divine friend.*

One scene best captures the depth of love between John and his father, and the power of the impact on John's life of uncompromising courage and purity. The time came in his early twenties for the young Paton to leave home and go to Glasgow to attend divinity school and become a city missionary. From his hometown of Torthorwald to the train station at Kilmarnock was a forty-mile walk. Forty years later, Paton wrote:

My dear father walked with me the first six miles of the way. His counsels and tears and heavenly conversation on that parting journey are fresh in my heart as if it had been but yesterday; and tears are on my cheeks as freely now as then, whenever memory steals me away to the scene. For the last half mile or so we walked on together in almost unbroken silence—my father, as was often his custom, carrying hat in hand, while his long flowing yellow hair

---

* James C. Paton, 8, 21.

(then yellow, but in later years white as snow) streamed like a girl's down his shoulders. His lips kept moving in silent prayers for me; and his tears fell fast when our eyes met each other in looks for which all speech was vain! We halted on reaching the appointed parting place; he grasped my hand firmly for a minute in silence, and then solemnly and affectionately said: "God bless you, my son! Your father's God prosper you, and keep you from all evil!"

Unable to say more, his lips kept moving in silent prayer; in tears we embraced, and parted. I ran off as fast as I could; and, when about to turn a corner in the road where he would lose sight of me, I looked back and saw him still standing with head uncovered where I had left him—gazing after me. Waving my hat in adieu, I rounded the corner and out of sight in an instant. But my heart was too full and sore to carry me further, so I darted into the side of the road and wept for a time. Then, rising up cautiously, I climbed the dike to see if he yet stood where I had left him; and just at that moment I caught a glimpse of him climbing the dike and looking out for me! He did not see me, and after he gazed eagerly in my direction for a while he got down, set his face toward home, and began to return—his head still uncovered, and his heart, I felt sure, still rising in prayers for me. I watched through blinding tears, till his form faded from my gaze; and then, hastening on my way, vowed deeply and oft, by the help of God, to live and act so as never to grieve or dishonor such a father and mother as he had given me.*

The impact of his father's faith and prayer and love and discipline was immeasurable. Let every father read and be filled with longing and firm resolve to love like this.

---

* Paton, 25–6.

112

HELPING PEOPLE HAVE THE ASSURANCE OF SALVATION
We Can Be Sure and Not Waver

C hristians are called to help fight for their own assurance and to help others fight for theirs. God means for us to know we are saved and to enjoy that bold confidence in the face of opposition and threat. "These things I have written to you who believe in the name of the Son of God, so that you may know that you have eternal life" (1 John 5:13). What then shall we say to each other to help maintain the assurance of salvation? Here's what I would say.

1. Full assurance is God's will for us.

> And we desire each one of you to show the same earnestness to have the full assurance of hope until the end. (Hebrews 6:11)

2. Assurance is partially sustained by objective evidences for Christian truth.

> To [his apostles] he presented himself alive after his suffering by many proofs, appearing to them during forty days. (Acts 1:3)

3. Assurance cannot neglect the painful work of self-examination.

Examine yourselves, to see whether you are in the faith. Test your-selves. Or do you not realize this about yourselves, that Jesus Christ is in you?—unless indeed you fail the test! (2 Corinthians 13:5)

4. Assurance will diminish in the presence of concealed sin.

When I kept silent about my sin, my body wasted away through my groaning all day long. (Psalm 32:3, NASB)

5. Assurance comes from hearing the Word of Christ.

So faith comes from hearing, and hearing through the word of Christ. (Romans 10:17)

These are written so that you may believe that Jesus is the Christ, the Son of God, and that believing you may have life in his name. (John 20:31)

6. Repeated focusing on the sufficiency of the cross of Christ is crucial for assurance.

Since we have a great priest over the house of God, let us draw near with a true heart in full assurance of faith. (Hebrews 10:21–22)

7. We must pray for eyes to see the truths that sustain assurance.

I pray that the eyes of your heart may be enlightened, so that you will know what is the hope of His calling, what are the riches of the glory of His inheritance in the saints, and what is the surpassing greatness of His power toward us who believe. (Ephesians 1:18–19, NASB)

8. Assurance is not easily maintained in personal isolation.

And the eye cannot say to the hand, "I have no need of you." (1 Corinthians 12:21)

Exhort one another every day, as long as it is called "today," that none of you may be hardened by the deceitfulness of sin. (Hebrews 3:13)

9. Assurance is not destroyed by God's displeasure and discipline.

Rejoice not over me, O my enemy; when I fall, I shall rise; when I sit in darkness, the LORD will be a light for me. I will bear the indignation of the LORD because I have sinned against him, until he pleads my cause and executes judgment for me. He will bring me out to the light; I shall look upon his vindication. (Micah 7:8–9)

10. We must often wait patiently for the return of assurance.

I waited patiently for the LORD; he inclined to me and heard my cry. He drew me up from the pit of destruction, out of the miry bog, and set my feet upon a rock, making my steps secure. He put a new song in my mouth, a song of praise to our God. Many will see and fear, and put their trust in the LORD. (Psalm 40:1–3)

11. Assurance is a fight to the day we die.

Fight the good fight of faith. Take hold of the eternal life. (1 Timothy 6:12)

I have fought the good fight, I have finished the race, I have kept the faith. (2 Timothy 4:7)

12. Assurance is finally a gift of the Spirit.

The Spirit himself bears witness with our spirit that we are children of God. (Romans 8:16)

Whoever believes in the Son of God has the testimony in himself.... And this is the testimony, that God gave us eternal life, and this life is in his Son. (1 John 5:10–11)

113

SIN, CIVIL RIGHTS, AND MISSIONS

The Amazing Role of Sober Truth

The biblical doctrine of human depravity is a great antidote to racism. I have seen this recently in two very different articles. One is by Andrew Walls called "The Evangelical Revival, the Missionary Movement, and Africa" (*The Missionary Movement in Christian History* [Maryknoll, NY: Orbis Books], 79–101). He points out that the Great Awakening in America and England (1730s and '40s) gave rise to the modern foreign missionary movement. One of the ways it did so was by clarifying the unity between the sinful homeland and the sinful heathen.

> There was no difference between the spiritual state of a pleasure-seeking duchess (though baptized and adhering to the prevailing religious system of the higher and middle classes) and that of a South Sea Islander. That spiritual parity of the unregenerate of Christendom and the heathen abroad had important missionary consequences.... A consistent view of human solidarity in depravity shielded the first missionary generation from some of the worst excesses of racism. (79)

In other words, a dark view of our own depraved hearts, and a sense of brokenness before God, and a dependence on mercy in Christ make it harder for us to view other humans—whatever race—as less advantaged before God. The doctrine of total depravity unites us in desperate dependence on mercy. The early missionaries—with all their flaws and biases—knew this. And it helped them count others better than themselves for the sake of Christ (Philippians 2:3).

The other illustration of how the doctrine of depravity works against racism comes from a review of the book *A Stone of Hope: Prophetic Religion and the Death of Jim Crow* by David L. Chappell. Elisabeth Fox-Genovese shows how the theological convictions of the black leaders of the civil rights movement were very different from those of the white liberals who supported the movement. Liberalism as a movement has a high degree of confidence in human reason and in the inevitability of human progress away from barbarism. So they saw the civil rights movement in those terms and supported it.

But Martin Luther King and most of the other black leaders were cut from another cloth. They "believed that the natural tendency of this world and of human institutions (including churches) is toward corruption." This did not produce despair, but a "hopeful pessimism." Humans are bad, but God is good and powerful. He can and will establish justice. The bond of human depravity among all humans and all races, linked with the hope of redemption in Jesus Christ, provided a deep and powerful impulse for the civil rights movement that many of its white liberal participants did not understand.

> Seen through the lens of the leading black activists' view of the
> fallen and depraved character of human nature, liberal optimism
> seemed more than slightly facile, especially liberal views about
> the natural—indeed, inevitable—improvement of the position of
> minorities in general and black Americans in particular.... It is
> common to assume that southern blacks readily saw whites as
> sinful—and often with good reason. It is much less common to
> recognize that leaders like [Martin Luther] King also acknowl-
> edged the inherent sinfulness of black southerners. For all but

racists on either side, the conclusion is inescapable: if, "of one blood He made them," then it inexorably follows that sinfulness adheres to the human condition shared by people of all races. The whole point of the civil rights movement was to affirm that fundamental equality of condition, yet many find irresistible the temptation to paint one side as entirely good and the other as entirely evil.... A heroism grounded in optimism is admirable and uplifting, but a heroism grounded in the pessimism of prophetic faith is decisively more impressive and moving. (Elisabeth Fox-Genovese, "Hopeful Pessimism," in *Books and Culture*, July/August 2004, 9)

Stop and ponder these amazing illustrations of the role of sober truth—even truth about total depravity—in the global missionary movement and the civil rights movement. Oh, let us hold fast to the truth of Scripture! It will break out and do its good work in ways we never dreamed.

114

GOD WORKS WONDERS

In Steady-State Obedience and in Total Disobedience

1. Don't dream too small or pray too small about what God may do to save sinners and glorify his name in the midst of steady-state obedience.

God ordinarily works his wonders of mercy and salvation in the midst of our steady-state obedience. For example, in 2 Timothy 2:24–26 Paul says:

> The Lord's servant must not be quarrelsome but kind to every-one, able to teach, patiently enduring evil, correcting his opponents with gentleness. God may perhaps grant them repentance leading to a knowledge of the truth, and they may escape from the snare of the devil, after being captured by him to do his will.

Our duty is steady-state obedience: don't be quarrelsome, be kind, teach well, be patient, don't return evil for evil, correct with gentleness. In the midst of this steady-state obedience, "God may perhaps grant them repentance." We should not assume that nothing extraordinary will happen while we persevere in daily faithfulness. That is where God loves to act in supernatural ways.

Therefore, we should pray: "O Lord, make the fruit of our lives utterly disproportionate to the measure of our faithfulness."

2. Don't dream too small or pray too small about what God may do to save sinners and glorify his name in the midst of total disobedience.

God is not limited to work only where we are obeying and praying and dreaming of his intervention.

For example, in Acts 22:5–8 Paul tells us about how Christ broke into his totally disobedient life when no human being had planned or dreamed it.

> I journeyed toward Damascus to take those also who were there and bring them in bonds to Jerusalem to be punished. "As I was on my way and drew near to Damascus, about noon a great light from heaven suddenly shone around me. And I fell to the ground and heard a voice saying to me, 'Saul, Saul, why are you persecuting me?' And I answered, 'Who are you, Lord?' And he said to me, 'I am Jesus of Nazareth, whom you are persecuting.'"

In the midst of Paul's total disobedience God broke in and made Paul into a great missionary. Here's a contemporary version of God's inbreaking power: D. James Kennedy, pastor of Coral Ridge Presbyterian Church, tells the story of his conversion in *Indelible Ink*, edited by Scott Larsen (WaterBrook Press, 2003):

> At the age of twenty-three, I was a spiritual derelict. Worse than that, I was thoroughly satisfied with my secular lifestyle as a ballroom dance instructor in Tampa's Arthur Murray Studio. I was a college dropout, but making good money in a job that I immensely enjoyed. I was single, popular, and pretty well unhampered by moral restraints. Nor could I recall ever having heard the gospel....
>
> That was before my clock radio, in my rented apartment on South Boulevard in Tampa, threw me a curve. I had come in

from an all-night dance party and thought I had set the appliance to wake me at the proper time with appropriate music for a soothing return to consciousness. But what I heard that Sunday afternoon was…the thundering voice of Dr. Donald Gray Barnhouse, pastor of Philadelphia's Tenth Presbyterian Church. I jumped out of bed to switch the dial but was stopped almost in mid-flight by a question I couldn't brush aside.

In the penetrating, stentorian tones for which he was famous, this great preacher and broadcast evangelist asked, "Suppose that you were to die today and stand before God, and He were to ask you, 'What right do you have to enter into my heaven?'—what would you say?" I was completely dumbfounded. I had never thought of such a thing as that, and my nonchalance suddenly evaporated into thin air.

I sat on the edge of my bed, as though transfixed, groping for an answer to this simple question. I had enough common sense to realize that, even though I had no background in the Bible, this was the most important question that had ever entered my mind. (69–70)

In mercy, God led Kennedy to a nearby corner newsstand where he asked simply, "Do you have any religious books?" He was given Fulton Oursler's *The Greatest Story Ever Told*. In this way, with no human design or dream, God saved D. James Kennedy.

Therefore, let us pursue steady-state obedience, but let us also pray, "O Lord, grant new life, and glorify your name, where no human has dreamed it or designed it."

115

SURRENDERING AND DEMANDING RIGHTS: TWO KINDS OF LOVE

Thoughts on Mercy and Justice in
2 Thessalonians 3:6–15

> *Now we command you, brothers, in the name of our Lord Jesus*
> *Christ, that you keep away from any brother who is walking in*
> *idleness and not in accord with the tradition that you received*
> *from us. For you yourselves know how you ought to imitate us,*
> *because we were not idle when we were with you, nor did we*
> *eat anyone's bread without paying for it, but with toil and*
> *labor we worked night and day, that we might not be a burden*
> *to any of you. It was not because we do not have that right,*
> *but to give you in ourselves an example to imitate. For even*
> *when we were with you, we would give you this command: If*
> *anyone is not willing to work, let him not eat. For we hear*
> *that some among you walk in idleness, not busy at work, but*
> *busybodies. Now such persons we command and encourage in*
> *the Lord Jesus Christ to do their work quietly and to earn their*
> *own living. As for you, brothers, do not grow weary in doing*
> *good. If anyone does not obey what we say in this letter, take*
> *note of that person, and have nothing to do with him, that he*
> *may be ashamed. Do not regard him as an enemy, but warn*
> *him as a brother.*

By surrendering and demanding a right at the same time, Paul modeled two forms of love.

In verses 8–9 he surrendered the right to be paid by the church for his ministry: "With toil and labor we worked night and day, that we might not be a burden to any of you. It was not because we do not have that right, but to give you in ourselves an example to imitate." So Paul has the right to be paid simply for preaching. But he surrenders that right in this case to accomplish something else: giving an example to the church of secular work for self-support.

But Paul also demanded a right in verse 10—the right to receive work for pay: "If anyone is not willing to work, let him not eat."

Both of these—the surrender of a right, and the demand of a right—are forms of love. Surrendering a right is love because Paul sacrifices his own right in order to model a productive way to live. Demanding a right is love because it aims not at self-aggrandizement, but at the good of the brother. This is what verses 14–15 make plain:

> If anyone does not obey what we say in this letter, take note of that person, and have nothing to do with him, that he may be ashamed. Do not regard him as an enemy, but warn him as a brother.

The aim is not alienation, but restoration from destructive behavior through tough love that insists on change.

Another way to say it is that Paul was modeling mercy and justice. Mercy: because, in working a secular job for his bread, he gave more time and effort than was required and demanded less than he had a right to receive. Justice: because, in demanding that others work, he was forbidding them to demand mercy from the church and insisting that they earn their food.

Now when should we do which? How do you know when to love with mercy and when to love with justice? Three guidelines:

Know your personality well, and be vigilant not to indulge your bent carelessly. If you are naturally merciful, consider justice seriously. If you are naturally judicial, consider mercy seriously. We are very likely to indulge our natural bent at the expense of love.

The more personal and private a matter is, the more likely surrendering rights will be the loving way. But the more communal and public a matter is, the more likely demanding rights will be the loving way. The reason for this is that, in public, demanding rights can be seen as a way of caring for others, not just yourself, but in private a demanded right will almost surely communicate self-aggrandizement and a failure to treasure Christ above all.

Be sure in either case—loving with mercy, or loving with justice—that your burden is the greatest good for the greatest number. That is, seek to help the greatest number enjoy making much of Christ forever.

116

IF CHRIST PREDICTED WAR, MAY CHRISTIANS PRAY FOR PEACE?

Distinguishing God's Work and Ours

I ask this question because some Bible-believing Christians feel that prayer for peace in these "last days" would be contrary to God's will, since Jesus said, "When you hear of wars and rumors of wars, do not be alarmed. This must take place, but the end is not yet" (Mark 13:7). If war "must take place," how can you pray for peace without opposing God?

Our prayers should be guided by what is morally right for men to do, not by what God, in his sovereign providence, may will to take place. Rarely, if ever, should we pray for moral evil to take place, but God may will that moral evil prevail for a season. For example: (1) God willed that Christ be crucified. Many of the necessary acts involved in crucifying Christ were morally evil. Therefore, God willed that this moral evil prevail for a season (Acts 2:23; 4:27–28). (2) God willed that Joseph's brothers sell him into slavery in Egypt, even though this was evil for them to do (Genesis 50:20). (3) And God ordains the sinful ravages of the end times (Revelation 17:17).

In other words, God ordains and predicts that moral evil prevail for certain seasons, but this does not mean we should pray for moral evil to happen. We should pray according to the way God has commanded us to live—in righteousness and love. We should pray that God's will be done on earth the way it's done in heaven by the perfectly holy angels (Matthew 6:10), not the way it's done on earth through the agency of sinful men.

In fact, Paul teaches us to pray for peace among nations for the sake of the gospel. The crucial text relating to prayer and peace is 1 Timothy 2:1–4. "First of all, then, I urge that supplications, prayers, intercessions, and thanksgivings be made for all people, for kings and all who are in high positions, that we may lead a peaceful and quiet life, godly and dignified in every way. This is good, and it is pleasing in the sight of God our Savior, who desires all people to be saved and to come to the knowledge of the truth."

Notice the link between praying for (1) national leaders, (2) the preservation of peace and order, and (3) the "desire for all to be saved." There is a connection between (1) national leadership, (2) peace, and (3) evangelism and missions. It is true that the church may grow in times of hostilities and war. But it is also true that wars have devastated the church in many areas. It is not our business to decide the sovereign purpose of God in ordaining that some wars happen. Our business is to pray that justice, peace, and the proclamation of the gospel prevail. Our business is to pray that the Christian church not be complicit in national affairs as if nation and church were one. Ours is to pray that the church be seen as aliens in the cause of Christ-exalting love and justice with no supreme allegiances to any nation.

This leaves open the possibility that Christians might support a just war. God has given to the governing authorities the right to bear the sword (Romans 13:1–6). There are occasions when justice and love painfully call for military force for the sake of opposing aggression or liberating the oppressed. In such cases our prayers would be for the minimizing of misery and the speedy triumph of justice and the restraint of animosities and cruelties.

So let us pray for the love and wisdom and courage and power and fruitfulness of the church of Jesus Christ around the world. Let us plead that she would be distinct from all the nations and all the national and ethnic manifestations of pride. Let us plead that she would be a peacemaking presence of salt and light everywhere. And that she would be unafraid to call every nation into question for the sake of justice and humility. And that Jesus Christ would be magnified as no national deity but as Lord of lords and King of kings. And let us pray that all lords and all kings see this and humble themselves and make way for the Lord of glory.

117

THE GREATEST EVENT IN HISTORY

Two Paradoxes in the Death of Christ

Not surprisingly, the greatest event in the history of the world is complex. For example, since Jesus Christ is man and God in one person, was his death the death of God? To answer this we must speak of the two natures of Christ, one divine and one human. Ever since AD 451 the Chalcedonian definition of Christ's two natures in one person has been accepted as the orthodox teaching of Scripture. The Council of Chalcedon said,

> We, then,…teach men to confess:…one and the same Christ,
> Son, Lord, Only-begotten, to be acknowledged in two natures,
> inconfusedly, unchangeably, indivisibly, inseparably; the distinc-
> tion of the natures being by no means taken away by the union,
> but rather the property of each nature being preserved, and con-
> curring in one Person and One Subsistence, nor parted or divided
> into two persons, but one and the same Son, and only begotten,
> God, the Word, the Lord Jesus Christ.

The divine nature is immortal (Romans 1:23; 1 Timothy 1:17). It cannot die. That is part of what it means to be God. Therefore, when Christ died, it was his human nature that suffered death. The mystery of the union between the divine and the human natures, in that experience of death, is not revealed to us. What we know is that Christ died and that in the same day he went to Paradise ("Today you will be with me in Paradise," Luke 23:43). Therefore there seems to have been consciousness in death, so that the ongoing union between the human and divine natures need not have been interrupted, though Christ, only in his human nature, died.

Another example of the complexity of the event of Christ's death is how God the Father experienced it. The most common evangelical teaching is that the death of Christ is Christ's experience of the Father's curse. "Christ redeemed us from the curse of the law by becoming a curse for us, for it is written, 'Cursed is everyone who is hanged on a tree'" (Galatians 3:13). Whose curse? One could soften it by saying, "the curse of the law." But the law is not a person to curse anyone. A curse is a curse if there is one who curses. The one who curses through the law is God, who wrote the law. Therefore, the death of Christ for our sin and for our law breaking was the experience of the Father's curse.

This is why Jesus said, "My God, my God, why have you forsaken me?" (Matthew 27:46). In the death of Christ, God laid on him the sins of his people (Isaiah 53:6), which he hated. And in hatred for that sin, God turned away from his sin-laden Son and gave him up to suffer the full force of death and cursing. The Father's wrath was poured out on him instead of us so that his wrath toward us was "propitiated" (Romans 3:25) and removed.

But here is the paradox. God deeply and joyfully approved of what the Son was doing in that hour of sacrifice. In fact, he had planned it all together with the Son. And his love for the God-Man, Jesus Christ, on earth was owing to the very obedience that took Jesus to the cross. The cross was Jesus' crowning act of obedience and love. And this obedience and love the Father profoundly approved and enjoyed. Therefore, Paul says this amazing thing: "Christ loved us and gave himself up for us, a fragrant offering and sacrifice to God" (Ephesians 5:2). The death of Jesus was a fragrance to God.

So here we have one more glorious complexity. The death of Christ was the curse of God and the wrath of God, and yet, at the same time, it was pleasing to God and a sweet fragrance. While turning from his Son and giving him up to die laden with our sin, he delighted in the obedience and love and perfection of the Son.

Therefore, let us stand in awe and look with trembling joy on the death of Jesus Christ, the Son of God. There is no greater event in history. There is no greater thing for our minds to ponder or our hearts to admire. Stay close to this. Everything important and good gathers here. It is a wise and weighty and happy place to be.

118

A CALL FOR CHRISTIAN RISK

*How the Removal of Eternal Risk Creates
the Call for Temporal Risk*

By removing eternal risk, Christ calls his people to continual temporal risk. For the followers of Jesus, the final risk is gone. "There is now no condemnation for those who are in Christ Jesus" (Romans 8:1). "Neither death nor life...will be able to separate us from the love of God in Christ Jesus our Lord" (Romans 3:38–39). "Some of you they will put to death.... But not a hair of your head will perish" (Luke 21:16, 18). "Whoever believes in me, though he die, yet shall he live" (John 11:25).

When the threat of death becomes a door to paradise, the final barrier to temporal risk is broken. When a Christian says from the heart, "To live is Christ and to die is gain," he is free to love no matter what. Some forms of radical Islam may entice martyr-murderers with similar dreams, but Christian hope is the power to love, not kill. Christian hope produces life-givers, not life-takers. The crucified Christ calls his people to live and die for their enemies, as he did. The only risks permitted by Christ are the perils of love. "Love your enemies, do good to those who hate you, bless those who curse you, pray for those who abuse you" (Luke 6:27–28).

With staggering promises of everlasting joy, Jesus unleashed a movement of radical, loving risk-takers. "You will be delivered up even by parents...and some of you they will put to death" (Luke 21:16). Only some. Which means it might be you and it might not. That's what risk means.

It is not risky to shoot yourself in the head. The outcome is certain. It is risky to serve Christ in a war zone. You might get shot. You might not.

Christ calls us to take risks for kingdom purposes. Almost every message of American consumerism says the opposite: Maximize comfort and security—now, not in heaven. Christ does not join that chorus. To every timid saint, wavering on the edge of some dangerous gospel venture, he says, "Fear not, you can only be killed" (Luke 12:4). Yes, by all means maximize your joy! How? For the sake of love, risk being reviled and persecuted and lied about, "for your reward is great in heaven" (Matthew 5:11–12).

There is a great biblical legacy of loving risk-takers. Joab, facing the Syrians on one side and the Ammonites on the other, said to his brother Abishai, "Let us be courageous for our people...and may the LORD do what seems good to him" (2 Samuel 10:12). Esther broke the royal law to save her people and said, "If I perish, I perish" (Esther 4:16). Shadrach and his comrades refused to bow down to the king's idol and said, "Our God whom we serve is able to deliver us.... But if not, be it known to you, O king, that we will not serve your gods" (Daniel 3:16–18). And when the Holy Spirit told Paul that in every city imprisonment and afflictions await him, he said, "I do not account my life of any value nor as precious to myself, if only I may finish my course" (Acts 20:24).

"Every Christian," said Stephen Neil about the early church, "knew that sooner or later he might have to testify to his faith at the cost of his life" (*A History of Christian Missions*, Penguin, 1964, 43). This was normal. To become a Christian was to risk your life. Tens of thousands did it. Why? Because to do it was to gain Christ and not to was to lose your soul. "Whoever would save his life will lose it, but whoever loses his life for my sake will find it" (Matthew 16:25).

In America and around the world, the price of being a real Christian is rising. Things are getting back to normal in "this present evil age." Increasingly, 2 Timothy 3:12 will make sense: "All who desire to live a godly life in Christ Jesus will be persecuted." Those who've made gospel-risk a voluntary lifestyle will be most ready when we have no choice. Therefore, I urge you, in the words of the early church, "Let us go to him outside the camp and bear the reproach he endured. For here we have no lasting city, but we seek the city that is to come" (Hebrews 13:13–14).

When God removed all risk above
He loosed a thousand risks of love.

The Satisfied Soul

119

Do Jews Have a Divine Right in the Promised Land?

How Christians Should Think About the Jewish-Palestinian Conflict

How should Bible-believing Christians align themselves in the Jewish-Palestinian conflict? There are biblical reasons for treating both sides with compassionate public justice in the same way that disputes should be settled between nations generally. In other words, the Bible does not teach us to be partial to Israel or to the Palestinians because either has a special divine status.

I do not deny that Israel was chosen by God from all the peoples of the world to be the focus of special blessing in the history of redemption which climaxed in Jesus Christ, the Messiah. "The LORD your God has chosen you to be a people for his treasured possession, out of all the peoples who are on the face of the earth" (Deuteronomy 7:6).

Nor do I deny that God promised to Israel the presently disputed land from the time of Abraham onward. God said to Moses, "This is the land of which I swore to Abraham, to Isaac, and to Jacob, 'I will give it to your offspring'" (Deuteronomy 34:4).

But neither of these biblical facts leads necessarily to the endorsement of present-day Israel as the rightful possessor of all the disputed land. Israel may have such a right. And she may not. But that decision is not based on divine privilege. Why?

First, a non-covenant-keeping people does not have a divine right to hold the land of promise. Both the blessed status of the people and the privileged right to the land are conditional on Israel's keeping the covenant God made with her. Thus God said to Israel, "If you will indeed obey my voice and keep my covenant, you shall be my treasured possession among all peoples" (Exodus 19:5). Israel has no warrant to a present experience of divine privilege when she is not keeping covenant with God.

More than once Israel was denied the experience of her divine right to the land when she broke covenant with God. For example, when Israel languished in captivity in Babylon, Daniel prayed, "O Lord...we have sinned and done wrong.... To you, O Lord, belongs righteousness, but to us open shame...to all Israel...in all the lands to which you have driven them, because of the treachery that they have committed against you" (Daniel 9:4–7; see Psalm 78:54–61). Israel has no divine right to be in the land of promise when she is breaking the covenant of promise.

This does not mean that other nations have the right to molest her. She still has human rights among nations when she has no divine right. Nations that gloated over her divine discipline were punished by God (Isaiah 10:5–13).

Second, Israel as a whole today rejects her Messiah, Jesus Christ, God's Son. This is the ultimate act of covenant-breaking with God. God promised that to Israel "a son is given; and the government shall be upon his shoulder, and his name shall be called Wonderful Counselor, Mighty God, Everlasting Father, Prince of Peace" (Isaiah 9:6–7). But with tears this Prince of Peace looked out over Jerusalem and said, "Would that you...had known on this day the things that make for peace! But now they are hidden from your eyes.... You did not know the time of your visitation" (Luke 19:42–44).

When the builders rejected the beautiful Cornerstone, Jesus said, "The kingdom of God will be taken away from you and given to a people producing its fruits" (Matthew 21:43). He explained, "Many will come from east and west and recline at table with Abraham, Isaac, and Jacob in the kingdom of heaven, while the sons of the kingdom will be thrown into the outer darkness" (Matthew 8:11–12).

God has saving purposes for ethnic Israel (Romans 11:25–26). But for now the people are at enmity with God in rejecting the gospel of Jesus Christ, their Messiah (Romans 11:28). God has expanded his saving work to embrace all peoples (including Palestinians) who will trust his Son and depend on his death and resurrection for salvation. "Is God the God of Jews only? Is he not the God of Gentiles also? Yes, of Gentiles also, since God is one. He will justify the circumcised by faith and the uncircumcised through faith" (Romans 3:29–30).

The Christian plea in the Middle East to Palestinians and Jews is: "Believe on the Lord Jesus, and you will be saved" (Acts 16:31). And until that great day when both Jewish and Gentile followers of King Jesus inherit the earth (not just the land), without lifting sword or gun, the rights of nations should be decided by the principles of compassionate and public justice, not claims to national divine right or status.

120

A Prayer for Our Church

Asking God to Build a Certain
Kind of Men and Women

Oh, Lord, by the truth of your Word, and the power of your Spirit and the
ministry of your body, build men and women at _____
who don't love the world more than God,
who don't care if they make much money,
who don't care if they own a house,
who don't care if they have a new car or two cars,
who don't need recent styles,
who don't care if they get famous,
who don't miss steak or fancy fare,
who don't expect that life should be comfortable and easy,
who don't feed their minds on TV each night,
who don't measure truth with their finger in the wind,
who don't get paralyzed by others' disapproval,
who don't return evil for evil,
who don't hold grudges,
who don't gossip,
who don't twist the truth,
who don't brag or boast,
who don't whine or use body language to get pity,
who don't criticize more than praise,

who don't hang out in cliques,
who don't eat too much or exercise too little;
But
who are ablaze for God,
who are utterly God-besotted,
who are filled with the Holy Spirit,
who strive to know the height and depth of Christ's love,
who are crucified to the world and dead to sin,
who are purified by the Word and addicted to righteousness,
who are mighty in memorizing and using the Scriptures,
who keep the Lord's Day holy and refreshing,
who are broken by the consciousness of sin,
who are thrilled by the wonder of free grace,
who are stunned into humble silence by the riches of God's glory,
who are persevering constantly in prayer,
who are ruthless in self-denial,
who are fearless in public witness to Christ's lordship,
who are able to unmask error and blow away doctrinal haze,
who are tough in standing for the truth,
who are tender in touching hurting people,
who are passionate about reaching the peoples who have no church,
who are pro-life for the sake of babies and
moms and dads and the glory of God,
who are keepers of all their promises, including marriage vows,
who are content with what they have and trusting the promises of God,
who are patient and kind and meek when life is hard.

⚹ desiringGod

Everyone wants to be happy. Our website was born and built for happiness. We want people everywhere to understand and embrace the truth that *God is most glorified in us when we are most satisfied in him*. We've collected more than thirty years of John Piper's speaking and writing, including translations into more than forty languages. We also provide a daily stream of new written, audio, and video resources to help you find truth, purpose, and satisfaction that never end. And it's all available free of charge, thanks to the generosity of people who've been blessed by the ministry.

If you want more resources for true happiness, or if you want to learn more about our work at Desiring God, we invite you to visit us at www.desiringGod.org.

Subject Index

everlasting, 255
God's glory and, 16–20
indomitable, 168
rejoicing, 46
worship and, 269–272
Judgment, final, 175–178
Justice, 29, 308–309, 332–334, 379–381
Justification, 167–169

Kindness, 95–96

Lamp of the body, 188–190
Language, 40–43
Law
   curse of, 65, 103, 185
   dying to, 235–237
   sin and, 320–322
   written on every heart, 140, 157
Leisure time activities, 329–331
Liberalism, 374
Life, God's plan and, 191–193
Light and darkness, 30–32, 130–132, 188
Listening, 115–116
Losses, 45–46, 52–54
Love
   of Christ, 24–26
   demanding rights, 379–381
   dying to the law, 235–237
   glory of God, 16–20

for God, 136–138
of God, 335–337
God-centeredness of God's love, 16–17
intensity of God's love, 27–29
meaning of, 93–96, 198, 267
Muslim neighbors, 88–92
never ending, 40–41
in people, 206
surrendering and, 379–381
Lust, 323, 350–352
Lying, 49–51, 205–206

Manners, 144
Marriage
   anger and, 196–198
   as covenant, 33
   priorities and, 44–45
   relationships, 75–78
Mary, mother of Christ, 121–123
Mealtime prayers, 326–328, 353–355
Media-driven celebrity, 118–120
Meditations, 1–2
Mental warfare, 323–325
Mercy, see also Sin
   eye as the lamp of the body, 189
   forgiveness and, 197
   justice and, 332–334, 380–381

Person Index

SCRIPTURE INDEX